My First Last Day at School

Daily Devotions for Living in the Real World

Al Cadenhead, Jr.

OS

Smyth & Helwys, Inc.®
Macon, Georgia

ISBN 1-57312-011-1

My First Last Day at School
Daily Devotions for Living in the Real World

Al Cadenhead, Jr.

Copyright © 1995
Smyth & Helwys Publishing, Inc.®
6316 Peake Road
Macon, Georgia
31210-3960
1-800-747-3016

The paper used in this publication meets the minimum requirements of American Standard for Information Sciences—Permanence of paper for Printed Library Materials.
ANSI Z39.48–1984.

Scriptures are taken from the New Revised Standard Version (NRSV) unless indicated otherwise.

Library of Congress Cataloging-in-Publication Data

Cadenhead, Al
    My first last day at school: daily devotions for living in the real world/by Al Cadenhead.
    vi + 186 pp.   8" x 8"
    ISBN 1-57312-011-1
    1. Devotional calendars.
    BV4811.C331995
    242'.2—dc20   94-41133
                                                                             CIP

One of the worst "sound bytes" of heresy is the idea that only ordained ministers are "all-the-time Christians." Actually, all Christians are full-time. There is no such thing as a day off from commitment by those who belong to Jesus Christ. Every one of us is enrolled in the same rigorous course: Discipleship 101. We cannot miss a single day from class.

Al Cadenhead is a busy pastor beset, as others, by the peril of pace. Yet, he has seen the need personally to nourish his spirit daily and provides in this volume resources for all of us who would do likewise. He counsels in one of the January devotionals (the eleventh), "Speed should not cause us to ignore personal time in our daily schedule. A twenty-minute period is worth its weight in gold when it is used for prayer, meditation, or just listening to the wind."

Our television screens confront us constantly with the emaciated forms of persons who are hungry. Famine in Somalia, war in Rwanda, and disruption in Haiti reduce multitudes before our very eyes to skin and bones. There is a worse plight for Christians, however: to suffer spiritual malnourishment—to go for days, weeks, months, or years without any food for the soul.

These morsels of "daily bread" will prevent such hunger. They will nourish from within. The devotionals are bite-sized, simply profound—wrung out of a real observer's experience with real people involved in real lives. They will guard us from the certain vanity that tries to do too much, too fast, too soon, all without a proper spiritual diet.

These daily devotionals are pithy and remind us that God constantly creates by way of the principle: out of little, much. Acorns yield oaks, if they are good acorns. Here are some good acorns—cracked, salted, roasted, and served piping hot. They reflect the economy of Jesus who saw the greatest of kingdom forces unleashed in a pinch of leaven, a shaft of light, a mustard seed, a widow's mite. These daily morsels are sent forth by a friend to his friends whom he hopes will be fed by them as he has been.

So, dear reader, slow down; listen, taste, and eat. Al Cadenhead has set an appetizing table for all who would nourish their souls daily.

W. Randall Lolley

The respected Christian psychiatrist Paul Tournier was once asked the reason for the wholeness he seemed to possess in his life. He responded, "I attribute it to a decision I made some fifty years ago to get up early each morning and spend time listening to God." Paul Tournier was certainly not the first to practice this discipline.

Jesus was always able to cope with the pressures and hardships that came his way because his life was nourished by a habit of retreating to certain places for prayer and thought. This pattern was so obvious and, yet, most of us have never learned this valuable lesson. We know from our experiences with our automobiles that fuel is necessary for the engine to operate, and good fuel is an even better advantage. Far too many of us "throw" ourselves at the world each day with tanks that are very close to empty, if not altogether dry. I offer two suggestions to those who would seek to enrich their lives with a quiet, regular, reflective time each day.

First, one must be intentional and make this need a priority. Unless one genuinely makes this a part of the daily routine, normal pressures and demands will inevitably crowd it out of the day. A meaningful devotional life is never an accident. It happens because one recognizes the need and is willing to make it a priority. The choice time of day for meditation will vary from person to person. Some people do best in the early morning; others cannot help but fall asleep. For some persons, the late evening before retiring to sleep is best. One's personal schedule and physical chemistry must determine the best time.

Second, the use of devotional and study helps can stimulate thinking and guide one's thoughts. The Bible is the most important tool, but other materials can be extremely valuable in using this time. One of the most important books for me was given to me by my first grade school teacher. It was printed before the turn of the century but has become a cherished possession. It is a part of my daily meditations.

Obviously, I hope that this volume will become an important part of your daily devotional material. Let it be a partner with your Bible, and remember that it is to stimulate your thinking. I do not claim this book to be the last word on anything, but as you read each day, you will be sharing the thoughts and observations of one who is doing exactly what you are doing and taking a similar journey. As you read, we will become partners in our walk through the days of this year. I like the way that sounds: partners. Partners are important in our journey. Remember, this is not an uncharted journey. Our mutual partner will be there to meet us each day whether we seek God in the early hours, or late evening, or whenever we have the wisdom to recognize our need for that divine presence.

Al Cadenhead, Jr.

Dedicated to my congregations, present and past

First Baptist Church, High Point, North Carolina
The Hill Baptist Church, Augusta, Georgia
First Baptist Church, Vienna, Georgia

"Giving thanks to God the Father at all times and for everything, in the name of our Lord Jesus Christ." (Eph 5:20)

My wife, Suzanne, teaches kindergarten. On the last day of a school year, a mother of one of the children shared an interesting experience that occurred on the way to school that morning. The mother noticed that her little girl seemed distraught, even to the point of tears in her eyes. The mother asked why she was crying. The little girl thought for a moment and, with all of the contemplation possible for a six year-old, said, "I am crying because it is my first last day of school." The little girl somehow knew that this was a significant day but also a day of mixed emotions. She was not quite sure how to handle this day mixed with joy and sadness. What a wise assessment!

Aren't most days like that? Seldom do we have a day that is all good or all bad. Life is a mixture of that which we like and that which we do not like. The key is recognizing not only the existence but the necessity of both. How do we remain open to all that life brings? "Give thanks always to the Father for all things." Does any other option make sense? Accept the good and ignore the bad? Claim the good and do battle with the bad? Can it be that what seems bad today may be for our good tomorrow?

God has done a lot of magic with what seems to be bad for those persons who remain open "by giving thanks to God for all things." We have all been where the little kindergarten girl was. Every day is a first last day in one way or another, filled with mixed experiences and mixed blessings.

"As your days, so is your strength." (Deut 33:25)

January 2

The words of the ancient writer of Deuteronomy were echoed later by the poet J. E. Saxby:

> Oh, ask not thou, How shall I bear
> The burden of tomorrow?
> Sufficient for today, its care,
> Its evil and its sorrow:
> God imparteth by the way
> Strength sufficient for the day.

Both of these writers demonstrated true wisdom. We can know that as we begin this new year, it will be filled with both good and bad. We will have positive and negative experiences, joy and pain. If we allow, the negative can so occupy our conscious minds that our joy is ignored and overlooked. Even when we have so many sources of joy, we can be very much in love with sorrow and peevishness if we lose these pleasures and choose to sit on a little handful of thorns.

One of the toughest disciplines we must learn is to enjoy the blessings of this day when God sends them and bear the evils of the day patiently. This day alone is ours. Yesterday is dead and gone. Tomorrow is not yet born. It is possible for us to look around and bring into our thoughts all of the evils and uncertainties in our world so that our load for today becomes intolerable.

January 3

"My presence will go with you, and I will give you rest." (Exod 33:14)

What a comforting thought! This short verse in Exodus hooks me every time I read it. I have no doubt that many of us long for that promised rest. How shall you rest in God? By giving yourself wholly to God. If you give yourself by halves, you cannot find full rest; there will ever be a lurking disquiet in the half that is withheld. Martyrs, confessors, and saints have tasted this rest and "counted themselves happy in that they endured."

A countless host of God's faithful servants have drunk deeply of this rest under the daily burden of a weary life, even moments that were dull, commonplace, painful, or desolate. All that God has been to them, God is ready to be to you. Once the heart is fairly given to God with a clear conscience and steadfast purpose of obedience, you will find a wonderful sense of rest. As the poet Jean Nicolas Grou wrote,

> Thy presence fills my mind with peace,
> Brightens the thoughts so dark erewhile,
> Bids cares and sad forebodings cease.
> Makes all things smile.

January 4

"Everyone who loves is born of God and knows God." (1 John 4:7b)

The writer of 1 John offers words that sound easy until we try to live them out in our daily life. More than just a little effort is required. We may, if we choose, make the worst of one another. Everyone has weak points and faults, and we may fix our attention upon these constantly. We also have the option of making the best of one another. We may forgive, even as we hope to be forgiven. We may put ourselves in the place of others and ask what we should wish to be done to us and thought of us, were we in their place.

By loving whatever is lovable in those around us, love will increase by flowing back from them to us, and life will become more pleasurable rather than painful. Then, earth becomes a little more reflective of heaven, and we become more reflective of the one whose name is Love.

Like the eighteenth-century minister John Keble, may we pray for the sensitivity to lighten the load of those around us.

Oh, might we all our lineage prove,
Give and forgive, do good and love;
By soft endearments, in kind strife,
Lightening the load of daily life.

"My way is hidden from the Lord, and my right is disregarded by my God." (Isa 40:27b)

January 5

The prophet Isaiah may have been talking about his own people and situation, but he points a finger at our day and age as well. He was referring to the people of his day who were becoming discouraged. They felt that God was ignoring their plight and had possibly forgotten them altogether. They were becoming weak and frustrated. Their goals were not being accomplished.

Although failed goals are always very painful, Isaiah reminds us that the day will come when we will "soar like eagles, and run and not be weary, and walk and not faint." These are very simple but comforting words. Yet, take note that Isaiah says all of this comes on the other side of a bridge, a bridge of waiting. Soaring, running, and walking come after we are willing to wait.

For some of us, waiting is tough. I don't like to wait. I hate lines and stop lights. I much prefer God to work on my schedule, but to my advantage God sometimes chooses to do what I need rather than what I want. I have trouble admitting that when I feel my way is hidden from God's sight, it could be that I just haven't waited long enough. Waiting was not easy for Isaiah's day, and it has not gotten any easier in the twentieth century.

"The Lord has heard my supplication; the Lord accepts my prayer." (Ps 6:9)

January 6

I am astounded how often we ignore objects of great value that are at our fingertips. Opportunities are frequently overlooked simply because they are so accessible. One example might be prayer. It certainly is not new. As a practice it has been around since humankind became aware of some power behind all things and a source beyond our own capacity. We have always had an inherent need to call on a power greater than our own.

Prayer has a special place for those of us who follow Christ. Jesus provides for us the very best example of the results of a proper kind of prayer life. One of the secrets of his power can be found in the channel that was always open with his heavenly father. We all have access to that same kind of power and peace. Our problem is that we do not take advantage of our opportunities. All of the equipment needed is already built in. The only requirement is a little time and energy. We are the losers when we fail to pray as we should.

One issue stands in the way for too many of us, however. To develop the right kind of prayer relationship with God is to recognize our dependency upon God, and that is where our pride stands in the way. Our own feelings of arrogance and an unrealistic estimate of our own adequacy often leads us down the road to unhappiness. If the fear of God is the beginning of all knowledge, then arrogant independence must be the epitomé of ignorance.

January 7

"Whatever is true, . . . , honorable, . . . , just, . . . , pure, . . . , pleasing, . . . , commendable, . . . , think about these things." (Phil 4:8b)

The mind is one of God's greatest gifts. The quality of the human mind sets us apart from the lower forms of animal life, at least most of the time it does. The mind is given to us to serve us and, like all of God's gifts, the key is in our stewardship. One of the intriguing aspects of the mind is the fact that it always seems to be active. Try not to think. I remember as a child playing a game called "Trying Not to Think about Anything." At a given moment I would make an earnest effort to draw a total blank in my mind, but in trying not to think I had to think in order to do so. (What used to be a game for me now occurs regularly in the pulpit!)

The mind is constantly working. One of the keys to a joyful life is keeping it moving in the right direction. We have the power and ability to direct our thinking. We can use our mind in positive, healthy ways or allow it to run free and make a slave of the rest of our body. Jesus said if we think something, we may as well have committed it. I believe Jesus knew that if we think on some thought long enough, we will eventually convince ourselves it is right, whether it is or not. Consider a little hurt you may have received. You can nurse it and make it bigger, or you can forget it as a part of life. Your mind is a gift; your happiness depends on how you use it.

January 8

"The creation waits with eager longing for the revealing of the children of God." (Rom 8:19)

As we begin a new year, the time is right to consider something known as the "self-fulfilling prophecy." It is a theory that has been around for a long time and has wide application to almost every area of our lives. At the risk of oversimplification, the theory is founded on the assumption that we tend to get what we expect. The expectation helps to create the conditions to make it become a reality. For example, in the work setting, our co-workers are very much affected by our expectations of them. If we expect them to be cooperative and creative or, on the other hand, lazy and apathetic, they probably will be.

This principle is also true at home. Consider our children. Within certain limits we tend to get what we expect from them. If we expect an uncooperative spirit, behavioral problems, and a difficult attitude, we will not be disappointed. On the other hand, if we expect them to be caring and conscientious, they probably will be. The same idea holds true in marriage. I have known very few people who expected their spouse to be worthless to be disappointed. The same principle can be applied to almost any relationship. We tend to get what we expect. This is a good time of the year to take a look at what we expect from the people around us.

"Moses' hands grew weary; so they took a stone *January 9*
and put it under him, and he sat on it." (Exod 17:12)

Depression is so common today. Research indicates that it may be related to a number of factors rather than one single source. It may be caused by a chemical imbalance in the body. Other researchers point toward vitamins and hormones. There is also the more well-known association with stress and anxiety.

Given enough time, stress and anxiety can do a number on anyone. We feel it from so many directions, day after day. This buildup eventually creates the condition for one of the biggest causes of the "blues." It is a very simple thing called fatigue. Vince Lombardi one said, "Fatigue makes cowards of us all." This is so true! Most of us are over-committed and have truly accepted more demands than we can possibly handle. The result is fatigue—physical, mental, and emotional fatigue.

I am not saying that fatigue is the only cause or even the primary cause of depression, but it is right there on top. We must rest if we are to function properly. Otherwise, we lose our effectiveness, and eventually our body will rebel and get what it needs. Even in the process of creation, God felt the need to rest. Are we better than God?

"Who am I, that I should go to Pharaoah and *January 10*
bring the Israelites out of Egypt?" (Exod 3:11)

Have you ever dealt with the feeling that you are unimportant, if your life really counts for anything? Many years ago God spoke to Moses from a burning bush and essentially said, "I am concerned about my people. I'm sending you to Pharaoh to tell him to let my people go." (Excuse me, Lord, would you repeat that?) Moses made the usual statement, "But I am a nobody," although he did as he was told.

Life has a way of bumping us around. We reel from blow after blow until we lose confidence in our own abilities to accomplish anything of value. We can learn two quick lessons from Moses. First, we need to affirm the difference that one person can make. Everett Hale once wrote: "I am only one, but still I am one. I cannot do everything, but I still can do something. I will not refuse to do the something I can do." The second lesson is found in God's reply to Moses' statement, "I am nobody." God answered, "I will be with you." Here is the key to heroic living. Claim God's promise.

The world desperately needs persons who will make a difference and respond to the cries that surround us. Maybe we cannot do everything, but we can do something. We may not have to go to Egypt (thank God!), but we will discover that we can make a difference.

January 11

"Be still, and know that I am God." (Ps 46:10)

Speed is a problem today, and I do not mean the drug. Another form of speed is injuring far too many people. It has to do with our pace. Part of the problem is that many of us have not made the effort to find out how God wants us to use our time. We need to put God in our timetable and seek divine guidance each day as we make choices about our time. Speed causes us to do foolish things.

Speed should not cause us to ignore personal time in our daily schedule. A twenty-minute period is worth its weight in gold when it is used for prayer, meditation, or just listening to the wind. Speed should not blind us to the number of demands that we take on each day. We can do a few things, but we can't do everything.

Speed should never be a substitute for common sense. God will give us special insight when we really try to slow down and listen. There is a certain vanity in trying to do too much, too fast, too soon. There may be some "look-at-me-how-busy-I-am" syndrome that ought to be handed over to the owner of all time. Slow down; the race will be over soon enough. Enjoy the ride.

January 12

"The small and the great are there, and the slaves are free from their masters." (Job 3:19)

Strange how we remember experiences that are relatively insignificant! For example, I remember an evening many years ago when my children were young. We had all collected in the kitchen, anxiously awaiting mealtime. Melody, my daughter, was about four years-old at the time and possessed patience as measured in seconds equal to her age. She was hungry and began to cry. I opened the cabinet door and found a box of saltine crackers. In an act of desperation I handed her one cracker. The sobbing stopped, and she smiled. I thought, "The power of one small cracker!" Even then I knew that the day would come when it would take a lot more than a cracker to satisfy a growing daughter. (How right I was!)

That experience reminds me again of a very important fact. Although our needs and requirements increase, the value of little things does not decrease. Little things make a difference. They make or break relationships. They strengthen or weaken marriages and friendships. They are important on the job and make all the difference at home. Although big things can split up homes, the usual cause is the accumulation of a "bunch" of little things. Big gifts seldom keep couples together, but a few simple gestures can bridge some troubled waters. Little things are very important. Never underestimate their potential!

"Blessed are your eyes, for they see, and your ears, for they hear." (Matt 13:16) *January* 13

I like this thought the journalist Joseph Wood Drutch wrote: "The rare moment is not the moment when there is something worth looking at but the moment when we are capable of seeing." Jesus often spoke of people who have eyes but do not really see, and those who have ears but do not really hear. Life is what we are, what we perceive, and what we are attuned to.

An art student saw the brilliant colors used by a master painter, which opened up a whole new world for him. He put the revealing experience this way: "He skinned my eyes. I had never seen color before; nothing will ever again look the same to me."

The great moments in our lives are not the moments when we have great experiences; we have them all the time. The great moments are when we can see for real. How that lesson applies to each of us will vary from person to person, but just think of the sadness of our missing so much that surrounds us everyday because we have our hands over our eyes and our fingers in our ears.

"Forgive us our debts, as we also have forgiven our debtors." (Matt 6:12) *January* 14

The teachings of Jesus are so filled with practical wisdom. They may be other-worldly in origin, but never in application. For example, Jesus talked a great deal about forgiveness because he knew that broken relationships and hostility reduce the meaning of life for all persons involved. Part of being human is that we are full of contradictions. We live separate lives and at the same time want to be close. Our communication sometimes falters, and we end up misunderstanding, frustrating, and hurting one another. Resentment turns to anger. We end up doing and saying things that separate us.

Forgiveness, as Jesus used the term, does not mean forgetting. Rather, it means "we shall not let this separate us." Forgiveness is the refusal of love to let anything separate us from another human being. The Hebrew word for forgiveness means "lightness" or "lifting up." In short, forgiveness is the removal of the effect of the past on the present. Those who forgive no longer carry the burden or resentment of the past into the future. They are free to live in the present with the load taken off their shoulders. We have heard the expression, "Forgive and forget." We have to forgive because we cannot forget.

January 15

"Do you not know that you are God's temple and that God's Spirit dwells in you?" (1 Cor 3:16)

The apostle Paul was talking to us as well as the people in Corinth long ago. How does it feel to be called God's temple? Do you realize what that means? Allow me to answer the question with a very simple story that I heard long ago.

A young lad in Poland lived on a farm. One day some gypsies traveled by his house and asked if they might drink from the well. Having drawn the water, they stood looking intently into the well. The lad was curious and asked them what they saw. "Do you know who lives down there?" said the gypsy leader. "God," the leader continued. The boy peered down into the well at the water and saw his own reflection. "But that's me!" the boy said. The gypsy replied, "Now you know where God lives."

The story may be quite simple but serves as a reminder that God really does seek to live in us. We are God's temple, or at least we should be. Someone told me once that God has two dwelling places: in heaven and in a believing heart. When you look into the mirror today, can you honestly say that you are looking at God's temple? For this to be the case we must first open ourselves to God and truly allow God to live not only in us but through us. Remember also that this kind of temple has a door that can only be opened from the inside. We have to let God in. It is always our choice.

January 16

"O Israel, hope in the Lord! For with the Lord there is steadfast love." (Ps 130:7a)

A man who had been confined for many years in a cell had given up all prospects of ever being free. When the slightest glimmer of hope would rise in him, he would quickly put it out of his mind. One day, however, he tried the door of his cell and found it unlocked, as it likely had been for many years. He opened the door and walked out into the light of freedom.

We live in a time when hope is almost gone for many people. Yet, we also know that without a sense of hope and promise for the future, life loses its vitality. When there is no hope for the future, there is no power in the present. Hope is never stolen from us; we give it up. Whenever we live our lives void of hope, it is of our own choosing. Like the prisoner, we are choosing not to try to turn the handle on the door that can lead us to freedom.

An empty tomb is always an unforgettable reminder that the door is unlocked and a wide world of hope awaits us. How sad to be imprisoned by a door that is not even locked! Today may be the very day when you need to reach out and push the door. Only the Lord knows what is on the other side. Push and see what happens.

"Do not be grieved, for the joy of the Lord is your strength." (Neh 8:10b) *January* 17

Once I heard a preacher say in a sermon that the most predominant characteristic of any Christian should be a sense of joy. He was probably right. Christians should possess joy. Joy is not a phony grin, for some days even Christians do not feel like smiling. Joy is much deeper.

Joy comes from knowing that what we see, taste, and touch is not all there is. It is a sense that comes from believing there is a design to the universe and a purpose in what happens to us each day. It is acknowledging that we are not at the mercy of some impersonal cosmic force. Joy comes from understanding that even though life may at times become rough and rocky, it will never utterly destroy us or separate us from the one who is behind and beyond it all. This joy comes from recognizing that we are not left to face life alone because, through God's spirit, we are given companionship every moment of every day.

So, I agree with the wise minister who pointed to joy and labeled it as one of the important characteristics of the Christian life. Joy is not a goal. It is an indirect result of a life that is founded on the "Rock."

"Whatever you ask for in prayer with faith, you will receive." (Matt 21:22) *January* 18

One day I was traveling on the interstate highway toward Atlanta and passed a very intriguing sight. I noticed a tractor-trailer parked on the other side pointing in the opposite direction. The driver was doing something strange. He appeared to have his shoulder to the left front wheel and was actually trying to push the thing. Now, I've done some pushing in my life. I had a 1947 Studebaker that was pushed about as far as it was driven, but I have never pushed an eighteen-wheeler. Everything seemed to be alright, and the trucker was simply giving it all he had. I thought to myself, "That is confidence par excellence." He was giving it his best shot.

I couldn't help but think also that most of us need some of that man's confidence to put our shoulders to some tasks that need to be addressed. Too often we look at our challenges ahead of time and decide too soon that we can do nothing. Then we sit back and wait for someone to send the wrecker and pull us out.

Just a little bit of positive thinking goes a long way, and many of us need it. Regardless of who we are, we all face some difficult tasks, tasks that require some confidence and the power of a little positive thinking. It is mighty easy to sit down and write them all off as hopeless. Nevertheless, to the trucker with his shoulder to the wheel, you get the blue ribbon for confidence this week. Most of us are not even in your league!

January 19

"If I but touch his clothes, I will be made well." (Mark 5:28)

Many years ago, as a chaplain in a hospital, I observed a very moving experience. A little four-year-old girl was dying from a brain tumor. Her pain was unbelievably intense. No medication or procedure made a difference. A chaplain named John was visiting patients on the floor. Not seeing me in the room, he walked in and sat by the girl's bed without saying a word. He gently took her hand and held it. Almost like magic her crying ceased, and she quietly went to sleep. Without saying a word, John left the room.

I have thought about that experience many times, and it always reminds me of the importance of a simple touch. It can do wonders, even in situations that seem to have no solutions. Jesus had a habit of touching people. He could have performed his miracles from a distance, but most of the time they were accompanied by some form of touch. Our society does not touch much anymore. Yet, children and adults alike need it. Some children will misbehave because a spanking is better than no contact at all.

A simple touch can bridge the generation gap. It can comfort a domestic flare-up. It can help a skinned knee and soothe the most anxious mind. I can think of few things that families need more today than a little touching, but don't take my word for it. The next time you pass your child, or spouse, or parent, or sibling, hug that person's neck and watch what happens.

January 20

"If you continue in my word, you are truly my disciples." (John 8:31b)

A man cut off a dog's tail and buried it, but the dog dug it up and brought it back. The man buried it again. In a few minutes the dog dug it up again and brought it back to the man. Can you guess the moral of the story? You got it! The dog was faithful to the "end." A bad joke, but a good point because most of us are not so faithful to the end.

Our Lord said, "If you continue in my word, you are my disciples." Continuance in his word may not be the condition of salvation, but it is the proof of discipleship. When Christ spoke of continuing in his word, he was talking about more than just reading the Bible. He was talking about all that flows from him as the lord of life. It is not just a picture of inactivity while reading, but the entire picture of our lives. If we continue in his word, our conduct, thoughts, and motivation will reflect a Christlike character that is embraced by his word. Commitment is vital to begin the process, but we must keep on growing. Like the dog we must be faithful to the end.

"As I live, says the Lord, every knee shall bow to me, and every tongue shall give praise to God. " (Rom 14:11)

We have a parrot named Garrison who is an intriguing character, to say the least. He spends the vast majority of his time in a small cage and sits in the same place on his perch almost all the time, even when he is sleeping. I have always been amused that a bird can sit on a perch during sleep and not fall off when I have trouble staying in a big bed. Recently I read something that explains it. The tendons of the bird's legs are made so that when the legs are bent at the knee, the claws contract and grip like a steel trap. The claws refuse to let go until the knees are unbent. The bended knee helps the bird to hold on.

The same theory is true for Christians, to a degree. When we pray on bended knee, literally or figuratively, we find strength to hold on—and certainly there are times when we need to hold on. When we are frightened, sad, lonely, or anxious, we need strength beyond our own. To bow down is as much a mental attitude as it is a physical posture. To acknowledge one's need and to bow before the right source is the key. So, the next time you are really troubled, remember how a bird holds on so tightly to a perch. The bent knee gives the bird very unusual strength. The same is true for us.

"In all your ways acknowledge him, and he will make straight your paths." (Prov 3:6)

January 22

A group of sailors became lost at sea due to a storm. After the storm ceased, they were arguing about their location. One sailor had become skilled in the science of navigating by the stars. He argued: "They are fixed. We can navigate in the darkness based on their location in the heavens." The other sailors would not agree. The group decided to light a lantern and hang it from the ship's bow, thinking, "The lantern will light our way."

We all recognize the folly of the latter choice. A lantern will only light the way one has already chosen. The same truth can be applied to our own lives. Too many of us want to hang a lantern to point the way we have already chosen to travel, and life remains just that: our own choosing.

We need something far most fixed to guide us. We have to establish our direction by a point of reference that does not change and is capable of navigating through the inevitable troubled waters. We are all navigating, whether we care for the term or not, and we desperately need a sense of direction. We would be wise to become familiar with the stars of the heavens and trust the one who holds them in place.

January 23

"Since it is by God's mercy that we are engaged in this ministry, we do not lose heart." (2 Cor 4:1)

One of life's great risks is to lose heart, to reach a point where we become cynical and discouraged. Often in his letters to young churches, Paul urged his people to keep their spirits up and not let the difficulties of the day cause them to lose their spirit.

How do you keep heart? One way is to avoid piling up disasters so that they form a wailing wall. Centuries ago Jeremy Taylor put this advice picturesquely: "How many people are busy gathering thorns to sit on?" They multiply the obstacles so that they lose heart before the heart really has a chance to get into the battle. We need to keep our heart fortified. Paul asked: "If God is for us, who can be against us?" We keep heart by remembering that our labor is not in vain in the Lord. The steady and continuous stroke counts.

In our world there are a variety of ways to lose heart, but a strong personal faith can give us the hopefulness and resilience needed to move forward through gloom and despair. Do not forget Paul's advice to the Corinthians: "By God's mercy . . ., we do not lose heart."

January 24

"Do not worry about tomorrow; for tomorrow will bring worries of its own." (Matt 6:34a)

Jesus continually tried to help people open up to the possibilities of each moment. He knew life was not forever, so every moment of every day should be made to really count. The Romans had a phrase for it: *in hoc hora est eternitas*, which means "in this hour dwells eternity." The medieval monks wrote the phrase on their sundials to remind them that the briefest moment in this life is not a private possession to be disposed of glibly.

We make today count by allowing the past to be the past and leaving behind the bitter memories that fester in us. Jesus bids us to release the excess baggage of guilt, to dispose of yesterday's regrets and missed opportunities and disappointed dreams—all of which prevent us from fully experiencing the present. Jesus also reminds us that we make today count by cutting off our worries. The interest rates on borrowed trouble are too high. Worry is essentially egocentric and blocks genuine sharing with others. When we worry, we cannot enjoy being with others; but the greatest price we pay is losing the magic of the present moment.

Jesus bids us to be open and greet life with expectation, reverence, and wonder. Only when we are in this frame of mind can we treat each day with respect and make each day count. To worry is to borrow from tomorrow at a very, very high interest rate.

"Do not lag in zeal, be ardent in spirit, serve the Lord. Rejoice in hope, be patient in suffering, persevere in prayer." (Rom 12:11-12)

January 25

A common desire among those of us who have been believers for a long time is the desire to rekindle the excitement for God's call in our lives. A student of nature who has written vividly of the Arizona desert said not long ago, "The best way to see a thing is to see it for the first time or to show it to somebody else." Both of these ways of "seeing" apply to the truth of Christianity.

To prevent our losing the wonder of the gospel, we should try to see it as though it is for the first time. Again and again, we should try to look at it as though we have never seen it before. The habit of daily meditation will help this attempt greatly. The surest way of seeing something clearly is to keep showing it to other people. This is why a regular work of teaching others or communicating our beliefs is not only a fine gift for "others," but it is a great thing for ourselves. It sharpens our own awareness and deepens our appreciation. Do your fires need to be rekindled? It might be a good project.

"The kingdom of heaven is like a mustard seed that someone took and sowed in his field." (Matt 13:31b)

January 26

The parable of the mustard seed is a good anecdote to our addiction to size, noise, and power. In the story, Jesus lifted up the vitality of the silent and unseen forces in life. So often God works in ways that are not visible and perceptible to us. The Bible is repleat with examples.

The great forces of life are the silent and unseen forces. What about the power of influence? What about the way a simple example can touch a life and make all the difference in the world in the direction someone is taking? One theologian has stated it this way: "Moral education is impossible apart from the habitual vision of greatness."

When Jesus talked about the great plant that came from a tiny seed, he was giving encouragement to all of us regardless of how few our talents might be. We are to use what we have in a committed way and not sell ourselves short. In our efforts to do God's will, we have more than our own strength; we have the power that comes from aligning with divine purposes. A mustard seed is a very small seed, but never forget the tree that springs from it.

"I tell you, this poor widow has put in more than all of them." (Luke 21:3)

January 27

One afternoon as Jesus was watching people who came to make their offerings for the temple, one particular contributor caught his attention. A widow dropped in two copper coins, the least valuable

Jewish money in circulation at that time. Jesus was deeply moved. He beckoned the disciples to him and pointed out her deed. Jesus lifted up this poor widow in her generous act as a model for what thankfulness to God really means. Her quiet gesture of sacrifice is a lasting example of how God is praised when we, in humble trust, give ourselves because we are grateful.

Two insights about gratitude come from this story. First, giving thanks is always voluntary. No one can compel anyone else to be thankful. You can't pass laws to create this emotion. It must come from the heart. Next, to give thanks is natural for the human spirit; complaint is unnatural. A cantankerous, negative person who is always finding fault is a perversion. When praise and thanksgiving rise from the heart, we find our highest art and richest gift. A spirit of thanksgiving is appropriate for any season of the year.

January 28

"As they go on their way, they are choked by the cares and riches and pleasures of life, and their fruit does not mature." (Luke 8:14)

We could all benefit by paying attention to the wisdom of those words of Jesus. Anything allowed in the heart that is contrary to the will of God, even if it seems insignificant or deeply hidden, will eventually cause us to stumble and fall. Any root of bitterness cherished toward another, any harsh judgments indulged in, any slackness in obeying the voice of God, any doubtful habits—any one of these can cripple and paralyze our spiritual life.

We are not at the mercy of chance at this point, however. The Holy Spirit is always working with us to assist us in discovering these negative traits by permitting the continual little twinges and pangs of conscience. Consider the words of Charles Wesley written long ago:

> Preserve me from my calling's snare,
> And hide my simple heart above,
> Above the thorns of choking care,
> The gilded baits of worldly love.

January 29

"Jesus heard that they had driven him out, and when he found him, he said, 'Do you believe in the Son of Man?' " (John 9:35)

I can honestly say that as many times as I have read this passage and preached from it, I have never really paid any attention to this verse. The "him" in the verse was a blind man that Jesus had healed. He was the man born blind, the one of whom the disciples had asked, "Who had sinned to cause it?" Jesus had replied that no one had sinned, but the man was blind that the works of God might be made manifest. The end result was that Jesus healed him so that God might be revealed.

The healing caused trouble for the man. The Pharisees were hostile that Jesus had been given credit for the healing, and they cast the man out. In other words, the work of Christ caused the man problems even if it had been caused by his sight having been restored by Jesus. The scripture indicates that Jesus, upon hearing of the man's trouble, found him and asked him if he believed in the Son of Man.

What strikes me most are the words, "Jesus found him." I am impressed that Jesus was so sensitive to the man's plight even after he was healed. He did not just heal the man and forget him. He found him, checked with him, talked to him, affirmed him, made sure that he understood what had happened. I am glad that I believe in and worship a savior who is sensitive to the needs of people. He really does care for all of us, you and me.

"As servants of God we have commended ourselves in every way: through great endurance . . ." (2 Cor 6:4)

January 30

A framed quote hanging on the wall of my study has offered some advice to me through the years. So many times I have found myself with persons in the midst of some type of trying circumstance, and there appears to be no relief in sight. I then offer the quote on my wall that reads, "When you get to the end of the rope, just tie a knot in it and hold on." Sometimes holding on is all we can do, not necessarily the best option but often the only option.

As Paul penned today's verse, he was offering a window to his readers into his own life. He had experienced beatings, disappointments, and many frustrations. In spite of many struggles, however, he continued to hold fast to his faith, and his faith continued to give him strength. In the letter to the Galatians, Paul had to defend his own apostleship. His opponents had accused him of peddling a second-hand gospel. In 2 Corinthians he was also trying to give his main credentials for being a Christian. In fact, one way of proving he was authentically Christian was to point out his ability to just "hang in there" and not give up as others might do.

Paul's faith did not protect him from hardships and struggles. One might ever raise the case that his faith caused him more than a few problems. The flip side of it was that his faith gave him the grace to endure. What about you? Is your faith strong enough to help you endure or rather hold on to the knot?

January 31

Most of us discovered long ago that a dollar can only be spent once, in spite of our wish to the contrary. This particular fact forces us to make decisions. If we have one dollar, we must decide how we will spend it. When it is gone, it is gone.

We forget, however, that our time has that same characteristic. From somewhere we have developed the attitude that time is unlimited and, therefore, our usage of it is not a big issue. Unfortunately, time is a commodity like money in that it can be used only once. When it is gone, it is gone. That moment of time deserves the same respect and careful stewardship as a dollar bill. Again, we are forced to make decisions.

Some of these decisions take on ethical dimensions. Just as we can choose to spend the whole dollar on ourselves, we can do the same with our time, or we can choose to spend some of that time for concerns other than our own. Again, when it is gone, it is still gone, and we can't always spend it again on someone else or on ourselves. Time is a valuable gift from God. Like our money it can only be spent once, and at times in our lives (daily, in fact) we must decide on whom a given moment of time will be spent.

February 1   "In the shelter of your presence you hide them from human plots." (Ps 31:20a)

Have you ever looked out over the duties of the day, or even worse looked out over a period of days, and wondered how "in the world" you could get it all done? Anxiety is always the result of more to do than one can, or so it seems at this point.

If we could make up our minds, with God's help, never to undertake more work than we can carry on calmly, quietly, and without anxious haste, we would find this simple, common-sense rule can do for us what no plans or tears could ever accomplish. The instant we feel ourselves growing nervous and out of breath, we should stop and breathe deeply with the assurance that God finds no pleasure in confusion. Anxiety and confusion honor neither God nor ourselves. Don't brag about burnout. It is not a spiritual gift!

February 2   "All things work together for good for those who love God." (Rom 8:28a)

Few verses in the Bible have been quoted and misquoted as much as the above verse. To understand the verse, we must first recognize that all things are not good. Even the most faithful Christians may suffer when other persons or natural forces do harmful things to them. God is not pleased with some of the things we do to one another. God finds no sadistic pleasure when a child suffers and is in pain. God neither causes nor takes delight in a person's hunger and thirst. While all things are not good, persons who love God and have responded to the divine call to salvation may discern God's hand working to turn bad situations into something good.

I firmly believe that God is busy and at work in the process of changing the bad into good. The most serious inhibitors of the process are people. The limits that appear are usually of our own doing. To believe that all things work together for good implies a certain trust in God as to what "good" really means. Our limited and narrow perspective may see "good" as slightly different from the divine perspective. Without a sense of trust, the verse cannot be understood. Remember that this "good" is perceived by those who are called to God's purpose. The verse can become a bridge over troubled waters, but without a sense of trust the bridge can never be built.

"It is that very Spirit bearing witness . . . that we are children of God." (Rom 8:16) *February 3*

Have you thought recently about the security that this verse offers? To be told that I am a child of God leaves me with a pretty good feeling. None of us should take that compliment lightly.

One of the special memories I have of my early childhood is of my great-grandfather on my dad's side. We called him Poppa Bishop. I never knew him as anything else. In fact, I could not tell you right now what his real name was. He was just Poppa Bishop.

He was not a gentle man. He was hardened by life and circumstances. He outlived four wives and a lot of unhappiness. Finesse was not his long suit. He smoked a pipe all his life. I think mostly of him sitting on my grandmother's front porch, rocking and coughing. He had an enormous cough. You could hear him in the next county, but he didn't seem to mind.

Occasionally a warmer, lighter side of Poppa Bishop would surface. For example, when I was around him and left to go somewhere that seemed important to him, he would frequently stop me on the way out and say, "Don't forget to tell them whose boy you are." That was as close to a compliment as I would get from him, but it was indeed a nice compliment.

We should live every day with the same confidence in our relationship with God. In fact, the verse reminds us that the Spirit tells us every day, "Don't forget to tell them whose boy you are."

"Let the prophet who has a dream tell the dream." (Jer 23:28a) *February 4*

There are many lessons we need to teach our children. One lesson that frequently is pushed aside or forgotten in lieu of others is to teach our children to dream. Certainly dreaming can be an escape from reality, but when used correctly it can guide us and motivate us far beyond our normal limits.

I like what Lou Brock once said. He was batting .320 at the time and setting new standards for excellence in baseball. He said, "Psychologists say we are the products of our environment. Why can't we be products of our dreams?" As long as the obstacles in our lives are not greater than our dreams, we can overcome, grow, and be happy.

Successful people are usually the product of dreams. While our environment certainly has its influence upon us, we are much more prone to be shaped by our dreams. And if we are to dream, why not dream big dreams? We cut ourselves short when we aspire to half of what we could have done. We neglect our children's welfare when we allow them to aspire only to a little of what could be so much more.

Needless to say, dreaming can be taken to an extreme. It can be an avoidance of reality, and unrealistic dreaming can set up the conditions for a great deal of frustration. I fear that our problem, however, is not aspiring for too much but settling for too little.

February 5

"Do not be children in your thinking; rather, be infants in evil, but in thinking be adults." (1 Cor 14:20b)

Jesus frequently commended a childlike spirit to people. There is a big difference between a childlike spirit and a childish attitude. The Christian life is a continuous struggle between the child and the adult within us, between childishness and maturity.

There are many distinguishing features of childishness. One characteristic that is easily observed is the tendency to blame all of our faults on others. As a character in a contemporary novel explains it, "Society would be all right if it were not for other people." Children will quickly try to blame other people for their shortcomings. We occasionally laugh because we expect this kind of behavior from them. They will inevitably point a finger at someone else as the guilty party, and we frequently think this behavior is cute.

When as adults we behave in such a manner, we are a source of embarassment to ourselves and the one who designed us with growth as our goal. Claiming responsibility is an adult characteristic. Paul called the Christian community to a mature faith, one that enlarges our perspective rather than narrows it, one that keeps challenging us to continued growth and understanding.

February 6

"We are afflicted in every way, but not crushed; perplexed, but not driven to despair." (2 Cor 4:8)

We all experience interruptions and detours. Someone has suggested, "Life is what happens when you have made other plans." While Paul may have stated it a little differently, he knew first-hand the frustration of dealing with interruptions. At every turn he met some kind of surprise or difficulty.

He experienced imprisonments, beatings, storms at sea, shipwrecks, times of rejection, and the pain of being totally misunderstood. He survived all of these trials with a positive attitude because his faith gave him the balance and perspective he needed.

Paul used interruptions as opportunities. Instead of taking the "poor me" or "why me?" route, he tried to turn negative situations into something positive. He had the discipline to look beyond the disruptions and find openings for growth. His frustrations did not cease; but the deeper they became, the more open he became to the will and presence of God. In his second letter to the Corinthians he said, "Yet, we believe now that we had this experience of coming to the end of our tether that we might learn to trust not in ourselves alone but in God." Like Paul, we might find this to be a good day to depend on our faith for a little balance and perspective.

"For the Son of Man came to seek out and to save the lost." (Luke 19:10) *February 7*

Recently my dad and I were talking about how important it is to have a purpose for our existence. Something must call us and motivate us to produce day after day. Unless there is some reason for our activity, it just doesn't make much sense. Jesus possessed this singleness of purpose. He made it clear that he had come "to seek and to save the lost." This purpose allowed him to move through some terribly troubled times. When life became difficult, he seemed to remember the reason for his existence. This purpose kept him from being sidetracked into lesser pursuits and kept him moving onward.

Each of us needs a reason for living, a sense of purpose. That purpose may not be handed to us on a silver platter; we might have to struggle to discover it. If we seek it, however, we will find it. At best life is difficult. We must have something that motivates us to stay in the thick of it all. There must be a reason. None of us are on this earth by mistake. We are no accident. We are part of a total plan. This belief is crucial for a healthy attitude toward life. Otherwise, nothing makes sense. What is your reason for existence? What calls you today?

"Neither to forget the things that your eyes have seen nor to let them *February 8*

slip from your mind; . . . make them known to your children." (Deut 4:9)

A friend was recently sharing with me over the phone his concern that his schedule did not allow much time with his children. I immediately came to his rescue because my own guilt was triggered. I gave him my standard lecture on "It's not the quantity of time but rather the quality that counts with one's family." I was seeking to make us both feel better. But, in all honestly, what happens when you apply this analogy to other areas of life?

You are in the desert, no water for days. A stranger offers you water. He gives you a teaspoon of water but tells you it is the purest quality available. You've been looking forward to a good meal at the close of the day. You sit down to a finely decorated table. The waiter places before you a piece of steak one-inch square but reminds you that it is the finest beef that can be bought.

We could cite a few more examples, but let's return to the issue of relationships. They need time to grow, especially when we're talking about family. When it comes to our children, a quick ten-minute game of checkers one night a week before bedtime does not fit the bill. Brief periods of concentrated time are not wrong, but never let them be cop-outs for the quantity of time that family relationships need for growth. To my good friend over the phone, I was not totally honest; my own guilt got in the way.

February 9

"He took them with him and withdrew privately to Bethsaida." (Luke 9:10)

A certain perspective of life comes to us only when we are willing to back away from the tireless circles in which we move. Unquestionably, activity is vital, and accomplishments result from hard work. But a certain kind of strength comes only when we separate ourselves from those things. In silence and the quietness of heart we discover ourselves and the God who created us. History is full of holy men and women who found it necessary to regularly flee worldly living and make their choice to serve God in the secret of their heart.

If Jesus needed those times of silence and withdrawal, how much more do we mortal people need them? At times we feel that God is far away, that a great gulf of distance exists between us. The problem is not with God, but rather within ourselves. God is always closer than a breath. The problem is that we are too busy to notice. There is indeed a perspective of life that comes to us when we are willing to back away and allow peace a proper place in our hearts. It will not always happen in the rush of the world; it comes through peace of the spirit.

February 10

"For you, O God, have heard my vows; you have given me the heritage of those who fear your name." (Ps 61:5)

There have been many philosophers over the years, but I know of no one more in touch with reality than Charles Schultz. In one of his comic strips, he defined happiness in a unique way. Charlie Brown was quoted as saying, "Happiness is having three things to look forward to and nothing to dread." How true!

Most of us are never more alive than when we have something exciting to anticipate. In fact, one of the capacities that separates us from the lower animals is our ability to anticipate and expect.

Expectation makes tough days tolerable and gives us hope for tomorrow. Expectation for tomorrow gives ease to today.

Our capacity to expect is very fragile, however, and that ability can be threatened. For example, the routineness of life may lull us to sleep and cause us to quit expecting anything new or different. Order makes life tolerable, but it does not preclude the emergence of something new that we did not anticipate.

We should be careful not to let the pessimism of our day and age rob us of our ability "to expect." It will happen if we are not careful. Many peoople anticipate absolutely nothing good in the future, and we can easily catch their disease. Our ability to expect is a gift from God, and I encourage you to protect it with all of your might.

"Do not remember the former things, or consider the things of old." (Isa 43:18) *February* 11

The past and the future can be real friends. If we allow, however, they can become real problems. The water of life touches our boat in only one place: the present. We have to do our living there if it is to take place at all. The past is a big temptation, however. Once I heard a man say about New York City: "It is a nice place to visit but I wouldn't want to live there." I think the same thing could be said about the past. Much about the past can capture our attention. Sometimes we may want to relive good experiences in our memories, but the past should never freeze us and make us unaware of events of the present. The past memory could be an unpleasant one. In fact, it may have been a very frightening experience that hangs over us like a dark cloud.

The temptation may be just as great to try to live in the future. We all have the ability to anticipate and plan, which helps to make us human, but the future always takes the shape of mystery. The future can be frightening. What will happen to me, my family, my career, my health? The apprehension can go on and on. We can become so tied up with our future that we lose touch with where it is all happening, the "here and now." Remember that the past and future are gifts from God. They are good places to visit but not to live.

"For God alone my soul waits in silence, for my hope is from him." (Ps 62:5) *February* 12

During World War II, a German psychiatrist named Viktor Frankl was imprisoned in a Nazi concentration camp. During those days of horror, Dr. Frankl watched everything that was important to him be taken away. He lost his family, possessions, even the clothes on his back. He watched many people give up and die. Others seemed to have more residual strength. He began to ask himself why some prisoners seemed to give up and die sooner than others. He determined without a doubt that the one irreducible difference was the element of hope. Those who were able to sustain hope were the ones with the best chance of surviving.

When a person quits hoping, he or she can be written off. There must be a future and a reason for living. With a reason to live and hope for tomorrow, one can move through the hard times and the good times. Meaning can even be found in suffering. Even as one moves through the "valley of the shadow," there is strength to move forward. An old hymn echoes something very similar:

> My hope is built on nothing less
> Than Jesus' blood and righteousness;
> I dare not trust the sweetest frame,
> But wholly lean on Jesus' name.
> On Christ the solid rock I stand;
> All other ground is sinking sand,
> All other ground is sinking sand.

February 13

"Love one another with mutual affection; outdo one another in showing honor." (Rom 12:10)

With Valentine's Day a few hours away, romance is an appropriate topic. Stories of fantasy such as "Cinderella" are great for children, but if you apply them to real life, problems emerge. Mythical romances paint a picture of marriage that is not necessarily true. In the fantasy world, when the stars are in place and conditions are right, the characters fall in love and "live happily ever after."

We know that people don't fall in love because the stars happen to be in a certain place; they fall in love because in God's grace they meet each other's needs. They don't just automatically live happily ever after, either. A good marriage happens because two people are constantly working like crazy to make it happy. I refuse to believe that we are so naive to think that marital bliss comes from anything less than hard work. When a marriage is happy, I can point you to two people who are working. When it is not happy, I can point you to at least one and possibly two persons who have ceased working at the relationship.

Two people fall in love because they do something for each other. They meet needs; and when they quit working to meet those needs, problems arise. People don't accidentally fall in love and stay in love. If you do not believe that work is a requirement for a happy marriage, you had better stay in the land of fairy tales.

"Do not forsake her, and she will keep you;

love her, and she will guard you." (Prov 4:6)

A good friend shared a delightful experience of her five-year-old son. For a long time her son had a crush on a little girl at kindergarten. The two young sweethearts evidently had been having trouble, and he had taken the matter quite seriously. His description to his mother of his love life was very revealing when he said, "We just done faded away."

While this experience was concerning a five-year-old, it really describes what happens to us in adulthood. Whether in friendship or family relationships, breakups and rifts occur, not instantaneously but as a result of "fading away." Few relationships break up overnight; usually they occur after a time of drifting apart.

In business we are concerned about daily crises, but we are even more concerned about the trends that occur. If this is true in business, it is even more so in marriage. We should be even more concerned about the trends in a relationship. Relationships never stand still. The persons involved are either moving closer or further apart. In my little friend's words, "You are either growing closer, or you are fading away." I heard a man say recently, "Marriage ain't no big thing. It's just a whole bunch of little things."

I am indebted to the wisdom of my five-year-old friend. People don't just break apart. They fade away. Trends may be important in business, but they are vital in the home. How are you trending?

"Forgive us our sins, for we ourselves forgive

everyone indebted to us." (Luke 11:4a)

I was listening to an unknown radio preacher the other day, and he made the statement that "to be forgiven we must also forgive." I first thought that this guy ought to read his Bible because the Bible makes it clear that God's forgiveness is conditioned only by our willingness to accept it. Yet, there is some truth to what he said. The contingency of our being forgiven is not a theological issue. In other words, we do not have to prime the divine pumps of heaven to receive drops of mercy. More than anything else, it is a matter of either buying into a system of forgiveness or not. You can't receive something from a system that you don't participate in.

Forgiveness is both real and fluid. It is like trying to deliver water through a hose pipe that is stopped up at one end. If it is blocked on one end, you can't get it into the other end. So, our willingness to be forgiven relates directly to our willingness to offer forgiveness. Our own forgiving spirit has a direct bearing on the gift of forgiveness we accept. Do you have a forgiving spirit? It is not an insignificant question. Maybe the radio preacher was right after all.

February 16

"Are not all angels spirits in the divine service, sent to serve for the sake of those who are to inherit salvation?" (Heb 1:14)

One of the real beauties of creation is the way God designed everyone to have a part in the overall plan. Everyone—regardless of age, position, or status—has a role to fulfill. I like the sound of the verse from Hebrews, "Are they not all ministering spirits?" (KJV). With that question in mind, one point needs to be made: the most active people are not the ones to whom we owe the most. Rather, as Phillips Brooks once said, "It is the lives, like stars, which simply pour down on us the calm light of their bright and faithful being, up to which we look and out of which we gather the deepest calm and courage."

We find reassurance in these words for many persons who seem to have no chance for active usefulness. Still it is good to know that we can be something for them; to know that no man or woman of the humblest sort can really be strong, gentle, pure, and good without the world being better for it, without somebody being helped and comforted by the very existence of that goodness.

February 17

"Do not remember the sins of my youth or my transgressions; according to your steadfast love remember me." (Ps 25:7)

Karl Menninger asked a question in one of his books: "What ever happened to sin?" His implication was not that we have become so good that sin is no longer a part of our lives, but rather that we apparently have lost our consciousness of sin that obviously exists. Unfortunately, losing our awareness does not do away with sin nor its destructive impact on our lives. The sad part is that one of the fringe benefits of our faith is that we do not have to carry that burden with us.

We need to know that our sins are forgiven. How shall we know this? By feeling that we have peace with God; by feeling that we are able to go to God at any time and be embraced by divine tenderness and compassion; by saying to God when we commit a sin, "I have sinned; forgive me"; by looking at God's love until it sinks into our heart; by waiting on God until we find peace and our conscience no longer torments us; by feeling that our sins, great as they are, cannot keep us away from our heavenly father.

The eighteenth-century words of Thomas Haweis are appropriate here: "When on my aching, burdened heart my sins lie heavily, my pardon speak, new peace impart, in love remember me."

"The Lord is in his holy temple; let all the earth keep silence!" (Hab 2:20) *February* 18

I have great appreciation for a book written about twenty years ago by Wayne E. Oates entitled, *Nurturing Silence in a Noisy Heart*. I struggle with silence a great deal myself. Dr. Oates reminds his readers that silence is like growing camellias. Camellias must be given proper care, nurturing, and the opportunity to grow. Then, they do the rest themselves.

Silence, too, must be given proper nurturing and the opportunity to grow. Sound silly? I hope not because dealing with silence is a very important part of anyone's life. Otherwise, we will never get in touch with a part of our existence.

Most of us are afraid of silence. It makes us confront ourselves, and most of us structure our lives so that we can avoid that most feared of all persons. Who knows? Maybe we will not like ourselves. Then, what would we do? Without dealing with ourselves, we are only half alive. We do not fully exist. Silence gives perspective.

Even Jesus recognized the need in his own life for silence and often retreated from the noise of the moment. Are you afraid of silence? If you are, don't be. Silence can be beautiful and vital to happiness. Most of all, silence can be your friend. Nurture it carefully like a flower.

"Jesus told his disciples, 'If any want to become my followers, let them *February* 19
deny themselves and take up their cross and follow me.' " (Matt 16:24)

There is a certain risk in trying to reduce the Christian gospel to a few words. If one should be bold enough to try, however, two words that are descriptive to its nature must be included: simple and radical. The gospel is as simple as responding to the command, "Follow me." We have for hundreds of years tried to make the gospel into a complicated program of doctrines and theological puzzles. Any complexity comes out of our own doing, not God's. We have been given an example and a request to follow. It is simple enough for any child to respond.

Yet, while following is a simple request, it brings about radical changes in life. The more I study the New Testament the more I am convinced of its radical nature. We are far more involved in games with Jesus than taking his demands seriously. The teachings of Jesus radically impact our attitudes, values, priorities, prejudices, passions, likes, dislikes, and every aspect of life. Multiple choice is not the format. To follow means to change the very roots of our existence. Even scripture reminds us that the way is narrow and straight. Even a passing observation of the human race indicates that the majority of us are not willing to embrace the gospel and its radical nature.

February 20

One night recently a strange event occurred in our home. Our daughter was studying for a test. I had some writing to do. Suzanne was reading. We went an entire evening without turning on the television, a rarity in our home. Now, I am not one to heap coals of condemnation upon the world of television. The "tube" has a profound effect upon us. It can educate us, entertain us, and inform us of events in a matter of seconds. Our world has become much smaller because of television. My problem with television is that most T.V.'s have no "off" button. In fact, many of them seem to come on automatically. In our house you can walk in the door, and the T.V. knows to come on!

Television becomes a problem when it interferes with family life. Time for talking is limited to the commercials. Families go days and sometimes weeks without carrying on a meaningful conversation. There is no way to nurture relationships without talking. Family members can become strangers to each other. Therefore, I am not advocating that we lable television as immoral or illegal. I am saying that we need to be careful not to allow it to make strangers out of family members. Occasionally, just turning it off rather than trying to talk above it is much more comfortable.

February 21

If asked, most of us could list several ways in which certain individuals should love us. For example, if my wife really loves me, I expect her to express that love to me in certain ways. The rub comes when that love does not come exactly in the avenues we expect. We expect one thing and sometimes get something entirely different. We then play the tune that the other person doesn't love me because, if s/he did, s/he would give us what we want or need.

At this point, the pressure of proving one's love is completely on the other person. That person must validate his/her love, whether the expectation is realistic or not. We may be waiting for proof in ways that are beyond the other person. As trite as it might sound, one of the most loving things we can do for others is to let them love us through ways in which they are capable.

For example, John and Sally have an argument due to an insensitive remark made by Sally. John waits for an apology. No apology comes. Yet, at supper time Sally prepares a favorite dish of his that she doesn't even like. They eat in silence. John is still waiting for something she has already done, as best she could. In other words, the question of love has suddenly shifted to John. Is he willing to love Sally enough to let her love him in the way that she is capable of at the moment, even if it is not according to his plan? We can love others by letting them love as they are capable.

"Where there is forgiveness of these, there is no longer any offering for sin." (Heb 10:18)   *February 22*

The Peanuts characters say so well what many of us feel. In a television special, Charlie Brown was lamenting over a problem he was having with Snoopy. As he and Lucy were walking along the beach, Charlie picked up a rock and threw it into the water. Lucy immediately scolded him for throwing the rock. She told him, "That rock spent 4,000 years trying to get to land, and you just threw it back into the water." Charlie, who was already in the pits, lowered his head and said, "I always feel so guilty."

What Charlie Brown was describing was a state of mind that many of us are far too familiar with. So many people carry around a sense of guilt that is heavy and burdensome. For some it is the result of specific deeds. For many of us, however, it is simply a free-floating sense of guilt for our human inadequacies. Regardless of its source, guilt is so useless and unnecessary. A believing Christian has a distinct advantage at this point.

If one is truly sorry for his/her misdeeds and recognizes them as wrong, there is a simple solution for the problem. The simple act of honest confession can bring relief like waters to a thirsty man. One of the most important "fringe benefits" of being a Christian is our access to God's forgiveness. If God can forgive us, surely we can forgive ourselves. There is no need for a burden of guilt. It is a simple matter of owning and disowning.

"O magnify the Lord with me, and let us exalt his name together." (Ps 34:3)   *February 23*

I remember a very important lesson that I learned many years ago. Our daughter, Melody, was only two years-old. My wife enjoys playing the piano, and in those days Melody would always sit beside her and play along. One morning Melody got up early and took advantage of the empty piano bench. She began to bang around and started to sing. To us the tune was not recognizable, but to her it was probably a symphony. The striking part of this concert was that she kept singing over and over again, "Today, today, today . . ." She never changed the lyrics. She just seemed excited about the fact that it was early morning and a new day was ahead.

Melody's concert then and even now makes me feel a little guilty. I don't always get up feeling excited about the prospects of a new day. All too frequently I am anxious about either what happened yesterday or what I think will happen today. A new day is God's gift, and I should never take it for granted. Now, I know that some of us are just not the kind of folks who feel like turning cartwheels in the morning, but that should not keep us from facing a new day with positive anticipation. Time is a gift from God and should never be treated as a burden. I wish I could do a better job of singing Melody's old tune, "Today, today, today . . ." It has to be a better way to start the day.

February 24

"When he is quiet, who can condemn? When he hides his face, who can behold him?" (Job 34:29)

I have never been much on just opening the Bible and blindly pointing to a verse of scripture and then assuming that it is God's direct message to me for the day. Yet, in all honesty, it appeared to happen that way one morning. Normally I have my quiet time early in the morning. Only that particular morning was not very quiet, at least not internally for me. There were no great crises pending, just a number of the usual "open-ended" and normal tasks of the next few days, but for some reason, all of the anticipated responsibilities were getting to me more than usual.

I happened to open my Bible to this passage from Job and realized that my problem was not the next few days but the way that I was preparing to meet them. We need to primarily be mindful of the present and not even permit our minds to wander with curiosity into the future. The future in not yet ours; perhaps it never will be. It is exposing ourselves to temptation to wish to anticipate God and prepare ourselves for things that God may not destine for us.

If such things should come to pass, God will give us light and strength for the need. Why should we desire to meet difficulties prematurely when we have neither strength nor light as yet provided for them? The present duties are those that are pending. Indeed, our fidelity to the present prepares us for fidelity in the future.

February 25

"Whoever speaks the truth gives honest evidence, but a false witness speaks deceitfully." (Prov 12:17)

A number of years ago John Drescher, writing for a Pittsburgh newspaper, wrote a series of articles about things he would do differently if he were starting his family again. For one, he said that he would seek to be more honest. The honesty he spoke of was much deeper than returning a nickel that isn't rightfully yours. Many of us, particularly as parents, practice another form of dishonesty. It is one that pretends perfection or implies conduct beyond reproach.

Consider the father who was pressing his son for better marks in spelling. In spite of scoldings and extra study, the boy could not pull up his grade. One day his son told his teacher, "When my dad went to school he got all A's in spelling." "How do you know? Did he tell you that?" the teacher asked. The boy replied, "No, but I know he did by the way he scolds me." Dad's behavior conveyed an untruth. In fact, the father finally admitted that he also had trouble in spelling when he was young. From that moment on the boy did much better. With dad's honesty the son could have hope that since dad made it, he could too.

This does not imply a "show-and-tell-all" type of honesty. Rather, letting a child know that his or her problems are not unique may be welcomed news by an anxious young mind. A well-adjusted child does not come from a home where everything is perfect, just open and loving . . . and honest.

"And this is love, that we walk according to his commandments; this is the *February 26* **commandment just as you have heard it from the beginning." (2 John 1:6a)**

Does love exist in your home? Most of us very quickly would answer yes, of course! But, just exactly what kind of love lives within those walls? Unfortunately, most of the love we give and receive is a "conditional type" of love. That may sound a little blunt, but generally speaking it is true. While an underlying affection tends to hold people together, most of us give the impression that our expressions of love are conditional in regard to our spouses as well as our children and friends.

We may say in some very subtle ways to our children, "Take care of your rooms, make good grades, and never embarrass me in public, and you can have my love." "Be an 'A' student, make the football team, meet my expectations, and I will give you my approval." "If you will get your homework done, I will give you a little of my time before bedtime." We give the message that our children must earn our love. They must meet the conditions. The same message may be given to our spouse. "If you will just do things my way, I will give you all kinds of love."

Examine the pages of the New Testament, and you will discover the unconditional nature of Jesus' love. It was always a gift. One never had to earn it. What a difference if we practiced that kind of love!

"You shall not take vengeance or bear a grudge against any of your people, *February 27* **but you shall love your neighbor as yourself: I am the Lord." (Lev 19:18)**

One author wrote of visiting two rooms that deeply impressed him. One was the "Hall of Mirrors." In this hall he could see nothing but repeated images of himself. In one look he could see himself seven times at a single glance. Another room was so full of windows that he called it the "Room of Windows." He could not see one single image of himself. His compensation for the loss was the fact that he could look out and see the wide world.

There has been a popular trend in the past few years to turn "inward." Bookstores are filled with reading material on this subject. Various titles deal with the same area as the book, *The Art of Being Selfish*. This trend toward introspection has legitimacy. It came as a healthy revolt against society pulling at us from every side, a reaction against the guilt we feel when we refuse even one call to service.

I am afraid that now the pendulum has swung too far. Some people insist that happiness is found by saying "no" to all but self. We need to remember that both aspects of living have their place. We must learn how to say "no" and "yes." While Jesus taught us to give ourselves away, he also taught that we should be wise in the way we use our gifts. It is not a matter of either the wide world or ourselves, but both. The real art of living comes from spending ourselves in such a way that our lives and the lives of others are enhanced.

February 28   **"If a widow has children or grandchildren, they should first learn their religious duty to their own family and make some repayment to their parents." (1 Tim 5:4)**

The family unit is a part of God's plan and, when it is functioning well, can provide many important elements in the process of our individual growth and nurture. One valuable factor is the way it speaks to our need to belong. We are social creatures by nature and, while we like periodic moments of solitude, our human needs are met in the process of social interaction. Therefore, belonging to a group is so important for most of us. A sense of security comes from belonging, and fulfillment results from interaction with one another.

The family should provide a sense of belonging. If children do not feel that they belong in the family and that loyalty and love flow to and from them there, they will soon find their primary group elsewhere. When a sense of belonging is absent, a feeling of lostness, loneliness, and lack of love pervades. When children feel a sense of belonging, they enter the world much stronger and better equipped to relate to other people. The give-and-take of normal relationships become an opportunity for growth. Also, children can experience a natural step from knowing that they belong to a loving, earthly family to the assurance that they belong to a loving heavenly father and the family of God.

February 29   **"Those who find their life will lose it, and those who lose their life for my sake will find it." (Matt 10:39)**

Why do we do things we know are not good for us? Why do we hold on to habits that weaken us and attitudes that can destroy us? Why can we not turn loose of old securities and patterns that we know are binding us and give ourselves the freedom to grow and experience newness of life?

A family had one expensive possession: a rare vase. One day the young son, who had been cautioned never to touch the vase, got his hand caught inside. The upset parents applied soap suds and cooking oil with no success. Then they thought of calling the doctor to see if he could help. The doctor worked with his delicate instruments but finally said, "It is no use. I'll have to break the vase." The frightened little boy looked up and cried, "Would it help if I turned loose of the penny that I am holding?"

Sometimes our holding on to old ways of possessiveness and self-centeredness keeps us from experiencing the abundant life of which Jesus spoke. He said that in order for us to really find life, we must be willing to lose it for his sake. Sounds like a pretty fair trade!

"God gives the desolate a home to live in." (Ps 68:6a)   *March 1*

With a little luck, spring is just around the corner, and then spring is hardly here before we are in the heat of summer. People begin to think "outdoors." Thoughts turn to trips, vacations, and outings. After all, the winter has been tough; now it is time to stretch and move around.

Even though the schedule during the winter is busy, the pace always picks up with spring and summer. To accomplish everything we want to do, we must make plans. Right now, before things get too hectic, make some commitments to family time—not just one big trip but some regular times together when things are "low-keyed" and relaxed, times when your family might even do nothing. Unstructured time together doesn't necessarily equal boredom. We need time to be together, to talk, to share, and actually get to know the people with whom we live.

"He must manage his own household well, keeping his   *March 2*
children submissive and respectful in every way." (1 Tim 3:4)

I know a man who swears that in his twenty years of marriage he and his wife have never had a fight. I will be the first to give them credit for a good marriage, but give me a break! Not one fight in twenty years? And one of the best parts of fighting is making up! Marriage is too complicated to avoid conflict. With intimacy there is always that potential. The only way I know to avoid conflict is to completely avoid each other. A good marriage is not necessarily one free from conflict; the real test is found in the way we handle it. By conflict I am not referring to a fist fight, but when two people do not agree and a resolution is needed.

Through the years I have observed couples who, in the midst of some heated conflict, would handle the whole thing with a great deal of love and concern. Oh yes, they were genuinely mad, but nothing underhanded was happening. They were attacking a problem and not each other. Then I've watched others who intensely disagreed and spent most of their time going for the spouse's throat. Their fighting was vicious and underhanded. Handling conflict in a healthy way is essential to any good relationship, especially marriage. There is most definitely a good way and a bad way to fight.

March 3

"But Jesus called for them and said, 'Let the little children come to me; and do not stop them; for it is to such as these that the kingdom of God belongs.' " (Luke 18:16)

Prior to his retirement, my father-in-law worked on the administrative staff of the county schools in Greenville, South Carolina. He was in a different school almost every day and usually ate in the cafeteria. One day while he was in the lunch line, a class of young students lined up behind him. A cute little girl stepped out of line and walked up to him, reached up, hugged him like a long lost friend, and then stepped back in line. He was surprised by it all. In a few minutes the teacher of the class came to my father-in-law and asked if he was really Sally's grandfather, as the little girl had told her friends. He admitted that he had never met Sally before in his life, but he was honored by her temporary adoption. He hasn't seen her since.

I have thought about that experience many times. Grandfathers almost symbolically equal love. Evidently, little Sally needed a grandfather that day, even though she had to produce him in her mind. Who knows? Maybe her day wasn't going well. What better person to call on than a grandfather? There must be a message. In our world today many pressing needs make demands on our time. In the midst of all these important demands, we need to remember that there are a lot of little "Sally's" who need a hug. It may be our "Sally" or someone else's. Take a minute to hug a child today. It may be the most important thing that you do all day.

March 4

"Happy are those who trust in the Lord." (Prov 16:20b)

I was recently standing in front of a store looking at some items in the window. While standing there I began hearing a very strange sound in the distance. It was getting closer and closer. My intrigue came from the fact that it had been so long since I last heard this sound. It was so pleasant to hear and so nice to know that it still existed. I had wondered lately if it had gone out of style or if people had forgotten how. It was coming from a man walking down the street. He was whistling. I didn't know people whistled anymore. Maybe it had gone out when canned biscuits, instant pudding, and riding lawn mowers appeared.

Evidently no one had told this old gentleman that you aren't supposed to whistle anymore. He seemed determined, but not in a frenzy—very normal by all other standards. Why don't people whistle anymore? It's not hard to learn. Maybe it is because you can't talk and whistle at the same time. Maybe we don't have time to whistle. You can't grit your teeth and whistle, either. Do people whistle when they are happy, or does whistling help to make people happy? By the way, the man was whistling the hymn "Amazing Grace." Maybe he just had something worth whistling about. One thing for sure, even though he never knew it, he made me feel a little better by simply walking past me.

"You must understand this, my beloved: let everyone be quick to listen." (Jas 1:19a) *March 5*

Several years ago a book was published entitled, *The Awesome Power of the Listening Ear*. The title alone speaks multitudes. Listening is an art and, like any other art, must be developed. To the casual observer, the achievements of an artist may seem effortless, the result of a gift. Yet, art work is the result of hours of practice. Of all the tasks you undertake, listening will be the most annoying if you are not sold on its importance. Just think of the people who consult with you, but as much as anything else just need a listening ear.

Listening is important in every profession. Lawyers may be concerned about legal matters but spend much time offering an ear. Physicians frequently discover patients asking for help through body pain when all they really need is someone to listen. Nurses may work with a sick person, but they soon find the patient just wanting to talk. Barbers and hairdressers may think they cut hair for a living, but they would be surprised how many people come to them just because they need attention. Spend five minutes in a nursing home, and you will quickly discover the urgent need of lonely people.

Even a casual reading of the Gospels indicates that Jesus was truly a gifted listener. We must understand, however, that there is no easy pathway to effective listening. It requires time and energy. Are you convinced? If so, make listening a goal. Consider how valuable this skill could be at home, at work, on the golf course, at church, or anywhere else.

"As the Father has loved me, so I have loved you; abide in my love." (John 15:9) *March 6*

Learning takes place in many ways, one of the most significant of which is by example or modeling. What we say around children is important. Sometimes they remember; sometimes they don't. But they seldom forget what they see.

In the book *If I Were Starting My Family Again,* John Drescher says that he would love his wife more. "That is, I would let my children know that I love her," he said. We talk about love so much. We say it ought to be the cornerstone of the family. But what does our example say? Is it visible? The way two parents express their love to each other is a big factor in how a child will express himself or herself to a future mate. Everyday we teach our children.

When was the last time your children heard you express your love to your mate? Even though they tease, children like to see their parents "in love." Our children need to see that the close relationship between a husband and wife is more than just a burden; it is a source of joy and excitement, something special. I can think of very few things that will do more to make a child feel secure than to see two parents who obviously and openly care for each other. What model are you setting?

March 7   **"Train children in the right way, and when old, they will not stray." (Prov 22:6)**

What are your children catching from you? For parents this is an extremely important question. Our children learn from our verbal instructions, but they learn and remember so much more from our behavior. They catch feelings and attitudes from us just as they would a germ or virus. Parents cannot instruct an attitude; it can only be demonstrated. What we say to our children is important, but what we practice in front of them is even more crucial. Let me explain.

When my son was about three years-old, I observed him doing a cute but frightening thing. He was playing in the yard with a toy lawn mower. He would push his toy mower a few feet, stop and act like he was cranking it, and then he would rare back and kick it very hard. He would go through this routine over and over, always concluding with a hard kick. Obviously he had observed that in someone—probably his mother! The experience caused me to wonder what else he was catching from me.

I am enough of a realist to know that there will always be some inconsistency between words and actions. The whole issue highlights the importance of one's example, however. Our children catch a great deal from us whether we are aware of it or not. I find this thought a little frightening.

March 8   **"Let us approach with a true heart in full assurance of faith, with our hearts sprinkled clean from an evil conscience." (Heb 10:22)**

In our age of behavioral science we have learned to explain our behavior. Certainly we need to know why we do what we do, but have we taken it too far? For example, we have accounted for the behavior of some criminals by pointing to certain factors in their background. Because of the deprivation of specific needs, they developed styles of behavior to compensate for the loss. Nevertheless, we must recognize the difference between explaining and justifying.

The same truth applies to those of us whose behavior is far less than criminal. Frequently we try to ease our guilt by attributing our bad acts to our background, hormones, or genes. We find relief in pointing our finger at something or someone other than ourselves. After all, if we can prove that our parents made some mistakes in raising us, we can "whitewash" our evil ways and say our problems are their fault.

We refuse to accept the consequences for our deeds. We rationalize until it feels better in our stomach. Soon we have convinced ourselves that all is okay regardless of how evil it may be. For a person or generation to accept the "rightness" or "wrongness" for behavior is a measure of maturity. To say "the devil made me do it" is not cute. Placing blame is a sickness that could destroy us all.

"The good leave an inheritance to their children's children, but the sinner's wealth is laid up for the righteous." (Prov 13:22)

In God's great plan of procreation, children are given for many reasons. I am convinced, however, that one of the foremost reasons for the gift of a child is that of joy. No matter how few or how many, children are given to be enjoyed. I think it must also be said that you might have to learn to enjoy children, whether they belong to you or someone else. I am not convinced that love of children comes naturally.

Take the example of the first child. Most of us are starting from scratch as parents. We are so concerned to do things right, to make sure our children are progressing normally, and that they be well-behaved and demonstrate to all who see them that we are adequate parents. Quite possibly we can become so preoccupied with the science of raising children that we miss out on the joy.

At best, parenting is tough. It requires energy, effort, time, money, and patience. It would be a shame to allow all of the pressures to get in the way of the pleasures, particularly the joy. Children can be among our greatest sources of therapy if we only allow them the chance. They are all a part of God's plan.

"Husbands, love your wives, just as Christ loved the church and gave himself up for her." (Eph 5:25)

When married couples say their love has died, I sometimes think it might be more accurate to say that they have killed it. I am not thinking of violent, brutal acts of dark betrayal. I just mean that the flame of love has gradually waned and burned out from sheer neglect.

Anyone can fall in love, I have been told, but to stay in love is another matter. One of the great illusions of our time is that love is self-sustaining. It is not. Love must be fed and nurtured, constantly renewed. Nurturing love demands creativity and consideration; but most of all, it demands time.

People are so busy that sometimes other things become more important than maintaining a relationship. Almost all couples could, if they really made up their minds about it, take time to sustain their love. If they are defeated, it is not because of fate but because of very poor planning on their part. "Get everything else done first, and then what is left is ours" seems to be the guiding principle.

Unfortunately, the time left over is usually no time at all. Love, which once came first, now comes last. When we make plans, almost anything can come along and spoil them. The idea that time alone together is an unnecessary selfish indulgence is a dangerous fallacy. It is all just a matter of priorities.

March 11

"I came that they may have life, and have it abundantly." (John 10:10)

I read an article not long ago that is worth considering. A study at Johns Hopkins University concluded that churchgoers live longer. A large sampling of the population indicates that the annual death rate for weekly churchgoers is about 500 per 100,000. The annual death rate per 100,000 of occasional churchgoers jumps to 900. This means that the death rate for non-churchgoers is nearly double that of their neighbors who attend regularly.

The study naturally could not delineate the reasons for these statistics, but the results should not be surprising. Persons who take time for church have learned to manage their schedules. They live and function in a more relaxed fashion. While not being totally free from anxiety, certainly churchgoers have access to a faith that provides trust and some lessening of daily tensions. The benefits of the scripture and music give hope and confidence and endless other sources of support and nurture.

Of course, the reason for attending church is not to live longer but to live better. Some people live long but poorly. There are those who realize that the good life has depth, height, and breadth, as well as length. Jesus said it best, "I came that they might have life . . ." Sounds like a good deal to me!

March 12

"Therefore encourage one another with these words." (1 Thess 4:18)

Can you remember times in your life when you felt tired or discouraged and ready to give up, and then someone came along at the right time to give you the word and the lift you needed to get back on your feet? One of the most important gifts we have to give to others is the gift of encouragement. Through this gift we have the power to lift people up and make a difference, not only in their day, but perhaps in their lives.

In his letter to the Thessalonians, Paul told some struggling Christians the importance of encouraging and building up one another. Sometimes the right words given in love can make the difference between victory and defeat in another's life. One of the best definitions of the church that I have heard is that the church—the body of Christ wherever the members might be—is a "mutual aspiration society" where we are accepted as we are and supported in the process of becoming what we can be. In these difficult times, we need to be aware of this opportunity continually.

Paul's words in today's verse have value for us. A little encouragement carefully placed can have enormous value. Beware of that which comes to you and, just as important, be alert to opportunities to offer a little of yourself.

"Can any of you by worrying add a single hour to your span of life?" (Matt 6:27)   *March 13*

A physician named William Osler was one of the founders of Johns Hopkins University. While he was still in school, he was filled with worry and anxiety about the future. His final exams were coming up, and he was uncertain about what would happen after graduation. One night he happened to pick up one of Carlyle Marney's books and read this sentence: "Our main business is not to see what lies dimly at a distance, but to do what lies clearly at hand." Those lines made a difference to Osler as he anticipated all that was before him. Years later when he returned to England to receive a high honor from the king, in his acceptance speech he said, "More than anything else I owe whatever success I have to the power of settling down to the day's work and trying to do it to the best of my ability and let the future take care of itself."

That is good advice: living each day one day at a time. We don't have tomorrow. We are only given this day and our daily bread. Could it be that the best thing we could do for ourselves right now is to just settle down to what lies before us between now and bedtime tonight? This little chunk of time may be all we can tend to for the time being.

"Then someone came to him and said, 'Teacher, what   *March 14*
good deed must I do to have eternal life?' " (Matt 19:16)

A young man with considerable resources asked Jesus, "What must I do to inherit eternal life?" Another way of asking might be, "What must I do to have a life that really matters?" The young man had evidently reached a time in his life when the things he had accumulated no longer brought him fulfillment. To put it another way, he was "stuck" and needed some forward momentum for his life.

The therapist Carl Jung once said, "We have an action-oriented side to our lives as well as a spiritual side." Frequently in earlier years the action side unfolds as we develop our job and acquire possessions, a home, and a family. This is often done at the exclusion of developing our spiritual side. In later years Jung observed that the spiritual dimension of our lives seeks fulfillment. An inner restlessness evolves, and we start asking questions about the meaning of our lives.

The wealthy man who asked the question of Jesus was at a point in his life when he was seeking meaning and purpose. Jesus told him to sell what he had and follow Jesus. The bottom line was a call to commitment, to use his life in a purpose that went beyond himself and gave him reason to get up every morning. Christ give that same call to us, to go beyond ourselves and follow.

March 15

"For we walk by faith, not by sight." (2 Cor 5:7)

The theologian V. A. Demant spoke a true word about life when he said, "Christian faith does not free me from perplexity. It does enable me to live with a lot of unsolved problems." We cannot understand many of the dilemmas in life. We may be struggling over some family problem that has no easy solution. We may be anxious about something related to our job. Or on a much more global scale, we may wonder how world peace can be secured. The list of possibilities is endless.

At times in life we have only enough light for the next step as the rest of the road is dark. We take that step in faith knowing that, while we are on the way, more light will be revealed. Sometimes we cannot see around the next turn, but in Christ we see a guide for the next step; in him we see the everlasting arms of a father's love, and that reassurance makes the difference. We can take the step in confidence.

Our faith does not promise us all of the answers, nor does it give us a guarantee we will be spared life's difficult moments. The promise of faith is that we will have the resources for whatever life brings.

March 16

"I am He who blots out your transgressions for my own sake, and I will not remember your sins." (Isa 43:25)

To the prophet Isaiah came the word of God: "I will not remember your sins." What sweet sounding words! I realize that such a statement might sound a little contradictory. How can a divine mind forget anything? Not a problem with my mind, but with God's? In this case, however, I will accept the words as stated. We also need to remember that forgetting implies how we to relate to others. We should learn how to forget.

When persons repent of their shortcomings, they should put the past behind and call their sins to remembrance no more. What a denial of faith to declare our trust in a God who forgives and forgets, yet carry with us a vast burden of unforgiven sin—our own and that committed against us!

Turning to the pages of the New Testament, we find Jesus telling people they were forgiven and urging them to lead a new life. Even Jesus recognized that this new life would be difficult for them if they still carried around the burden of guilt from past mistakes and also harbored the hurts of the past mistakes of others.

Our God is a God who is interested in new life. God wants us to come to terms with our past failures, but then to move beyond them and become the type of people we were intended to be: people with short memories—that is, the right kind of forgetfulness.

"Blessed are the meek, for they will inherit the earth." (Matt 5:5)   *March 17*

Even a casual observation of some people indicates that wherever there has been a faithful following of God in a consecrated soul, several things have inevitably followed. Meekness and quietness of spirit become in time the characteristics of the daily life.

A submissive acceptance of the will of God as it comes in the hourly events of each day, flexibility in the hands of God to do or endure the pleasure of the divine will, Christlikeness under provocation, calmness in the midst of turmoil and bustle, a yielding to the wishes of others and an insensibility to slights and affonts, absence of worry, deliverance from care—all of these and other similar graces are found to be the natural outward development of the inward life with Christ.

These words of the old hymn express well the hope of one who wishes to be meek in spirit:

> Take my life, and let it be
> Consecrated, Lord, to Thee.
> Take my moments and my days;
> Let them flow in ceaseless praise.

"For he knows the secrets of the heart." (Ps 44:21b)   *March 18*

The heavenly father alone knows how to lead His children in the paths of everyday living. God knows every aspect of your soul, every thought of your heart, and every secret of your character—its difficulties and hindrances. God knows how to mold you to the divine will and lead you in the right direction. God knows exactly how each event, trial, and temptation will tell upon you and disposes all things accordingly. The consequences of this belief, if fully grasped, will influence your thinking and your whole life.

You will seek to give yourself up to God more and more unreservedly, asking nothing but what God wills. It is conceivable to then take all of life joyfully, believing the "one step" set before you to be enough for you. Human nature is such that we want more in our sights. One step seems so little to know; and yet the beauty of faith is that trust takes the place of knowing, and peace takes the place of anxiety. You will be satisfied that even though clouds surround you and your way seems dark, God is directing all. That which seems a hindrance will prove to be a blessing because of divine allowance. Such sweet peace comes in the process.

March 19

"Clothe yourselves with the new self, created according to the likeness of God in true righteousness and holiness." (Eph 4:24)

I have always been intrigued by the way actors and actresses can put on a role and become somebody different. They have a real talent and ability to switch back and forth from the real self to the role they are pretending to be. Yet, the switch is only temporary and good only as long as necessary for the film or play.

Putting off the old nature and putting on the new, as Paul wrote, means more than just temporarily switching roles. Paul was talking about a permanent and complete change, one that takes place through and through. Our minds must be changed. Our central loyalties must be examined and reassigned. Our sympathies must be reconsidered, and our energies must be used in a different fashion. We accept our self-glorifying pride and willingly redirect our energies toward the will of God.

We as newly-created persons also recognize that we cannot do this alone. Normal strength is not enough. The very one whose image we seek to take on becomes the source of strength for all of these changes. So, today, what will you do? Will you just be an actor, or will you become more and more a real person?

March 20

"Surely goodness and mercy shall follow me all the days of my life, and I shall dwell in the house of the Lord my whole life long." (Ps 23:6)

Into all our lives, in many simple and familiar ways, God infuses the element of joy from the surprises of life that unexpectedly brighten our days and fill our eyes with light. The heavenly father drops this added sweetness into His children's cup and makes it to run over.

The success we were not counting on, the blessing we were not seeking, the melody of music in the midst of drudgery, the beautiful picture of sunset glow thrown in as we pass to or from our daily business, the unexpected word or encouragement or expression of sympathy, the sentence that meant for us more than the writer or speaker thought—these and a hundred other blessings that our experiences can supply are instances of the daily surprises of our God.

You may call it accident or chance, it often is; you may call it human goodness, it often is; but always call it God's love, for that is always in it. These are the overflowing riches of God's grace, free gifts to us.

"But now I am coming to you, and I speak these things in the world so that they may have my joy made complete in themselves." (John 17:13)

Recently in a conversation a friend told me that he was "working harder than ever before but enjoying it less than ever before." I wonder if by some chance that might describe you in regard to your personal walk, maybe even in your relationship with your church. You may be giving yourself generously and trying to make some good things happen, but are you experiencing joy in what you do?

Our Lord spoke frequently to this issue. He said he came that we might have joy. In fact, he went on to say that he came that our joy might be complete, not just any joy but one that is deep and genuine. Even with the cross in sight, Christ was concerned that we not forfeit a sense of joy in following him.

One of the growing edges for us is to recover a sense of joy in what we do. Consider the way our joy influences the way we are perceived by others, even those who are not believers. Just think of the impact on our outreach if we give people the impression that joy is the result of what we do. The opposite is true also. What will people think of our invitations to them to join us in this "pilgrimage" if they perceive us as unhappy and pessimistic? Today might be a good day to take a deep "spiritual breath" and remember that joy is a fringe benefit of our work for the Lord.

"Making every effort to maintain the unity of the Spirit in the bond of peace." (Eph 4:3)

Paul wrote to the Ephesians long ago, "Do your best to preserve the unity which the Spirit gives by means of the peace that binds you together" (KJV). Ephesus, the city to which Paul wrote one of his letters, was experiencing many diverse movements, doctrines, and philosophies that were pulling the Christians apart. Paul told the Ephesians to take pains to preserve the unity through the bonds of faith that tied them together. He called them to a common loyalty and hope and to reaffirm their commitment.

Commitment is a good word for our society, though often it is not practiced. A few years ago *Time* magazine carried an article titled, "The New Narcissism." The article was written by a journalist who was pointing out a trend in our society for people to pursue that which is for purely personal satisfaction. He went on to say there is so much emphasis on individual fulfillment that such things as altruism and relationships with others in the community are neglected. Do you agree with this analysis of our society? The New Testament speaks of personal fulfillment and abundant living, but this is a quality of life that comes only after we have made certain commitments.

March 23

"I am content with weaknesses, insults, hardships, persecutions, and calamities for the sake of Christ; for whenever I am weak, then I am strong." (2 Cor 12:10)

I tend to like this particular translation of this verse better than the King James Version: "I take pleasure in infirmities." From this verse one might get the idea that Paul had a sick need to experience pain, but that definitely was not the case. Paul found no more pleasure in suffering than any other person. Instead, he was able to grow from it and even become stronger than if he had not experienced hardship.

Several years ago, Dr. Marie Benyon Ray made an interesting study of the relationship between handicaps and achievement. She developed an assumption as a result of her study. "No one succeeds without a handicap. No one succeeds in spite of a handicap. Everyone succeeds because of a handicap." One might surmise from this study that attainment does not come from the absence of struggle but can always be traced to it. In other words, the things that work against us are sometimes good for us.

Paul made this discovery. Through his own experience he concluded that the limitations under which he labored were actually his assets. They pushed him forward. This is not to suggest that we go around seeking troubles, but rather that we should seek to let our troubles serve some kind of high end.

March 24

"The Lord said to Abram, 'Go from your country and your kindred and your father's house to the land that I will show you.' " (Gen 12:1)

In a recent biography of Alexander the Great, the writer described the panic the Greek army felt when Alexander died. The army had followed him across Asia Minor and faced the Himalaya mountains, which formed a natural barrier separating northern India from the plateau of Tibet in China. There they discovered they had marched clear off the map. Their only maps were Greek maps that showed only a part of Asia Minor. The rest of the map was blank space.

Marching off the map is a continuing human experience. Explorers such as Marco Polo, Columbus, and James Cook paraded off their maps when they went beyond the known world of their times. In our time astronomers hope to travel off their present maps of the sky. Information beamed back to Earth from powerful telescopes will rewrite our astronomical maps.

The most important maps are not those of the sky or of lands far away, but of our own lives. At times we must venture beyond our known territory. Don't forget that when Abraham left the ancient Babylonian city of Ur, he marched off the map of his familiar world and into the unknown. No wonder Abraham has become the example of faith. As Harry Emerson Fosdick wrote, "Life is a continuous adventure into the unknown."

"Be silent, all people, before the Lord; for he has
roused himself from his holy dwelling." (Zech 2:13)

The most important and productive moments of our day may be those very early minutes. The tone is frequently set during this time for all of the hours that follow. We essentially set the rhythm for the rest of the day.

Each morning compose your soul for a tranquil day, and all through it be careful often to recall your resolution and bring yourself back to it. If something shakes you, do not be upset or troubled; but having discovered the fact, humble yourself gently before God, and try to bring your mind into a quiet attitude. Say to yourself, no matter how frequently you fall, "Well, I have made a false step; now I must go more carefully and watchfully."

When you are at peace, use it profitably, making constant acts of meekness and seeking to be calm even in the most trifling things. Above all, do not be discouraged; be patient; wait; strive to attain a calm, gentle spirit. F. R. Havergal once wrote:

> Just to let thy Father do what He will;
> Just to know that He is true, and be still:
> Just to trust Him, this is all.
> Then the day will surely be
> Peaceful, whatsoe'er befall,
> Bright and blessed, calm and free.

"Do not worry about your life, what you will eat or what you
will drink, or about your body, what you will wear." (Matt 6:25a)

Each day we should repeat these words recorded by Matthew. So much difference would be made in our lives if we only believed that his words of instruction could be trusted. To "flesh" those words out in our daily life requires real effort.

It has been said well that no man ever sank under the burden of the day. Rather, the weight becomes more than one can bear when tomorrow's burden is added to the burden of today. If we find ourselves loaded, we should remember that the situation is our own doing. God begs us to mind the present and leave the future to God.

If only we could learn to cast our burdens upon God, the one who is quite capable of bearing them and sustaining us as well. I am convinced that trust is the critical issue of the Christian pilgrimage. We would do well to remember these words of the nineteenth-century poet Reginald Heber:

One there lives whose guardian eye
Guides our earthly destiny;
One there lives, who, Lord of all,
Keeps His children lest they fall;
Pass we, then, in love and praise,
Trusting Him through all our days,
Free from doubt and faithless sorrow,
God provideth for the morrow.

March 27

"Fight the good fight of the faith; take hold of the eternal life." (1 Tim 6:12a)

The humorist Roger Price stated that the world needs his new philosophy of "avoidism." He said, "The principle of avoidism is simple: simply avoid things. Non-avoiding leads to involvement, and all man's troubles grow out of involvement."

Price is half right. "Avoidism" is our safest defense against involvement, but involvement is not the source of man's troubles. Most of our troubles come from a lack of involvement. Too many Christians are natural avoidists, but this is contrary to the spirit of Christ. Persons who have accepted Christ have a mandate to be involved. True believers are constantly alert to ways of making their surroundings better. Believers take upon themselves the burdens of others, lift loads, help the weak, and stand with the forgotten.

Christianity can never be lived out on the sidelines. Life was not designed to be a spectator sport. When we try to get by with just being an observer, we will discover an absence of joy and meaning in life. Just as life is not a spectator sport, it is also not an intellectual game to be figured out. Understanding always comes on the other side of experience. An honest attempt to live out our faith demands involvement. If there is an absence of happiness and fulfillment in your life, you might want to take a look at what you are avoiding. You might be surprised.

March 28

"The Lord God said, 'It is not good that the man should be alone; I will make him a helper as his partner.' " (Gen 2:18)

Increasingly, mental health professionals are concerned about the problem of loneliness. In a world that is becoming crowded at an alarming rate, it seems paradoxical that loneliness is such a concern. Loneliness has been defined as a feeling of distress due to a lack of human relationships. Studies indicate that as much as a quarter of our population suffers from loneliness to the extent that it is a serious problem. Like hunger, loneliness is a signal that the body needs nourishment—emotional nourishment.

Loneliness may be transient, such as the occasional feeling we all have at times that usually lasts only a few minutes or a few hours. It may be situational, most often the result of a disruption in a social relationship such as divorce, death, or a move. It may also be chronic, which may be the most serious concern. For example, take note if you feel lonely for extended periods of time when no traumatic event has taken place. Chronically lonely people often have long-term difficulties relating to others.

Remember that loneliness is a signal that the body needs a certain type of nourishment. If you are dealing with such needs, do not ignore or deny them. Remember that the need to be with others was among the first that God addressed. Do not ignore this dimension of your life. God did not create us to live our lives in isolation. Reach out.

"I delight to do your will, O my God; your law is within my heart." (Ps 40:8) *March* 29

If we are sincerely and always ready to do whatever God appoints, all of the trials and annoyances arising from any divinely-appointed change become bearable and manageable. If God appoints us to work there, shall we lament here? If God appoints us to wait beside someone indoors, shall we be annoyed because we are not outdoors. Once we make our plans for the day, shall we grumble because God sends interrupting visitors, rich or poor, to whom we can offer help for their sake and for the sake of Christ? If we are truly at God's disposal, why should we be distressed over a simple task that falls before us instead of some seemingly more visible challenge?

Submitting our wills to the will of God means opening ourselves to the possibilities of each day whether those tasks are obvious to our colleagues or totally unknown to anyone except ourselves and God. To assume that kind of daily openness to God's will is to discover a type of freedom that is fresh and stimulating. To do so takes a little thought and effort. Long ago A. L. Waring wrote:

> I love to think that God appoints
> My portion day by day;
> Events of life are in His hand,
> And I would only say,
> "Appoint them in Thine own good time,
> And in Thine own best way."

March 30

**"Our struggle is not against enemies of blood and flesh, but against the rulers,
. . . the authorities, . . . the cosmic powers of this present darkness." (Eph 6:12)**

For nearly twenty years, I have enjoyed the hobby of growing roses. If you have had any experience with roses, you know that they require a lot of attention, or maybe I should say regular attention. Roses have a rather long growing season but require scheduled fertilizing, spraying for insects and fungi, and periodic pruning to keep the plants proportionate. Good intentions alone are not worth much when you raise roses.

A few weeks ago, most of my plants began to look unhealthy. Some of the stems were defoliating. Some leaves had an unwelcome yellow tint. Many of the stems had grown entirely too long. One night I tried to recall the last time I had spent some time in the rose garden. Weeks had passed since the roses were watered, sprayed, or pruned. No wonder they looked so unhealthy. I had all kinds of reasons for my neglect, legitimate reasons. The past few weeks had been very busy—easy to explain. The only problem was that good intentions and justifiable excuses are worthless to a rose. They still remained the victim of inattention.

Certain conditions are involved in raising a healthy rose. The productivity and beauty are in direct proportion to the attention given. The same is true of your spiritual life. If you think this dimension of your life can exist in a healthy state long without regular attention, you should take a slow walk through a rose garden.

March 31

**"Be content with what you have; for he has said,
'I will never leave you or forsake you.' " (Heb 13:5b)**

These words sound easy until we try to practice such an attitude on a consistent basis. If we could develop an attitude of contentment, our lives would change, our outlook would become brighter, and our physical health might even improve. If you really wish to gain contentment, let me suggest some guidelines to follow:

- Beware of the tendency to complain. Allow yourself to complain of nothing, not even the weather.
- Never allow yourself to envision or imagine yourself under any circumstances in which you are not. Life is tough enough as it is.
- Never compare your own lot with that of someone else. Great discipline is needed to follow such a practice.
- Be careful not to allow yourself to dwell on the wish that this or that had been otherwise. Playing the "if only" game is a definite road to frustration.

- Never dwell on tomorrow. Plan, yes, but do not "camp out" in a time that has not yet arrived. Tomorrow is God's, not yours. The heaviest part of sorrow is often the looking forward to it. The Lord will provide.

Paul said that in whatsoever state he was, he had learned to be content. With God's help so can we. We have everything to gain, including joy.

"I have said these things to you so that my joy may be in you, and that your joy may be complete." (John 15:11)

April 1

This day is often associated with a lot of foolishness. The theme is joy and frivolity. What a shame that many of us think we must step outside the gospel to experience a little bit of joy! In the fifteenth chapter of John, some of Jesus' last words with his disciples are recorded. He talked to them about abiding with him and love characterizing their behavior. He spoke of peace and many other vital issues. Couched in the middle of his words, however, was his desire for the disciples to have joy, his joy.

Christ still longs for us to experience joy in life. He takes no pleasure in our misery. It is sick theology to assume that if we are unhappy and miserable, we must be in the will of God. Yet, we must remember the nature of Christian joy. This joy is not based on external circumstances that always make joy a little more accessible, but comes from a much deeper level that continues even when things are far from perfect. This joy is from a relationship with God that is characterized by warmth and growth. It comes from remembering who we are, sinners saved by the grace of God, and what Christ has done to redeem us. A rainy day cannot steal such joy. That joy can help to balance the bumps and stresses of daily living. Today is April 1, a good day for joy.

"He is not here; for he has been raised, as he said. Come, see the place where he lay." (Matt 28:6)

April 2

During Napoleon's Austrian campaign, his army advanced to within six miles of Feldkirch. It looked as though Napoleon's army would take the city without resistance, but as Bonaparte's men advanced toward their objective in the night, the Christians of Feldkirch gathered in a little church to pray. It was Easter Eve. The next morning at sunrise, the bells of the village pealed out across the countryside. Napoleon's army, not realizing it was Easter Sunday, thought that in the night the Austrian army had moved into Feldkirch and the bells were ringing in jubilation. Napoleon ordered a retreat; the battle at Feldkirch never took place. The Easter bells caused the enemy to retreat, and peace reigned in the Austrian countryside.

Even with the Easter celebration in our thoughts, we must realize that enemies still surround us. When we ring the bells we give a message. Maybe the bells we need to ring are not necessarily of steel and iron. There can be a great deal of symbolism in the word "bell." What are our bells, and how do we ring them? Maybe there are some bells that need to be rung today. What might they be?

April 3

"In those days Jesus came from Nazareth of Galilee
and was baptized by John in the Jordan." (Mark 1:9)

Mark introduces Jesus by relating the experience of his baptism. This act was not just some hollow ritual; it was filled with meaning for his own ministry and is very instructive for our lives as well. Do not get caught up in the physical technique of the baptism. As a Baptist, I obviously vote for immersion, or as Grady Nutt used to say, "Dunk 'em til they bubble."

The importance of Jesus' baptism for us lies in the implication of the act. His baptism was a statement of what he believed. He submerged himself in the belief that God had chosen him and a commitment was necessary. He publicly made that commitment. Our own baptism represents a similar commitment.

He also made a statement about who he was. In the act of baptism he publicly claimed he was an obedient servant of a holy God. Baptism represents a giving of one's self. In our own act we are stating our belief in God's ability to forgive sins. Our baptism should represent a death to an old life where we were central and now we are raised to a new life where Christ is the focus of our life.

More than anything else, Jesus established his direction. Not even death would deter him. Our baptism is the same, or it should be. What is the direction of your life? Has the right direction been set? Is there a need for redirection? Today is a good day to begin.

April 4

"Saul clothed David with his armor; he put a bronze helmet on
his head and clothed him with a coat of mail." (1 Sam 17:38)

We can learn many lessons from the story of David and Goliath, but I will briefly point you to just one. You will recall that the Israelites were camped out and essentially feared the Philistine so much that no one would take his challenge. David stepped up and volunteered to take Goliath on.

I am intrigued every time I hear or read the story of Saul's attempt to get David to wear his armor. As the king, Saul had a massive amount of armored protection, which he insisted that David wear. David did, although he immediately took it off because it was too large. Instead, David picked up five smooth stones and used the very weapon that he had relied on many times in his life. With his sling he planted a stone into Goliath's forehead. David finished the task in the rather brutal act of cutting off Goliath's head. Don't overlook the fact that he used what was already accessible.

You and I must fight giants every day. They will not be the Philistines, but they will appear to be giants. We can't fight our giants in the manner someone else would. God has given us certain talents and gifts that will allow us to accomplish what we are called to do. Watch out for the giants today. With God's help just fight them in your own way.

"Go therefore and make disciples of all nations, baptizing them in the name of the Father and of the Son and of the Holy Spirit." (Matt 28:19)   *April 5*

An army colonel walked into a command post and said, "I'd like to talk to someone here with a little authority." The corporal at the desk answered, "Well, sir, you can talk to me. I have about as little authority around here as anyone."

The question of authority is one with which we always have to deal. Who has authority in our home? At our workplace? In our government? In our personal lives? The question of authority frames our entire lives. Who makes the decisions? Who exercises control? Who has the final say in our lives?

Jesus said that he was granted full authority by his heavenly father to send the disciples out with instructions as to how they were to live their lives. Another step was involved, however, and it is somewhat ironic. The authority given to Jesus by God can only be exercised in our lives when we grant him that authority. He never forces it upon us. With all the authority heaven can give him, our Lord becomes the influence in our lives only when we allow. Who is the authority in your life? Your life is your answer.

"Lord, help me to be honest about who is calling the shots in my life. Help me to grant you the same authority as does the Father in heaven."

"Not that I am referring to being in need; for I have learned to be content with whatever I have." (Phil 4:11)   *April 6*

I have long been a fan of "Peanuts." In one comic strip Charlie Brown was lamenting to his friend Linus, "I've always been criticized, right from the beginning. The moment I was born and stepped onto the stage of life, they took one look at me and said, 'Not right for the part!' " I think Charlie Brown put his finger on a source of anxiety for many of us. A feeling deep within of "not belonging" brings about a sense of discontentment that permeates all that we do.

Years ago the theory of transactional analysis came about as a result of this same issue. T. A. encouraged people to grow and mature to the point that "I'm not O.K." could be changed to "I'm O.K." In no way should we have the absurd perception of ourselves as sinless and perfect. That attitude would be an over-reaction in the opposite direction. Healthy contentment results from the feeling that being here is no mistake.

If, like Charlie Brown, we have decided, "I don't belong; I'm not right for the part," then nothing else will look right either. What happened to the day we were born? Was it something good? Was it something bad? You are no mistake! What you are, when you are, and where you are is no accident. Our being here is a part of the plan. To truly believe this fact can move us along toward the goal of contentment.

April 7

"Mary Magdalene went and announced to the disciples, 'I have seen the Lord'; and she told them he had said these things to her." (John 20:18)

What a beautiful season this is. The including of Easter as a part of the season only adds more beauty and meaning. Many people have attempted to determine the exact Sunday on which the resurrection took place, but the particular season that we have chosen to celebrate it is more than just coincidence.

The basis of Easter is a celebration of new life. This new life comes after darkness has been defeated. Again, the timing of this celebration is so great. It comes when the trees are issuing their buds, the grass is turning green, and the flowers are starting to bloom. It is a phenomenal time of year. Growth seems to be the goal of all living things.

Step outside during this time of year and just look around. Notice how much the trees have grown since last year. So much is happening with the shrubs and trees. When I look at my own back yard, I notice several shrubs that I considered cutting down that are now offering new growth and buds.

I read somewhere that growth is the only sure sign of life. If that is true, there is so much life around us this time of year. This time of year is also appropriate for inner reflection. Are we growing? Are we any stronger spiritually than last year? It would appear that if we are not growing, we are not totally alive. New life is all around us. Is there a sign of life within?

April 8

"What then are we to say about these things? If God is for us, who is against us?" (Rom 8:31)

One morning while living in Augusta, Georgia, I was driving on one of the major streets and noticed that in the intersection ahead something was interfering with the traffic. The cars were going around something. Finally I could see a man rolling his wheelchair right in the middle of the right lane. He was lined up in the street with the cars, rolling his chair with a fair amount of speed. As I passed him, I noticed that both of his legs were missing. His shirt was off, and his arms were enormous. He was not the least bit intimidated by the traffic. He claimed his right to be there and was even singing as he rolled. When I got a few yards away, I looked in my mirror and saw him give an arm signal, stop the traffic, and turn left into a side street. I was totally impressed.

This guy claimed his right to exist. He was not ashamed to be where he was. Persons who didn't like his presence could go around him. His power and confidence radiated from that well-worn chair. His confidence, his right to be in the road, and his nerve made me a little jealous. Confidence and nerve ought to be traits of a Christian. If we could only claim our place on the street! If it means that we must stop traffic to get the job done, so be it. Timidity is not a friend to the work of Christ. So, to the man with the powerful arms and no legs, keep it up. I will yield to you any day of the week!

"Pray without ceasing." (1 Thess 5:17) *April* 9

As I write this day's meditation, I have been on a new church field for only a few weeks. There are always a million things to learn and discover, some more important than others. The church I now serve has provided me with a beautiful office and study area. In the hallway outside the office is a nice sitting area, decorated with lamps and tables.

One lamp in particular always bothered me because it did not have a bulb in it. It was a beautiful lamp but was never turned on. I mentioned it several times to the housekeeping staff, but a bulb never appeared. Finally, after several requests, I noticed a bulb in the socket, and I could turn on the lamp. I turned the switch, but there was no light. Then I realized there was no receptable to plug the lamp in. The lamp looked nice and had a bulb, but there was no light. The lamp could not function because it was not connected to a source of power.

Too many of us are like that lamp. We really are not functioning because we are not hooked up to a source of power, causing us to do little more than just look good. We cannot function as designed. Our source of power is prayer. With it we can live out our lives with meaning and purpose. Without it we just sit there; and whether we even look good sitting there is questionable. Take a minute right now and connect. The plug is in front of you.

"Those who wait for the Lord shall renew their strength, they shall mount *April* 10
up with wings like eagles, they shall run and not be weary." (Isa 40:31)

I can think of very little that influences relationships more than our expectations of each other. What we expect from our marriage partner, our friends, our children, even our work associates has enormous impact on those relationships. Often when I am working with persons who are in conflict, I encourage them to stop and reflect on what they expect of each other. Are our expectations realistic or appropriate? We might discover that they are neither.

What do we expect from God? Such a question is quite appropriate when we are honest enough to admit that we are angry or frustrated with God. Isaiah said that God keeps promises, that we can count on our creator in the dark stretches of life. God may come to us in several different ways in those times, however. For example, God may rescue us from that which is binding us and we may feel like soaring with the eagles. Sometimes God enables us to solve the problem, and we run without being weary.

God is not limited to the rescue nor the collaborating with us to solve our problems, however. Sometimes God just helps us walk and not faint. When rescue is not possible, and when our fixing is not appropriate, God moves toward us and gives us strength just to hold on and not faint. That is a gift. God is faithful, either rescuing us, fixing the problem, or just helping us hold on.

April 11

"As for you, man of God, shun all this; pursue righteousness, godliness, faith, love, endurance, gentleness." (1 Tim 6:11)

Near the end of this very intimate and personal letter Paul makes his plea with young Timothy. At the risk of oversimplifying this speech, one might compare it to a half-time talk by a wise coach who has been in that position many times. After all, this exhortation is not addressed to a non-believer but to one who has already begun the Christian pilgrimage.

Precisely at that point when most of us are so susceptible to becoming lax and apathetic, Paul says, "Let's get with it. Let's get serious." Paul was suggesting a type of determination when he told Timothy to fight the good fight. He was talking about the good fight of being a worthy disciple of Christ. Discipleshp is not for sissies. It is for persons with drive and daring courage, faith and fearlessness.

What are the qualities of a determined disciple? First, discipleship means taking responsibility for your life. If you are to commit it, you must first claim it. Second, a disciple must understand the importance of the right kind of living. Don't desire to be superficial; just live a life that is right. Third, remember your own witness. We are representatives of Christ. We are disciples. Paul could just as easily be giving us a pep talk during half time—in fact, he was.

April 12

"So let us not grow weary in doing what is right, for we will reap at harvest time, if we do not give up." (Gal 6:9)

Persistence is one of the most important elements in the Christian lifestyle. We do not talk much about persistence as a virtue, but I am convinced that it may be one of the most highly valued of all our virtues. Are there not times for each of us when we must decide to stick to something or just give up? At times it is appropriate to quit, but not every time the going gets tough.

To persist means to continue in the cause, to remain, to endure. Too many Christians grow weary in well-doing too soon and really seem ill-prepared for the grind of the long haul. Some of our problems occur due to our expectations and impatience. In other words, we expect life to be easy and have little patience with it when it does not come that way. A good beginning is great, the big splash is great, the spectacular plunge is exciting, but in the end the battle is won by those with persistence.

According to our verse for today, persistence means keeping on when the cause is worthwhile. Paul adds that in due season we will reap, if we do not lose heart. How many battles for Christ could be won if we simply did not grow weary and lose heart? What really counts in the long run is if, with the help of Christ, we keep on when our prayers seem unheard and life is hard. Persistence means that when we fall, we get up because we believe in what we do.

"For this son of mine was dead and is alive again; he was lost *April 13*
and is found! And they began to celebrate." (Luke 15:24)

A teenager came to his pastor for advice. "I left home," he said, "and did something that will make my dad furious. What shall I do?" The minister said, "Go home and confess your sin to your father, and he will probably forgive you and treat you like a prodigal son." Later the boy reported to the minister, "Well, I told Dad what I did." "And did he kill the fatted calf for you?" asked the minister. "No," said the boy, "but he nearly killed the prodigal son."

Few stories in all of the world's literature are as well-known or as well-loved as the parable of the prodigal son. No portrait of God in any of the world's religions is more winning than this one. In the parable, Jesus was trying to answer the age-old question, "What is God like?" He painted a picture of a father who loves us enough to let us go. We are not created to be robots; we are free to choose our own destiny. Jesus also showed us a father who patiently waits for us to decide to come home.

The prodigal son abused his freedom, but one day he came to his senses and took responsibility for his own situation. The father welcomed him back unconditionally. The parable is a story of what grace is all about. It is about love that is more interested in redemption than judgment. The story is a reflection of the way God patiently waits for each of us, the first time, the second time, or whatever time. "Thank you, God, for your patient love."

"They do all their deeds to be seen by others; for they make *April 14*
their phylacteries broad and their fringes long." (Matt 23:5)

A Sunday School teacher asked, "Johnny, can you tell me who will wear the biggest crown in heaven?" Johnny said, "Sure, the one who has the biggest head." "Not so," Jesus said as he offered some very harsh words for the Pharisees. In fact, he called them frauds. He said, "They love the place of honor at banquets and the best seats in the synagogues, and to be greeted with respect in the marketplaces, and to have people call them rabbi."

In other words, the Pharisees had a bad case of the big head. Jesus called them blind fools because they were so puffed up that they had shut themselves off from the possibility of wisdom and truth penetrating from without. They were so full of themselves that they were unable to hear the truth. Not even God could get through.

Then Jesus laid out the truth for all to hear, including present-day readers of the verse, "The greatest among you will be your servant. All who exalt themselves will be humbled, and all who humble themselves will be exalted."

Where do the words of Jesus leave us? Is there any reflection of us in the lives and practices of the Pharisees? Have we conquered our need to be king of the mountain, or do we still struggle? The challenge of humbling ourselves is not a once-and-for-all experience. Such a challenge confronts us each day of our lives. Let's be alert. The Pharisees may be closer to "home" than we think.

April 15

"I give you a new commandment, that you love one another. Just as I have loved you, you also should love one another. (John 13:34)

I remember singing the song below while on a marriage retreat once. Within these four simple lines is a profound truth. The lines represent the progression from the way most of us interpret love to the meaning Christ gives to the word.

> Love is something we feel.
> Love is something that's true.
> Love is something that's real.
> But most of all, love is something we do.

Indeed love is something we feel. No one would want to remove that dimension of love. A heart that pounds with feeling is an asset to any relationship. Yet, there must be more than just feeling.

True love involves commitment. This is the love that binds people together and implies that giving must outweigh receiving. Love must be genuine and more than just an idea. Love joins people together in relationship. Most importantly, love is something that we do. Feeling and thinking love is where is must begin. If that is the end of it all, we have not come close to the meaning Christ gives to the word. Love, according to Jesus, is a command to act, to do, in love.

"For God so loved the world that he gave his only Son, so that everyone who believes in him may not perish but may have eternal life." (John 3:16)

Why does John 3:16 always seem to be the first Bible verse a child memorizes? Why is it the verse most often quoted? I have a hunch that if a poll were taken as to the first Bible verse that comes to mind, the overwhelming majority of people would select this familiar one. I suppose there are a number of reasons why it is so well-known. First, it is the best summary of the gospel ever stated in one sentence. How better can one sum up the story of the God of our Bible than in these few lines?

We are told that God loves us, that His love for us is great, so great that He would give His best for us. His best was none other than His only son. He gave His son to die for our sinful nature and set everything right for us. By simply accepting the gift of God's love for us through His son, we can have life that has no end, which means we do not have to experience the death that always results from sin.

Through the years we have made religion very complicated, as only humans can do, but the gospel is so simple. Even a child can understand the message of John 3:16. Don't worry about details that do not matter. Memorize the verse. Claim it. Accept it. Let it stay on your mind day and night. You will not find a better statement of what God feels for us, thinks about us, and has done for us.

"Someone asked him, 'Lord, will only a few be saved?' " (Luke 13:23)

Many years ago a man applied to an exclusive club for membership but was denied. The man became a famous comedian. Years later, this same club sent him an entrance form inviting him to join. The comedian wrote back, in a now-famous note, that he would not join any club that would have him as a member.

Our verse for today does not deal with a club but eternity, the key question being our acceptance into the kingdom of God. The text tells us that a man asked if those who are to be saved are few. How does one get in? In Bible times most cities were protected by a wall. Many cities had a night gate. This was a smaller gate within the larger one that was the only entrance into the city at night. Persons who wished to enter had to declare their business first. Jesus declared that entrance into the kingdom of God would be by such a narrow door and that many would not be able to enter.

How can we enter? We don't get in by way of church membership, although that is an honorable thing. We don't make the gate because we learn all the current religious language. Reading all the current religious books will not guarantee anything, either. Passing an entrance exam is not required. Entrance into the Kingdom is a gift of grace from God, a gift purchased by the sacrifice of Christ. Our only hope for making it through the door is by accepting the gift and responding with a life of obedience.

April 18

You will recognize this verse from the experience of Jesus appearing to some disciples on the Emmaus Road. The question has frequently been raised as to why they did not immediately recognize him. After all, he was no stranger to them. Numerous explanations have been given. Some scholars have suggested that the road might have placed the disciples in the westward sun, and their vision was impaired. Others have suggested that it was a matter of expectation. The disciples really did not expect to see Jesus again and naturally assumed him to be someone else. Still others have pointed to the transformed nature of Jesus' resurrected body that might have made him difficult to recognize.

During my seminary days, I heard John Claypool preach a sermon on this text in which he called attention to what has become the most revealing point of Jesus' encounter with the disciples. Claypool pointed out that the moment of recognition came as they invited Jesus in and heard him bless the bread. Just think about it. What a remarkable testimony to the gratitude of Jesus that his blessing of a simple loaf triggered their recognition of him! He never took anything for granted but related all good things to their source, God. Jesus was known for his gratitude. Will anyone associate us today with gratitude? Maybe lots of other possibilities, but probably not gratitude. Could we change that?

April 19

Would you agree that we live in a complicated world? The evidence of life's complications is all around us; much of it is our own doing. We seem to have this need to complicate life even if simplicity is the best way. Consider the pace of our living. Drive down the main thoroughfare of any city at 8:00 A.M. and observe our pace at its best, and return there at 5:00 P.M.

Consider our schedules. We can't even spell simplicity any longer. Our needs and desires require double time to maintain. There is no such thing as a simple business any longer. Before the ink on the letterhead is dry, we merge with a larger and more diversified group. Look at what we have done to religion. No longer is religion just a way of submitting to the will of God, but now it has become a whole complicated set of doctrines and guidelines.

Complexity has become a way of life. But does our faith have to be complicated? The answer is an emphatic "no." Faith is as simple as following the Word of God. What is demanded of us in our daily life? There is very little complication to the divine command to do justice, love kindness, and walk humbly. It could not be simpler. Uncomplicate your life today, and just do right.

"He also told this parable to some who trusted in themselves that   *April 20*
they were righteous and regarded others with contempt." (Luke 18:9)

One of the many things about Jesus that bothered the Pharisees was that he was not afraid to associate with sinners. He would not avoid the people whom the Pharisees totally ignored. Jesus continually shocked the authorities of his day, and he probably would shock the pious sophisticates of today as well. Why did he like sinners so much? Allow me to offer several suggestions.

- Sinners know that they still have room to grow. Jesus had not time to waste on people who thought they already knew it all.
- Sinners do not look down on others. If we are honest about the sin in our life, we realize that we are no better off than anyone else.
- Sinners know they must depend on God. The righteous Pharisees of Jesus' day felt so good about themselves that their dependence was upon themselves.
- There was no one else to love. We are all sinners. None of us are truly righteous.

Fortunately, Jesus likes sinners. How do we know that? Don't forget that he died for sinners. Just think about it. Jesus likes sinners, which includes you and me. I find comfort in that fact.

"He said, 'In a certain city there was a judge who neither feared God or had respect   *April 21*
for people. In that city there was a widow who kept coming to him.' " (Luke 18:2-3a)

Jesus told a story about a certain judge who feared neither God nor man, but a certain widow needed the judge to act in her behalf. At first he ignored her, but she kept coming to him with her request. When he could no longer ignore her, he refused her, but she kept coming back. She was so persistent that finally he relented for fear that she would wear him out. Then Jesus said, "Will not God grant justice to his chosen ones who cry to him day and night?"

Of course God will hear the cries of people and will answer. Jesus was not giving to us a methodology for prayer. He was not saying that if we want something to just keep asking until we wear God down. He was not describing God as an insensitive judge, but wanted us to know that by nature God does hear and care. We are not forsaken. If one who does not fear God nor man will give in to a little widow because she is persistent, will not a loving God hear the prayers of His children?

What is on your mind today? If it is important to you, it is important to God. You say that you have already brought it to God's attention. The parable indicates that you are to try again. God will hear and respond.

April 22

"The kingdom of heaven is like treasure hidden in a field, which someone found and hid; then in his joy he goes and sells all that he has and buys that field." (Matt 13:44)

Some things in life are worth any price. How much would you take for your health? For one of your children? For your good mind, more or less? Many of us do not appreciate the really important things in life until we lose them or are threatened with the possibility of losing them.

Jesus warned us on many occasions of the danger of forgetting the value of the Kingdom. He said that the Kingdom was like a treasure hidden in a field that a man found and covered up. Then in his joy he sold all that he owned and bought the field. The kingdom of heaven is like a merchant in search of fine pearls who, on finding one pearl of great value, sold all he had and bought it. In other words, no matter how much you know or own, if you have missed out on the kingdom of heaven, you have missed out on the one thing in life whose value exceeds all others.

Talk about the Kingdom sounds so "other worldly" or, at best, a little too religious to most people. Remember, though, that anything relating to Jesus also has to do with the Kingdom. He ushered in this kingdom to our midst and encouraged us to give our lives to it. Point to Jesus and you are pointing to the Kingdom.

What is important to you today? Do the life and teachings of Jesus have any influence upon your life? If not, you had better give an honest ear to the verse for today. We're talking pearls here!

April 23

"You do well if you really fulfill the royal law according to the scripture, 'You shall love your neighbor as yourself.' " (Jas 2:8)

As a minister I am frequently in the setting of funerals, much too often. I am always pleased to hear the good things that people say as they remember the one who has just died. Out of respect for the deceased, I seldom hear about the negative traits of that person. In fact, we go out of our way to say the very best, particularly as we encounter family members. Ministers are not immune to the temptation to build people up, however, sometimes to the point that it becomes a little hollow.

At a particular funeral the minister was just going on and on and on about all the good things the deceased had done. During the message one old buddy of the deceased left his seat, walked down to the casket, looked in, and explained that he just wanted to make sure they were talking about the same guy.

It is a sad weakness in us that the thought of a person's death hallows him/her anew to us—as if life were not sacred too. Why do we wait until someone cannot be encouraged by our positive opinions and then tell our thoughts only to a grieving family? We should be concerned to fulfill the royal law of love to grieving families, but families need our affirmation just as much while their loved ones are "alive and well."

"Now if I do what I do not want, it is no longer I that do it, but sin that dwells within me." (Rom 7:20)

Have you ever battled for control of your life? Some of us fight that battle every day, and the chances are good that today will be no different. The discouraging truth, however, is that our main adversary is not someone in our family, or someone at work, or someone who is angry at us. As Pogo once put it: "We have met the enemy, and he is us." A little boy scraped a chair across the kitchen floor and climbed on it to reach the cookie jar on the top shelf. His mother heard the noise and called out, "What are you doing in there?" With his hand in the cookie jar, the child replied, "I'm fighting temptation."

Can there be a more relevant passage of scripture for many of us? The writer John Milton once said, "He who reigns within himself and rules his passions, desires, and fear is more than a king." If so, how can we gain this control? At the risk of oversimplification, consider these suggestions.

- Claim the fact that no one can do it for us. We must claim responsibility for ourselves.
- We must really want to do better. Without some "want to" we are wasting energy.
- We must claim that we cannot do it alone. Paul asked, "Who will rescue me from this body of death?" Then he wrote, "Thanks be to God through Jesus Christ our Lord!"

"I am the Lord your God, who brought you out of the land of Egypt, out of the house of slavery; you shall have no other gods before me." (Exod 20:2-3)

Even though this particular verse is taken from a much larger and very well-known text, it holds the key for understanding all of the other commandments. It deals with the whole issue of where we put God in our lives. A better question might be what gods control our lives. In the text, God essentially said to Moses, "I am the only God. There shall be no other gods." Yet, will that be the case for us today?

Gods may appear in various forms. Possessions may seek to become the controlling force in our lives. In our abundance we have become very insensitive to and unaware of the influence of "things." Some of us may reckon with pride, appearing with many faces. It is healthy to feel good about ourselves, but pride can get in the way of Christ being Lord of our lives. Some of us will encounter pleasure. Like pride, pleasure appears with many faces and can be quite subtle. Some people worship another person—perhaps a sweetheart, a mate, a child, or anyone who steps ahead of God. In other words, almost anything can become a god if we allow. Let's be alert today—alert to gods.

April 26

The exchange that took place between God and Jeremiah on that day long ago sounds so human and so familiar. I do believe that I have heard parts of that conversation in my own life. God approached Jeremiah and broke the news that before he was even born God had chosen him to be a prophet. Jeremiah gave the classical response: "I am only . . ." In this case he said he was only a child. Faced with quite a challenge, Jeremiah felt he was not equal to the task.

At times all of us have been faced with a challenge from God—a task, an opportunity, an obligation, something that made us feel very inadequate even though we also felt it was something we really should do. The way God dealt with Jeremiah is quite instructive for us as well. In effect, God told Jeremiah, "Don't say I'm only . . . any more." That doesn't cut it. Next, God told him, "Just go to the people, and I will tell you what to say." Then God said, "I will go with you." That's it, Jeremiah; that's all you need!

The same is true for us. When we face challenges that we truly believe are given by God, the same advice applies. If we will just be faithful to the task, God will tell us what to do and will be with us in all that we attempt. "Lord, guide us each step, go with us, and that is enough. Amen."

April 27

I am not sure when Psalm 46 became my favorite psalm, but as far back as I can remember, it has been right there on top for me. For one thing, it describes in such vivid terms our world today. Roaring waters and trembling mountains are not daily occurrences, but they certainly represent the kind of unstable world in which we live.

The Psalmist also offers the reassurance that God is still in control of this world. That promise comes as good news to me. At times we need to be reminded of that fact, however. Life can be brutal. We experience grief and watch others experience sudden calamities. There are tornadoes, fires, and suffering. Broken dreams are common.

Behold there is hope. God is dependable through all of life's problems. In a society that declares that we can solve our own problems and urges us to pull ourselves up by our own bootstraps, we need to hear the psalmist declare that God is dependable. God is our shoulder to lean on through all of our difficulties.

So, today you may not hear any roaring waters or feel any mountains tremble, but there will be problems. You can bank on it, but you can also bank on the presence of God as your strength and refuge. "Lord, thank you for being there for us in this noisy world. Amen."

"Abram took his wife Sarai and his brother's son Lot, and all the possessions that they had gathered, . . . and they set forth to go to the land of Canaan." (Gen 12:5)

April 28

Abraham was such an important part of our spiritual heritage. The first time we encounter him in the book of Genesis he was living in southern Mesopotamia. Subsequently his whole clan moved north to Haran, and there the most formative event of his life occurred. He had an encounter with God and was given a most extraordinary promise. God offered Abraham a land and more descendants than the sands of the sea. Through his family all the earth would be blessed. To receive these blessings, Abraham had to do essentially one thing: leave where he was and set out on a journey.

Abraham would learn that God is dynamic and not static. One word would sum up Abraham's experience: "movement." There was to be no settling down with this kind of God. God is always out front, calling one forward. Abraham would also learn that perfection was not a prerequisite for God to begin working with an individual. God was willing to take Abraham where he was, then lead him toward the future. Abraham was a human being, far from perfect.

What can we learn from this spiritual forefather? The same truths apply to our lives. God is still a dynamic God, always calling us forward, always moving us toward a point. We do not have to be perfect to be used of God. Flaws do not make us unusable. We still can claim the promises of God, regardless of our weaknesses. The same God who called Abraham is calling us today. Just listen.

"Do not judge, so that you may not be judged." (Matt 7:1)

April 29

On more than one occasion Jesus cautioned against relating to others with a judgmental spirit. His teachings suggest that being judgmental has practical as well as ethical implications and that we should be easy on judgments. We can all agree with his teachings in principle, but carrying out such a lifestyle is not always so easy.

Jesus implied that we should be easy on judgments because, first of all, we seldom have all of the information we need to make accurate evaluations of another person. All we have is the observation we make from the outside. We seldom have enough information to really know what is going on. Even when people share their lives with us, we still only know what they have chosen to offer. Who really knows of the struggles and battles fought within the lives of those around us? We never truly know the mysteries of another person's life.

We should go easy on others because we are not free of error ourselves. Maybe it is just a characteristic of human nature, but we often require more forgiveness from others and God than we are willing to admit. We forget that we constantly stand in the position of being judged and that we are much quicker to ask for mercy than to offer it. Today, give evidence of God's grace by offering grace.

April 30

"My flesh and my heart may fail, but God is the strength of my heart and my portion forever." (Ps 73:26)

In recent years I have come to a point of appreciation of this verse, probably because I now realize that with the accumulation of years come more failures. The only way to avoid failure is to avoid life, and that does not seem like much of an option. I like what the famous inventor said: "All you have to do to be an inventor is to know how to fail intelligently. The only time you ever succeed when you are an inventor is the last time you try."

Failure can often be very painful, even embarrassing. At the time we can see little but the disappointment. Yet, the adjustments that come from our failures are precisely what bring about growth in our lives. Failures are opportunities in disguise if we have the courage to see them. If we are honest, we will admit that we tend to learn more from our failures than from our successes. New doors are opened to us that would otherwise remain closed. At least, we have the option.

We can also opt to pull in and refuse to try again. Growth is not guaranteed; it comes only when our attitude is characterized by courage and openness. When God is our partner, failure is never the end. It can even be the basis of a new beginning. Today may be a new beginning for you. That new beginning may come through some type of failure.

May 1

"A time to plant, and a time to pluck up what is planted." (Eccl 3:2b)

Spring fever seems to have moved in and done its damage, but now is on the down side. With summer just around the corner, everyone begins to think of trips, vacations, and other outings. After all, winter has been tough, and the time has come to stretch and move around. Even though the schedule during winter is busy enough, it tends to pick up even more with spring and summer. We realize that we must make plans now for much of what we will be doing in the months to come.

Right now, before things get too hectic, make some commitments to family time. I'm talking about more than just a one-shot, big-time trip together. Plan for some regular times together when activities are "low-keyed" and relaxed and you can just be "family." For some reason when we plan time together as a family, we feel like we have to structure every minute with some kind of action. Certainly every family needs to have experiences of doing things and going places together, but just as important are times of doing nothing together. Unstructured time does not necessarily equal boredom. We need time to just be together, to share, actually get to know each other, and—who knows—do the unheard: just talk!

"Give us this day our daily bread." (Matt 6:11) May 2

This particular petition from the Lord's Prayer has as much to do with patience and trust as it does the fulfilling of our bodily needs. "This day" is not an accident. The petition is not for this year's bread but this day's bread. In all honesty, I would much rather have an entire year's bread than just one day's amount, which extends me into a realm of trust.

One of the real secrets to life is learning how to settle down to the task before us and concentrate on the issue at hand. Bread for the year would be nice, but bread for the day is really all we need. Learning to trust in the source of the bread may be the toughest challenge of all. Talking trust is easy; living by it is something else. Today you may discover bread for the year. Then again, you may be given today's portion only. Enjoy it; it is enough for now.

"And the life I now live in the flesh I live by faith in the Son of God." (Gal 2:20b) May 3

Living by faith is not a trick. It is a discipline and requires some effort. Many people assume that the Christian faith frees us from perplexity. That is not the case. Instead as Christians, we are given the ability to live meaningfully in the midst of unanswered questions and unsolved problems. Our faith does not solve all of our problems, but its gives us a whole new perspective. There will always be times when we will not know the answers, but we are given strength and guidance to live with the questions and to move forward. In God's wisdom we are given the illumination necessary for those particular days.

Living by faith means walking in the light that we have. It means trusting in the goodness and wisdom of God that when we need more direction, we will be granted it. There is so much that we do not know and maybe will never know. Do we remain frozen until all our questions are answered and our path is fully illuminated? If we do, we will never move forward. Then, how is it done? It is called "walking by faith." Try it. You'll be surprised.

"Why do you call me 'Lord, Lord,' and do not do what I tell you?" (Luke 6:46) May 4

Recently I was interrupted in my study by my secretary who said that a transient had appeared at the church door, needing help. I first thought that I did not need the interruption. I was already having trouble producing Sunday's sermon, and I was more than just a little frustrated. I walked to the door and met the man. His need was legitimate. What he needed could be provided but would require a little time on my part. Without a lot of joy, I proceeded to work something out and managed to get the man on his way. I found pleasure in that he really was in need and did not represent the usual scam. I returned to my study and found a whole new burst of energy. I don't know where it came from, but I felt good about the moment and appreciated the opportunity to offer help to people. The sermon fell into place.

The gospel must be proclaimed, but at times it is to be done. Or in the words of the Nike commercial: "Just do it." The slogan implies that something is to be gained from just getting on with it. I don't want to relegate too much wisdom to a commercial, but I am wondering if there is not a message in it for our walk of faith. We are to be disciples. Discipleship certainly involves the head and brain, but it also employs the feet. To use Nike's phrase, "Just do it."

May 5

"A poor widow came and put in two small copper coins, which are worth a penny." (Mark 12:42)

Two dimensions of this story impress me: the widow's spirit and the fact that Jesus made such a big deal about her actions. He really held her up as an example. The widow dropped into the treasury two copper coins, the least valuable of Jewish money in circulation at that time. Jesus was so impressed by her spirit that he called for the disciples and said in effect, "You see that poor widow? She has given more than any of the others; for the others who have given have more than enough, but she with less than enough has given all that she had to live on."

Jesus lifted the widow up as a model of what being truly thankful to God really means. Her quiet gesture of sacrifice was an example of the joy God experiences when we give out of a spirit of gratitude. She did not give out of obligation; she was too poor to be obligated to give. Her gift was totally voluntary.

Today we will have opportunities to give. It may be our time, money, energy, or something important to us. Our gift will not be copper coins nor necessarily given in a temple. The question is not only if we will give, but if we will give out of a spirit of gratitude rather than obligation. The widow apparently found pleasure in doing so. We might find the same.

May 6

"Be careful then how you live, not as unwise people but as wise, making the most of the time, because the days are evil." (Eph 5:15-16)

The last part of this verse has always caught my ear. "Wise men make the most of the time." You cannot read these words of Paul without sensing his urgency about the work he was doing as an ambassador of Christ. He was strongly suggesting that the Ephesians look carefully at what they were doing. We also have much to do, and time is important. Unfortunately, too many of us have no sense of urgency in regard to our work for the Kingdom. After all, this work has been going on for a long time. Why get in a rush? We have an eternity to get the job done. On the other hand, we will live in a state of hurry for almost everything else in life. Matters of faith are different.

One of the greatest enemies of the Christian faith is apathy, the feeling of being lukewarm about our commitment and task. Paul was calling the believers at Ephesus to be alive to the moment and vital to the calling they had received. How invigorating to be committed to something for which you feel a sense of enthusiasm and urgency! Is there enthusiasm in your Christian walk? Do the matters of your faith have a sense of urgency about them? Paul would tell each of us today to be careful as we walk and to walk as a wise person and make the very most of our time. No sirens are blowing, but time is flying.

"Finally, be strong in the Lord and in the strength of his power." (Eph 6:10) *May 7*

I was watching a particular sports event recently and was impressed with the enthusiasm and energy with which the players entered the game. One of the players described to the sportscaster what the team members did in the final minutes before the game. He said they began chanting, cheering, clapping, and making all kinds of noise, and that the enthusiasm became almost uncontrollable. He said they were so fired up that they could just about do anything.

A lot of mornings I need some of that enthusiasm. "Game time" is upon me, and I am anything but fired up for what lies ahead. If I knew that chanting, cheering, and clapping would get me ready, I might try them; but I really don't think that is the answer. There must be a better way.

The kind of spiritual strength that we need comes from the opposite of making noise. Real strength for each day's game comes from those brief, quiet moments that fill us with the kind of energy that will get us through to the final whistle. The unfortunate truth is that most of us ignore that kind of pre-game plan in lieu of things that press us and demand from us. Discovering the power of God's presence comes from a pep talk, but it is a very quiet one.

I saw a phrase that said, "Seven days without a quiet time could make one weak." True indeed. Are you regularly making allowance in your schedule for a quiet time? Game time is just ahead.

"I have other sheep that do not belong to this fold. I must bring them also, *May 8*
and they will listen to my voice. So there will be one flock." (John 10:16)

This particular verse of our Lord has always caused me to scratch my head and even moreso to open my eyes. One of the real dangers we all face is the risk of tunnel vision. We see things one way to the point that we think that is the only way. Although in a few circumstances, our viewpoint may very well be the only way, in most cases the options are hidden from our superficial view. We need to be sensitive to the danger of a growing narrow-mindedness, one that develops into the condition of thinking that we possess, or our group possesses, all the wisdom about God or from God.

When I walk into the evening and look at the night sky, I am overwhelmed by how small I am and how limited is my perspective. From any point in my yard my perspective is different. Regardless of how many times I pause and look, I am seeing only a tiny fraction of what is out there. I try to remember this truth when I am expounding on what I know is the only way that something is to be. Most of the time, however, like the stars, the possibilities are quite open—just as the opinions and ways of thinking of people are limitless.

May 9 "Jesus turned about in the crowd and said, 'Who touched my clothes?' " (Mark 5:30b)

There are many consequences of our hurried lifestyle, one of which is the insensitivity that results from our preoccupation. When I observe Jesus in the New Testament, many dynamics strike me. For one, he maintained amazing sensitivity to the needs of people around him. Even when he was pressed from every side and the demands of people lay on his shoulders, he never lost his awareness of the most simple needs of persons he encountered. Can we say the same?

One of life's constant challenges is to not only maintain but to expand our awareness and sensitivity to those around us. Life can easily close in on us until our world contains only our own senses. In his ministry, Jesus continually challenged people to reach out to enter the lives of others with concern and caring. The verse for today is but a brief moment in a busy day of our Lord. The crowds were pushing and pressing him. He had every right to close in and protect himself. Yet, in the midst of noises and people, he was aware that someone in need touched him. I find that most remarkable!

Jesus provides for us a model of sensitivity as we go through this day. Demands will be all around us. Will we close in and forget those who touch us, or will we follow the clear example of the one who sets the pace?

May 10 "But this command I gave them, 'Obey my voice, and I will be your God, and you shall be my people.' " (Jer 7:23a)

In one sense God does not have to have our permission to be God. Yet, in another sense, to function as the divine, God must be granted that opporutnity by each of us as individuals. We are free creatures, and a part of that freedom is the right to refuse or reject God. Otherwise, we would not be creatures of free choice. How do we allow God to function as our God? What must we do? The verse for today gives us at least one way, one of the most important ways. We allow God to be God by simple obedience. Sounds simple, and it is.

66

Pray that God will give you what scripture calls "an honest and good heart," or "a perfect heart"; and without waiting, begin at once to obey God with the best heart you have. Any obedience is better than none. Occasionally in worship, we use the phrase, "Seek His face." The way we seek God's face in the world outside the walls of worship is by way of obedience. To obey God is to approach God. Every act of obedience brings the divine closer. That which so often hides from us is nothing less than our own imperfect heart. God wants to be our God today. The question before us is whether we will allow that.

"That which is, already has been; that which is to be,

already is; and God seeks out what has gone by." (Eccl 3:15)

May 11

Periodically we have a partial eclipse of the moon. I remember several years ago when there was a total eclipse. It occurred in the early hours of a Tuesday morning over a period of several hours. I remember the meteorologist saying that the last time this phenomenon accurred was in 1756. On that morning we set our alarm clocks and watched the entire show. I was intrigued that this particular event could occur only about every two hundred years.

While we were watching the darkness cover the moon, I could not help but think of all that has happened since the last total moon eclipse. Just think of the advances made during that time. We can travel faster than sound. People fly back and forth to the moon. A number of serious diseases have not only been discovered, but cures have been found. In many ways we have really progressed; yet, in some other ways, progress is not quite so obvious.

People still hate each other enough to commit murder. War is still our favorite past time. The world is no closer to a kindred spirit than it was in 1756. Poverty flourishes. Hunger continues as a fatal disease. People still struggle for hope that carries them beyond the present. It has been 200 years since that last eclipse. A lot has happened since that time. Then again, a lot is still the same.

"The exhorter, in exhortation; the giver, in generosity; the leader,

in diligence; the compassionate, in cheerfulness." (Rom 12:8)

May 12

The Bible never gives us a choice of separating the stewardship of our lives from our faith. By stewardship I am referring to much more than just the tithing of our financial resources, although that is a pretty good place to begin. Our attitude about stewardship finds expression in every dimension of our lives. The New Testament closely links giving and mercy to cheer. "The Lord loves a cheerful giver." With so many of us, however, giving fills us with a glee like a trip to the dentist, and extracting a coin becomes an operation like extracting a tooth without Novocain. Paul realized the need to stress a spirit of cheerfulness, without which there is no generosity.

A very important issue in regard to our giving is not just "how much" we give, but "how" we give. We can easily give an amount that is honorable but give in a spirit that reduces the joy our Lord experiences in our efforts. The cheerfulness that should go with mercy is not forced. It is unconscious and should flow out of an awareness that we give freely because we have received freely. We are neither heroes nor martyrs when we exercise good stewardship. Today might be just the right day to examine not just the "how much" but the "how" of our stewardship.

May 13

"You have made known to me the path of life; you will fill me with joy in your presence." (Ps 16:11, NIV)

The word "known" in this verse catches my attention. The psalmist said that the Lord has made certain things known about the path of life. Do you realize how important it is to make things known, not only in our relationship with God but with one another? More and more I encounter in families a rapidly spreading disease called the "mind-readers syndrome." By the way, don't check your medical dictionary; the syndrome is not included yet, though it may be before long.

The "mind-readers syndrome" creates a real problem. You see, it is the belief that if someone really cares about me, that person will know what I need without my ever telling him/her. As human beings we all share much in common but, as individuals, much about us is unique and distinctive. If we are to be fulfilled as persons, some very personal and well-defined needs must be met.

The problem comes when we depend on some significant person to meet a specific need without that person knowing it exists. We assume that if someone really loves us, he or she will give us what we need. I am not speaking of just material things but of essentials such as a touch, attention, and time—just to mention a few. If we were instructed by our Lord to ask for what we need, why should we assume that those closest to us should be different?

May 14

"Husbands, in the same way, show consideration for your wives in your life together." (1 Pet 3:7a)

I have a special word to married couples today. Back in the day when you decided to marry, you had some expectations of yourself and your spouse. These role expectations have been a very important influence on your marriage. Frequently partners bring into marriage differing expectations that can cause not only misunderstanding but occasionally a complete lack of understanding.

Because of the differential conditioning given male and female children, men and women have always had a difficult time understanding each other's behavior, and that conditioning differs from home to home. It is not unusual for a young man to say, "I don't understand the woman I married.

She expects me to do things for her that she could do for herself, and sometimes she expects me to do things that she has not even told me about."

Lack of understanding is by no means limited to men. A young woman may say, "I don't understand the man I married. He went out and bought a brand new car when we could hardly pay for the one we already had." This lack of understanding between men and women is a long-standing problem. Differing role expectations account for so many problems in the family. What can be done? To put it simply, you must be willing to talk. In other words, take out the secrecy.

"Those who are greedy for unjust gain make trouble for their households, but those who hate bribes will live." (Prov 15:27)

May 15

We face many crises as a country. One crisis hangs over us like a dark cloud, however. It should concern us all. In our country, everything sits on a foundation. Institutions, government, finances, business, and children depend on one groundwork: the family unit. In fact, I believe that "as the family goes, so goes the country." When families are strong and stable, husbands and wives are committed, children are raised in a healthy atmosphere, persons are motivated for a steady job, people pay taxes, money is borrowed to buy houses, and automobiles are bought and actually paid for. Our way of life depends on the family unit.

On the surface, at least, it appears that the family unit is in trouble. People are not in agreement about its value or future. It has been called everything from the backbone of civilization to an archaic institution that no longer has a place in our world. Yet, the story of broken homes continues to show its appalling increase. Our way of life depends upon the stability of the family unit. It is by far the most critical issue facing us as a country, and we had better get concerned. Or will we treat it like most other problems and put our heads in the sand with hopes that it will go away? Unfortunately, this problem is far too complex for that simple solution. Pray today for the families all around you. They need it.

"If one gives answer before hearing, it is folly and shame." (Prov 18:13)

May 16

Leadership is the key to success in any business or profession or even at home. When one begins to define leadership, however, it becomes a very illusive quality. Obviously, certain qualities are essential to a competent leader. A list would include such attributes as physical and nervous energy, a sense of purpose and direction, affection, integrity, decisiveness, and many others. Paramount in this list is the ability to give people what they need and want. How do you know what people need? By listening. Listening not only provides information and understanding but also indicates to people that one is concerned.

During the Bolshevik takeover in Russia, the revolutionary leader became ill and later died. Two persons, each representing a different approach to the task, contended for the position. One was a talker; the other was a listener. The talker was Tron Trotsky, an orator and organizer. Stalin was just the opposite of Trotsky. While Trotsky harangued the huge gatherings of people, Stalin sat and listened—his tongue still and his mind at work. Stalin won. I'm not making a model of Stalin, but we might learn something from him. Listening is an art and a key to success.

May 17

"I am the one who searches minds and hearts, and I will give to each of you as your works deserve." (Rev 2:23b)

According to this verse, the Lord searches our minds. (For some of us, that should not take long!) God gave us our minds to use, but often we bring shame to God by letting someone else do our thinking. One of our biggest dilemmas is allowing ourselves to be gullible to fads, ads, and gimmicks. Certainly, we should listen to and take advantage of good advice, but we ought to run it through our own mental computer a few times before we act. Our minds were given to use on a regular basis.

A lazy mind can be a source of embarrassment. For example, I enjoy working on automobiles, especially some old ones that I have. One car in particular has a big engine, so large that I can hardly afford to drive it. Since everything relating to cars is advertised as saving gas, I set out with the goal of increasing my gas mileage. I bought tires that were supposed to give me 10 percent more mileage. An engine tune-up was intended to increase mileage by 15 percent. The new oil I bought was guaranteed to add 5 percent more mileage. I got rid of unnecessary weight. I even thought about making my family walk beside the car to lessen the weight. Tire pressure was right. I bought correct air filters and even drove 55 m.p.h. The American market was guiding me. I figured my mileage should have been around 85 miles per gallon. I discovered that I had increased my mileage by 1.89 miles per gallon. In the meantime, I need to remember that my mind is a gift from God and that I should use it more than I do. Time will tell.

May 18

"You will be my witnesses in Jerusalem, in all Judea and Samaria, and to the ends of the earth." (Acts 1:8b)

We have a way of relegating this verse to another group in another place. After all, Jesus was talking to his disciples who were present with him on a day long ago. Or was he? Actually, he was talking to all of us, in this day and this time. He left us a big job, as big as the whole world—"to the end of the earth." If we are concerned with proclaiming the gospel, it is usually quite a provincial understanding of the gospel. In other words, we had just as soon not go out of our comfort zone with it. The verse implies that we are to look up and out, beyond our normal circles.

A schoolboy was given a problem to solve that required the use of a compass. He had lost his compass, so he went to his teacher's desk to borrow hers. Because he was a little anxious, he could not remember the name of the instrument. He said to her, "May I take your circumference?"

The question in that setting may have been a little embarrassing, but it is an appropriate question for us. What is our circumference? How large a circuit do we travel? What is the measure of our interest outside our backyard? No doubt, the place to begin is by having an interest in sharing the gospel. But does that interest take us beyond our own backyard? Remember, Jesus said "to the end of the earth." That command is for us today.

"A soft answer turns away wrath, but a harsh word stirs up anger." (Prov 15:1) *May 19*

Recently a friend sent me a copy of a quote he found in a professional journal. The quote, by Sir Harold George Nicholson (1886–1968), read: "The great secret of a successful marriage is to treat all disasters as incidents and more of the incidents as disasters." The more I think about this quote, the more convinced I am of its wisdom, not only for our marriages but for friendships and even work-related relationships.

No doubt, in the hustle and bustle of living, we are guilty of making nuclear explosions out of firecracker incidents. Little things that really should make no difference become magnified to the point that relationships are dangerously threatened. Because of pressures and the pace of our modern routine, most of us seem to be primed for the big explosion. The marriage relationship is the most vulnerable of all places for it to occur.

This is not to say that big problems don't occasionally arise. Most of our skirmishes are over relatively small problems, however. Mr. Nicholson's words should remind us that there is a real need to back off and observe ourselves when we start updating our arsenals for a fight. We need to make certain that the issue really is important enough to get out the big guns. If we are really honest and alert, we will discover that most of the seeming disasters are really incidents. The goal should be to keep the incidents as incidents.

"Let the wise hear and gain in learning, and the discerning acquire skill." (Prov 1:5) *May 20*

Recently my wife and I spent the day in Beaufort, South Carolina. This beautiful town is one of our favorite places. We usually look at a few antiques and then get on with the important activity: eating seafood. On that trip we ate at a really nice place on Lady's Island. The restaurant overlooked the marsh, and we had a ringside seat to the going and coming of the tide. We were there just at the right time to watch the tide reach the low point.

If you ever watch the tide go out into the marsh, you will see all kinds of things that are hidden when the tide is high. Shell banks and other natural obstructions become obvious, all of which would be very hazardous to a boater. When the tide is in, they lie just below the surface. To assume the water is clear and free could spell disaster. A wise man I once met in Charleston told me that you should always learn the marsh at low tide. This is when you can safely follow the channel and know where the deadly shell banks lie hidden. High water can be very misleading.

What is true of the marsh is also true of life. Life is made up of highs and lows. The highs make everything seem easy and clear, but beneath the surface are a lot of sharp and deadly obstructions that can spell disaster. None of us like the lows but, if we are careful and wise, we can learn where the real channels are. Life is not always high tide. Sometimes there are lows. Let's not forget what we learn in life's low moments.

May 21

"And this is the judgment, that the light has come into the world, and people loved darkness rather than light because their deeds were evil." (John 3:19)

Each Gospel in the New Testament has its own unique way of describing the entrance of Christ into this world. Matthew, Mark, and Luke have their very special and lovely way of sharing the role of Christ. John compares the appearance of Jesus in terms of light in the darkness. It is a very beautiful but descriptive way of pointing to the one who entered a world that was in a state of darkness.

Recently in a children's sermon in my church, I turned out the lights for a moment and then asked the children to describe their feelings. Their answers were predictable. Some of them mentioned loneliness. Others were afraid. Some said they could not see very well. Darkness can be a very frightening experience to both children and adults. The people of Jesus' day were in darkness. They were afraid, lonely, and confused. But according to John, with the Christ event light was brought into the darkness.

An artist painted a picture of dawn during the winter: the trees heavily covered with snow and a dark dreary house, lonely and desolate in the midst of a storm. It was a sad picture. Then with a quick stroke of yellow oils, the artist put a light in one window. The entire scene was transformed into a vision of comfort and cheer. Christ brought just such a light into our dark world. John said that this man named Jesus was the light that comes into our world and to our lives. Light is still needed for our darkness today—this day.

May 22

"We do see Jesus, who for a little while was made lower than the angerls." (Heb 2:9a)

Hebrews offers a solution to a very real dilemma: our limited understanding of so much that happens around us every day. Quite frankly, many things do not make sense. Many of us have the mistaken impression that a commitment of faith answers all of life's difficult questions. Look through the eyes of faith and we can see forever, so we may think. The truth is that even the strongest of believers must live with perplexity.

We want answers, and usually we want them right now. The writer of Hebrews acknowledged that we do not see everything, which is hard for many Christians to accept or to admit. We do not understand all mystery. We do not know why goodness often goes unrewarded and evil seems to do so well. If our eyes must see answers to life's greatest mysteries, then we will find little satisfaction in our living.

The writer offers the best alternative to complete understanding: simply keep your eyes on the one who understands all mysteries, for whom all questions have answers. We need direction and understanding in life. We cannot depend upon ourselves; we are too limited. We are to focus upon our Lord for our next step, knowing that he will undergird us every step along the way.

"The beginning of wisdom is this: Get wisdom,

and whatever else you get, get insight." (Prov 4:7)

May 23

If you could make a list of things that for some strange and mysterious reason could be granted, what would be on that list? To imagine that kind of possibility causes my mind to explode with requests that could change my life immediately. I would quickly list certain things among those guaranteed gifts. I would want to be out of debt. I would request good health for me and my family. As a preacher I would like every other Sunday off and no more church conferences. I would ask for future good mates for my children. Yet, in all honesty, would a request for wisdom be on my list? When Solomon approached God, his primary request was for wisdom. It certainly ought to be on my list, maybe even on the top, and it needs to be divine wisdom.

In a world that is fear-ridden, frustrated, and seeking answers, most of all we need the divine wisdom to know that life is possible only if it is built on spiritual wisdom. What our world needs most is not cheaper gasoline, more food, or more advanced technology. We need wisdom that is beyond our own. Today, as you pray, think about all the things that might be on a list of guaranteed gifts for you. Would wisdom be on that list, especially divine wisdom? If it isn't, it should be. Take a minute and do some rearranging of your list. Slip wisdom to the top.

"So that your days and the days of your children may be multiplied in

the land that the Lord swore to your ancestors to give them." (Deut 11:21a)

May 24

Recently someone referred to the television as the largest educator in America. I passed the statement off at first as a benign comment. Yet, if that statement is true, do you realize what is being taught?

Is the education our children are receiving from the magic tube a source of encouragement toward positive Judeo-Christian values?

Just think about what our children are exposed to night and day. Because of my work I am occasionally going in and out of homes during the day. I cannot count the times that I find young children glued to the television watching the "soaps." This is not a campaign agains the "soaps"; but let's face the fact that they give children a deformed image of marriage and family life. These programs are not harmless entertainment. They are teaching all of us that adultery, non-commitment, and dishonesty are acceptable simply because everybody does this.

While our family members are not great television watchers, at times we are all together around the same programs. It has become almost a joke in our home that when some less-than-decent scene comes on the television, we say to any younger members, "Close your eyes, or go brush your teeth." The way programs are trending, kids will brush all the enamel off their teeth! But, the real question is: If certain programs are unfit for children, why are they okay for us?

May 25   "Do you not know that in a race the runners all compete?" (1 Cor 9:24a)

If you've ever had any experience in track and field events, you know that a well-executed race has several important components. Preparation, a good start, concentration, and a good finish are just a few. As important as good starts may be, a good finish is even more important. Many races are won or lost in the last stretch before the finish line. One of the challenges that a runner faces is the temptation to lose "heart" and interest as fatigue becomes a reality. Questions and doubts flood the mind. One begins to ask if the race is worth the pain. Then the finish line comes into view, and the body mysteriously explodes with energy!

We are all running a race as we move into the future. Yet, I must be honest and admit that the finish could still be far ahead and we are far from the end. The end is in sight, however, and we already know how the race will end. Remember that a track meet is made up of many races, and you win a track meet by running every race as if it were the only one. As you run, don't let questions and doubts flood your mind. Concentrate, run hard, and feel the exhilaration of the moment. What God has called you to do today, do well. It is a small race in a larger track meet. Don't despair. The end is in sight, and the ribbon already has your name on it.

May 26   "You shall love your neighbor as yourself." (Matt 19:19b)

Holy Scripture reports very clearly that Jesus meant we should love others as ourselves. I can handle this command with some degree of success on one condition: that I be allowed to choose the person I classify as my neighbor. Yet, we know the truth. What is meant by our neighbor we cannot doubt;

it is everyone with whom we come into contact. Based on the assumption that most of us are not homebound, that opens up the range of possibilities to a significant number of people.

First, our neighbor is literally anyone who is next to us in our own family and household: husband, wife, parent, brother, sister, and so on. Then our neighbor is one who is close to us in our neighborhood, in our town, in our church, or on our street. With all of these, true charity begins. To love and be kind to these is the very beginning of all true religion. Our neighbor is also anyone who is thrown across our path by the changes and chances of life—he or she whom we have means of helping, the stranger, the deserted friend, even that person that we really don't like.

"Woe to you, scribes and Pharisees, hypocrites! For you **clean the outside of the cup and of the plate." (Matt 23:25)**

May 27

All of us have had the experience of trying to avoid a person with whom we feel some sense of discomfort. It may be someone with whom we have had a misunderstanding or an argument in the past. Possibly something embarassing has happened, and we don't want to be reminded of it. As a result, we go to all kinds of trouble to avoid this person. We will arrange our schedule, plan our activities, and alter our social life just so that we will not have to deal with this person who makes us feel uncomfortable. Then there are times when avoidance is impossible, and we are thrown together.

Many of us will go to great extremes to avoid one particular person. We are not really sure what is going on deep inside this person. Even understanding what makes this one tick is not easy. We try our best to structure our time and keep our world busy enough to avoid him or her. Keeping ourselves with other people at all times can protect us from encountering this person. Heaven forbid that we should be caught off guard! What would we discover? Would our worst fears be confirmed? Or would we discover that this person is not so bad after all? Could we finally feel comfortable? Could we save ourselves a lot of trouble? Who is this one we try to avoid? You guessed it; this person is our own self!

"And the doors of the house where the disciples had **met were locked for fear of the Jews." (John 20:19a)**

May 28

On the Sunday evening after our Lord's resurrection, the disciples were hiding behind locked doors. No one could blame them for their caution because there was ample reason to be fearful of the Jews and other authorities. All seemed lost. Their leader was dead. Their hopes were shattered. Their belief in a bright future was destroyed much faster than it had been created. Their discouragement and frustration were extreme. Then the scripture indicates that "Jesus stood in the midst." He showed them his hands and side. The disciples were filled with surprise. What seemed like the end suddenly became the beginning. An experience of tragedy became the fabric of a new beginning. We can hardly imagine how much the disciples needed that new beginning.

Is there a need for a new beginning in your life? From time to time we all need new beginnings, and some of those times are more intense than others. Something may be going on in your life that causes you to raise serious questions about the future. At one time or another we will all stand where the disciples were on that particular Sunday. All has gone wrong; we feel that all is lost. Then, invariably, one stands before us, offering us peace and saying, "It's going to be okay. Just hang on. All is well."

May 29

"Giving thanks to God the Father at all times and for everything in the name of our Lord Jesus Christ." (Eph 5:20)

Paul offered these words long ago when he was under less-than-perfect circumstances. Nevertheless, he said that we are to give thanks for all things unto God. To do so, at best, is a difficult challenge. Neither is thankfulness our natural tendency. Late in the 1800s, Orville Dewey expressed the sentiments of Paul:

Notwithstanding all the pain and weariness and anxiety and sorrow that necessarily enter into life, and the inward errings that are worse than all, I would end my record with a devout thanksgiving to the great author of my being.

Expressing "a thanksgiving for mercies," or the benefits of blessings that are peculiar to myself or my friends, is somewhat easier. The task is considerably more difficult to be grateful for all that belongs to my life, for joy and sorrow, for health and sickness, for success and disappointment, for virtue and for temptation, for life and death. Great wisdom must be found in Paul's words. Translating those words into daily life is a real need for us, not the least of which was his exhortation to give thanks always for all things.

May 30

"Pointing to his disciples, he said, 'Here are my mother and my brothers.' " (Matt 12:49)

The celebration of Memorial Day is a good occasion. Usually a few extra activities give people a reason to come together. The end of spring and the beginning of summer, the recognition of those who have made our way of life possible, and the celebration of sacrifice give a certain bond during this time of year.

This season of the year always causes me to think of community. Life is lived in the context of community. The interrelatedness of humankind cannot be ignored. Is that not what Memorial Day is all about, the recognition of sacrifices made on our behalf? The essence of community is that we do not experience life alone. What we do influences one another. Community is the opponent of isolation. Individual freedom is our right but is never to be lived out in isolation. My freedom has been bought by those who invested their lives in community.

As imperfect as our community may be, it is so much better than being alone. During this Memorial Day season, I am especially grateful for community. I am better off because of it. I think that is what Jesus had in mind when he was speaking to a crowd on a day when his family approached him. He pointed to his disciples and said, "Here are my mother and brothers." Life is bigger than just our own lives. In community we make life either better or worse for each other.

"No one has greater love than this, to lay down one's life for one's friends." (John 15:13)

May 31

We can very easily lose sight of the purpose for special holidays. Memorial Day should be one of the most important days on our calendar. For too many of us, however, the day is little more than the official beginning of summer. The day represents far more. It is a time when we pause and recognize those who have made our freedom possible.

As I write this page, I do so with the assurance that it will essentially be printed as written. Granted, my editor will play with it and make some life-threatening grammatical changes, but basically it comes out as I write it. No one will put me in jail for what I write and say. You too have a right to respond in like manner to what is written and said without fear.

Freedom of speech is only one facet of freedom, one of the many we take for granted. Most of us have never known anything but freedom and assume this is the way everybody lives. Not so. It comes with a high price. Memorial Day should cause us to stop and remember all those who have made our way of life a possibility, those who paid for it with their lives. As we pray today, let's thank God for sacrifices made for us.

"Trust in the Lord and do good; so you will live in the land and enjoy security." (Ps 37:3) *June 1*

Trusting in the Lord and doing good go hand in hand. Trusting is so easy to talk about, and yet living it out in the daily world is not quite so easy. If we could somehow say with the virgin Mary and mean it in the same spirit, "Behold the handmaid of the Lord," we would essentially be saying to God, "What would you have me do?"

Although yesterday we simply did not have enough light to approach the task, today the light seems to come from somewhere. When we bow our souls before God in total submission, God's hand will sustain us. We will find ourselves smiling at yesterday's fear as we discover strength and wisdom for today's challenge.

An eighteenth-century poet, Mary Frances Butts, offered these insightful words:

> Build a little fence of trust around today;
> Fill the space with loving works and therein stay;
> Look not through the sheltering bars upon tomorrow,
> God will help thee bear what comes, of joy or sorrow.

June 2

"Great is our Lord and abundant in power." (Ps 147:5a)

One morning several years ago I was determined to get a few things done in my yard before I put on my "uniform" and made my way to the office. The morning was beautiful, the air was cool, birds were singing, and the lawn sprinkler was doing its job with a nice rhythm. The moment was right for genuine worship of the creator. To be honest, though, I was so caught up in all that I had to do during the day that I was giving little inspirational thought to anything. I already knew of several problems that I had to face when I arrived at the church. At that moment a child became my teacher.

Our next door neighbors had three beautiful little girls, two of whom were identical twins. They were preschool age and loved to play outside. One of the twins, Rebecca I think, was out early. Unaware that anyone was around, she began singing as if the civic center were her audience. In typical childlike fashion, she made up her song. She might have heard something like it, but it was a genuine homemade version. The tune varied, but the words never changed. With great feeling she sang over and over, "My Lord, my Lord, my Lord." Her voice was so full of confidence that I stopped what I was doing and sat on the hood of my car and just listened. She continued, "My Lord, my Lord, my Lord." No worries or anxieties were in her voice. I turned off the sprinkler, put on my "uniform" and headed to the office, aware that I had been taught a lesson by one wiser than I.

June 3

"I have fought the good fight, I have finished the race, I have kept the faith." (2 Tim 4:7)

Scholars agree that Paul's letter to Timothy was one of his last letters and was written from prison. The purpose was to encourage Timothy and give him support during difficult days. Paul's words also address our own times. When Paul spoke about having fought the good fight and having kept the faith, he knew well the struggles of life. Remember first that he referred to life as a battle. Certainly life is filled with battles, some within us and others without. Possibly the greatest ones are those within. Paul then referred to life as a race. The type of race he was referrring to was not a quick sprint that requires a sudden burst; it was more like a marathon that requires endurance.

Most of all, the words of Paul remind us to keep the faith. He was able to fight the good fight and finish the race because he kept the faith. In his personal faith he found resources to face whatever and come out a winner. The good news of Paul's life is that we too can fight the good fight and finish the race if we only keep the faith.

"If the Lord had not been my help, my soul would
soon have lived in the land of silence." (Ps 94:17)

June 4

Another kind of silence is to be desired other than just the absence of noise. We all desire those moments of quietness, those sweet moments when we can separate ourselves from a loud world. The silence I am thinking of is a matter of personal discipline, restraining the imagination, not permitting it to work overtime on what we have heard or said, not indulging on the unnecessary "what ifs" of life.

Be sure that you have made no small progress in your spiritual life when you can control your imagination, fixing your mind on the duties actually existing, to the exclusion of the crowds of thoughts that constantly sweep across the mind. No doubt, you cannot prevent those thoughts from arising, but you can prevent yourself from dwelling on them. You can put them aside and check the self-complacency that feeds such thoughts. By the practice of such control of your thoughts, you will attain that spirit of inward silence that draws the soul in a close communion with God.

"A time to throw away stones, and a time to gather stones together." (Eccl 3:5a)

June 5

Most of us discovered long ago that a given amount of money can be spent only once. We may have tried to spend it twice, but we found out very quickly it can be used just one time. As a result, we are forced to make decisions. If we have one dollar in our pocket, we must decide how it will be used. When it is gone, it is gone. We forget, however, that our time has that same characteristic. Many of us have developed the attitude that time is unlimited and our usage of it is not a big issue. Unfortunately, time is a commodity like money in that it can be used only once. A given moment of time can be spent just one time. When it is gone, it is gone!

We must make decisions, some of which take on ethical dimensions. Just as we can choose to spend all of the dollar on ourselves, we can do the same with our time. The temptation is to do so, or we can choose to spend some of that time for concerns other than our own. We can't have it both ways. We cannot always spend it on ourselves and someone else. Time is a valuable gift from God. Many times each day we must decide on whom a given moment of time will be spent.

June 6

"O that I had wings like a dove! I would fly away and be at rest. " (Ps 55:6)

Occasionally, this seldom-read verse describes my own spirit and probably moves very close to many of you as well. The next verse continues, "I would flee far away and stay in the desert; I would hurry to my place of shelter, far from the tempest and storm." Have you ever experienced such a need and made a similar request, even if in the privacy of your own heart? Is there no means of escape for us when we are in trouble or distress? Is our only option to plod wearily through it all and hope for some kind of relief?

Each of us can escape if we will but mount up on wings and fly away to God. Isaiah has given us a hint in his well-known verse, "But those who wait for the Lord shall renew their strength; . . . they shall mount up with wings as eagles." All creatures that have wings can escape from the snare that is set for them, if only they will fly high enough.

What are these wings? The soul that waits upon the Lord, with complete surrender and perfect trust. If we will only surrender ourselves to God, with the trust of our entire being, we will find our spirits mounting up with wings as eagles. Hard times won't go away, but our perspective will undergo a radical transformation.

June 7

"My soul also is struck with terror, while you, O Lord—how long?" (Ps 6:3)

The Psalmist followed this verse with a plea: "Turn, O Lord, save my life; deliver me for the sake of your steadfast love." In a moment of raw honesty, the Psalmist offered his frustration to God. He opened the window to a room that was dark and cold. As we read his words many years later, he reminds us that it is okay to commune with God in moments that are not characterized as happy and bright.

If you enjoy the divine presence and feel drawn to God, communicate your delight and that you are happy and inspired. But what about those inevitable seasons of dryness when you are cold and weary, maybe even lonely and angry? Be honest with God. Express your feelings of distance, withdrawal, and a terrible void; tell God that at this present moment you do not feel moved or inspired. As one writer said, "O God, look upon my ingratitude, my inconstancy, my unfaithfulness. Take my heart for I cannot give it; and keep it, for I cannot keep it for Thee; and save me in spite of myself."

> I lay my head upon Thy infinite heart;
> I hide beneath the shelter of Thy wing;
> Pursued and tempted, helpless, I must cling
> To Thee, my Father; bid me not depart,
> For sin and death pursue, and Life is where Thou art!
> —Anonymous

"Well done, good and trustworthy slave; you have been trustworthy in a few things, I will put you in charge of many things." (Matt 25:21a)   *June 8*

These familiar words are taken from a larger discourse of our Lord on the subject of talents. The real issue at stake is faithfulness, being faithful in our use of resources and opportunities. To what duties are we to be faithful? Our first thoughts might be to some great and well-known task, a calling that requires great sacrifice. Indeed, those kinds of duties come our way. Most of us, however, live out our days in routine responsibilities. Does that mean that our lives are less ordered by the divine? Nothing is too little to be ordered by God; nothing is too little in which to see God's hand; nothing that touches our souls is too little to accept from God; nothing is too little to be done for God.

A wise man once said, "Whoso neglects a thing which he suspects he ought to do, because it seems to him too small a thing, is deceiving himself; it is not too little, but too great for him, that he doeth it not." Unquestionably, one who possesses great ideas best performs them through small duties. I find great comfort in knowing that God is dealing with us in the small as well as the large matters of life.

"Sons are indeed a heritage from the Lord, the fruit of the womb a reward." (Ps 127:3)   *June 9*

During some casual conversation at a meeting I attended, I made the statement that I had been gone every night that week and my family had not eaten an evening meal together all week. Later on, the more I thought about it, the more it bothered me. It was bad enough that my statement was true, but it was even worse that I appeared to be bragging about the situation. Ignoring the needs of my family was certainly not anything to brag about. I should have felt shame more than anything else.

The kind of world we live in does not enhance family life. Demands come from every direction, many of which are extremely worthwhile. The pace, schedule, and responsibilities tend to pull a family apart rather than forcing them together. Family relationships have to be built and nourished, which requires time. Yet, for some reason we tend to think that everything else is more important. Our towns and cities are full of families who don't even know each other. They may sleep in the same house and eat the same food, but they seldom sit and talk about personal things.

Today, more than ever, children are begging for their parents' time—time to talk, walk, kick rocks, and even do nothing together. When I come in from work, my family almost always asks, "How was work today?" I can think of so many times when I have hurried right past them because there was another meeting to anticipate. Never brag about how many nights you've been out. Guilt, not pride, should be the result.

June 10

"Evening and morning and at noon I utter my complaint and moan, and he will hear my voice." (Ps 55:17)

My dad has always advised me to be careful for what I pray because I might get what I request. A good feeling comes with an expectant prayer, the belief that prayer brings results. On the other hand, it is also very comforting to know that our prayers may not be answered because what we request is not for our good, even though we may not understand the reasons.

Surely in this reality there is no less love than in the granting of what we desire. Will not the same love that prompts us to give good prompt us to keep back evil? If in our blindness, not knowing what we ask, we pray for things that would turn in our hands to sorrow, will not our Father, out of love, deny us? How awful would be our lot if our wishes should pass straightway into reality, if we were endowed with a power to bring about all that we desire, and if sudden longings were always granted.

The process of acknowledging our indebtedness to the divine is an endless task. I am convinced that one day we shall bless God, not more for what God has granted than for what God has denied.

June 11

"We know that all things work together for good for those who love God, who are called according to his purpose." (Rom 8:28)

Possibly it is a commentary on the condition of our times, but I continue to hear more and more discussions, and in some cases questions, of whether things really do work together for good. Certainly the issue has to do with the desperate attempt by so many people to find purpose in their living, their work, and their existence in general. Paul's words to the Roman Christians provide a framework of faith that has gotten us through shadowy times.

We must not assume that all things are good. The verse must be seen as a whole and not chopped up and taken out of context. All things are not good, and God does not cause all things. To believe otherwise is a cop-out on our part and an attempt to credit God with some of our own blunders. The verse does not say that everything that happens to us is the direct will and intent of God. We have freedom in our existence, and many of the bad things that happen to us are a result of either our blunders or those of someone else.

The central issue is not who causes all things. The theme of the verse and the basis of our faith is that God is working through all things to bring about good regardless of who caused them. The person who has responded to God's call will discern the divine hand working continually to turn bad things into good, a small part of a larger work called redemption.

"Whoever obeys a command will meet no harm, and
the wise mind will know the time and way." (Eccl 8:5)

June 12

By procrastinating and putting off things beyond their proper time, one duty treads upon the heels of another, and all duties become heavy responsibilities. Such duties take away our peace. In most cases, the consequence is that we have no time to do the work as it ought to be done. We then become more concerned just to get the work done than to do it well. When just getting it done has become our goal, we become insensitive to the way God works through normal events. If we are terribly caught up in the anxiety of obligation, we may ignore the meaning to be found in a normal day.

I am not suggesting that every time we find ourselves in a mad rush, we are guilty of poor discipline. Yet, many of our "frenzied states" are brought on by poor time management and a lack of discipline. Disciplined management of our time is not the sole solution to our anxieties, but it is a good place to begin. Life presents us with enough variables without "making additional deposits in that account."

As I consider the issue of accomplishing our tasks through personal discipline, I remember the words of J. H. Thorn:

> We should do it once, and with our might, the merciful deed that our hand findeth to do, else it will never be done, for the hand will find other tasks. And every unconsummated good feeling, every unfulfilled purpose that His spirit has prompted, shall one day charge us as faithless before God.

"Be steadfast, immovable, always excelling in the work of the Lord,
because you know that in the Lord your labor is not in vain." (1 Cor 15:58)

June 13

The great Swiss theologian Karl Barth once spoke of the Christian faith as a matter of question marks and exclamation points. Barth's words were simple but quite profound. On one hand, life presents innumerable questions about ourselves and our world. The older we get the more we realize that easy, clear-cut answers are difficult to find. On the other hand, our faith offers statements punctuated by exclamation points that stand against our questions. In questioning death, we encounter a risen Lord. In every question mark, there is an exclamation point.

The Bible does not solve all of life's riddles, but it offers dramatic hope to persons who struggle to embrace its affirmations. The Christian journey is largely a process of discovering those exclamation points and holding fast to them. Saint Paul's call for steadfastness were right on target!

June 14

"The Lord is good to all." (Ps 145:9a)

"All that moves in the field is mine." (Ps 50:11b)

If we put these two verses together, we find ourselves with an interesting challenge. The psalmist declared that the Lord is good to all and "has compassion on all he has made." "Every beast of the forest" belongs to God. The tenderness of our Lord encompasses every creature. To follow the Lord means that we are to show the same tenderness as God did. This tenderness is so thorough and complete that there is a tenderness toward even the animal kingdom. Have you thought about the fact that one's Christianity should even influence one's attitude about animals?

The love of God should be reflected in the total picture of our life. No area is exempt. This concept applies to the way we relate and treat all of the created order. Certainly, it applies to the way we treat all people and even to the way we treat our dog and cat. To say that we love God and at the same time exercise cruelty in any form, even to animals, is a contradiction in itself.

Once I heard a man say that he "would give nothing for a man's religion whose very dog and cat are not the better for it." The next time you seek to harm one of God's creatures, remember the one who fashioned that creature.

June 15

Isaiah was having a hard time making the people of his day understand that God would see them through the hard times they were experiencing. A patient faith in an all-powerful God would carry them through to the other side. Patience is best invoked where there is a strong belief in a purpose that is larger than one can presently see.

When Isaiah said that God would make "mountains into a road," he was proclaiming the profound truth that God will make obstacles serve God's purpose. That which seemingly threatens or blocks our progress is often but a means of directing us in the divine way. The demands that weigh upon us, the problems at work, a daily cross that seems too heavy to bear all become an obstacle to our progress and happiness. We think that if somehow these dimensions of our life could change, we could live more joyful and productive lives. We pray for their removal.

We cannot see from our limited view that these very weights are necessary for our growth and development. They are a means to the graces and virtues for which we have been praying so long. We need to hear Isaiah and remember that these are God's mountains. We must submit ourselves and our burdens to God. Patience can be acquired only through that which seems unbearable. Trials not only test our worthiness, but also increase it. The tree is stronger when it has been toughened by the wind.

"Everyone then who hears these words of mine and acts on them will be like a wise man who built his house on rock." (Matt 7:24)

June 16

This is the season of the year when we applaud fathers and the contribution they make to the health of the family unit. While many perceptions in recent years have changed in regard to family life, the role of the father is still a vital one.

In 1225 the builders of the cathedral at Beauvals laid the foundation for a structure that would dwarf every other cathedral in Europe. Fifty years later, the choir vault was complete, and it was deemed a marvel. Twelve years later it fell. "Inadequate foundations and supports" was the verdict of architects who were called into analyze the mess.

When a life is built on inadequate foundations, that life is in danger of collapsing. How important it is to be able to ask some foundation-type questions such as: What is of ultimate significance for me? When or what do I really trust? What loyalty would move me to offer my life? What hastens my heart and evokes my strength and gifts? To answer these questions is to know if our foundation is solid.

Jesus taught that foundations were important. He told the dramatic story of the man who built his house on a rock and, because the foundation was solid, the house withstood every storm that came its way. How important it is for a father to be concerned about the spiritual foundations of his family and to exercise positive influence to assure that proper values and attitudes are communicated!

"God blessed them, and God said to them, 'Be fruitful and multiply, and fill the earth and subdue it.' " (Gen 1:28a)

June 17

The Book of Genesis depicts the creation of humanity as the climax of all that God created. We were created with relatively simple needs such as food, shelter, clothing, intimacy, and relationships. During the process of the years, we have fabricated all kinds of other needs and have allowed ourselves to submit to a giant that has changed every aspect of our lives. Call the giant what you like—advertising, marketing, conformity—but the game it plays is tragic. It teaches us to believe that if we work and buy, steal and borrow, we can meet these fabricated needs. The giant points toward happiness by presenting us with irresistible images that no one could doubt. In practice, expensive fun always blossoms into another full-blown need, which then calls for a more costly refinement of satisfaction, again failing us.

Do we have control over our lives, or does the giant? The giant is working day and night to present images of ourselves to drive, wear, eat, recreate, and even sleep in certain ways. Remember, "the lilies neither toil nor spin, yet even Solomon in all his glory was not clothed like one of these." We are much too subject to systems designed to create artificial needs and then satisfy them.

$\mathcal{June}$ 18   **"Fools think their own way is right, but the wise listen to advice." (Prov 12:15)**

In the process of growing more Christlike, there is one area especially in which I would like to grow. I would like to be a better listener. Most of us by nature are not good listeners, especially with our family. When we have to live with the demands and pressures of a job, we have a tendency not to listen when we arrive at home. If we are tired, we would like to forget about problems for awhile.

Often a spouse and children need our care and attention. Listening requires effort and energy while many other things compete for our time and ears. Our children want to talk to us, but usually we are too busy. Their talk is an interruption. It is believed that by the age of fifteen, a child asks 500,000 questions. On one hand, that is a lot of interruptions. On the other hand, that means a half-million opportunities to share something about the meaning of life.

We also need to hear with the third ear, or go beyond what is said and hear what is meant. Listening is an area in family living that concerns many of us. Particularly our children need an attentive ear. They are not around forever, and one day we will wish we had given more of ourselves. Listening is an investment that has tremendous payoff. I am convinced that we are all so busy that we just don't listen to each other enough.

$\mathcal{June}$ 19 **"Blessed be the Lord, the God of Israel, who alone does wondrous things." (Ps 72:18)**

Years ago my daughter taught me a lesson about being alive that I will long remember. My son, Chris, and I were making ready to go to the local high school football game. Melody, our four-year-old, objected to being left at home. We took her to her first football game. By the second quarter I was in trouble. We had gone through all of our peanuts; and Chris had gone for soft drinks twice, which caused me some concern. Melody discovered that the pom-poms were great for fanning people as they passed. In spite of it all, we had a good time. As I think about the evening, however, one thing stands out in my mind above all the rest. It had to do with her ability to be excited and surprised. She was electrified by the sights and sounds.

I've been going to football games for years. In fact, I don't even pay attention to a lot that goes on; but for Melody it was different. She noticed the lights and the people seated all around. She paid attention to the cheerleaders and became very excited as the band marched and played. I experienced the same sights but was oblivious to most of them. I had lost my ability to be surprised. Melody was like the Psalmist who was alive to his surroundings—sensitive to God's glory. When was the last time you noticed? Maybe we have been going to the game so long that we don't pay attention.

"I will quietly look from my dwelling like clear heat in sunshine." (Isa 18:4a) *June 20*

The heat of summer is upon us in more ways than one. While the temperature has been making its peaks, another type of heat involves us: the heat of activity. Summer has a way of sending people in all directions. One would think that with school being out and the adults taking a few vacation days, there would be plenty of free time. Somehow, that is not the case. Instead, everyone is intent on getting in all those plans they made at the beginning of the summer. With the realization that only a few weeks are left, we hurry around even more as we try to do everything we had planned.

You probably made plans for some family time together. It may have been a weekend trip, an outing for a day, or just some relaxed nights together. The chances are also good that a lot of those plans have been postponed, dropped, or changed. Many of those plans for family outings have been pre-empted by far less worthy adventures. Regardless of the preparation, you just can't get it all in.

The summer is not over. There is still time to make room for important matters that may have been pre-empted. They don't necessarily require money and a lot of time, but the investment is worth the effort. Summer is here and now. Don't cut important things. Families are not together forever. Do what you can while you can.

"Likewise the Spirit helps us in our weakness; for we do not know how to pray as we ought." (Rom 8:26a) *June 21*

In our personal lives spiritual progress can sometimes be painfully slow. Then at times spiritual awareness and our prayer life come alive in a vital and exciting way. Yet, there are those moments when the well seems to be dry and nothing is happening spiritually. The "drought" might be the result of a crisis when we feel alone and empty and try to reach out and pray but no one seems to be there.

In his letter to the Romans, Paul dealt with just such a time when he wrote, "Likewise the spirit helps us in our weakness; for we do not know how to pray as we ought, but that very Spirit intercedes with sighs too deep for words." This is an encouraging thought, to know that God's spirit broods over us when we cannot pray and responds with understanding and power until we can pray again.

Sometimes when we cannot pray, it is good to wait in silence so that we get in touch with our own deeper feelings, sort them out, and accept them for what they are and mean. At times we try to suppress our true feelings, thinking God will not accept them. We conjure up what we think are Christian feelings in order to pray, but this does not work. As we get in touch with our true feelings and offer them to God, the Holy Spirit moves and vitality returns to our prayer life. I am grateful for the ministry of the Holy Spirit who ministers to our needs when we are unaware.

June 22 **"A time to weep, and a time to laugh." (Eccl 3:4a)**

This verse serves a vital role in reminding me that there is a time to laugh. My family and I spend a week at the beach each summer. The time this year, as with all years, passed so quickly. We had hardly arrived there when it was time to go. A family vacation offers the chance for many kinds of experiences. One part of it I particularly wish we could continue when we are back in the saddle at home: the laughter. The different setting and routine certainly offer the chance for a more relaxed atmosphere. Somehow laughter comes easier. Experiences deemed silly at home become hilarious at the beach.

The merriment stands in stark contrast to the serious world that we live in. A free-floating mood of tension and apprehension seems to fill most of our days. As a result, we just don't seem to laugh much. The lack of honest laughter seems to be a by-product of the problem of taking ourselves so seriously. The proper kind of laughter is a gift from God. It breaks the spell of anxiety. At times it makes the difficult a bit more tolerable. We are so serious most of the time that laughter has become a luxury we evidently feel we can't afford. In a *Guidepost* article many years ago John Drescher made the statement, "If I were starting my family again, I would laugh more with my children." I wish I could can some laughter from our beach trip and then let it out on a gray Monday morning.

June 23 **"He began to speak and taught them, saying: 'Blessed are the . . . ' " (Matt 5:2-3a)**

As we follow Jesus through the pages of the New Testament, we discover that he did not take his signals from the world when he talked about finding happiness. According to the teachings of Jesus, happiness is always a derivative, a result of something else. Happiness is something that comes upon us, at times unexpectedly. I am convinced that happiness is not something we seek in and of itself. It cannot be negotiated, bought, or loaned. Happiness has a way of hooking up to something else.

As you read the Beatitudes, you get the idea that happiness comes as a result of humility, openness, and caring. It comes as a result of earnestly seeking the Father's will and being ready to even face persecution for it. Happiness comes when we seek peace and reconciliation. It is primarily a result of committing our lives to something beyond ourselves. It comes especially as we work for something that will outlive us. The feelings of joy and happiness are always a result rather than a goal.

Happiness is a spiritual issue. We discover that true happiness leads us to a new understanding of what Jesus meant when he said that we find our lives by losing them. If we seek happiness in any other way, we will discover that it is like trying to grab a "handful of smoke."

"Then the father said to him, 'Son, you are always with me, and all that is mine is yours.' " (Luke 15:32)

Jesus did not present a very attractive picture of the elder brother in the parable of the prodigal son. When the prodigal returned and the father gave a party, the older brother did not join the festivities because of his anger. He was very resentful of the attention that his brother received. He had serious question as to whether his brother deserved that special treatment. After all, look what the brother had done. The older brother also felt that he had been slighted since no one had thrown a party like that for him. He had remained in his responsible place and done all the right things, but the sorry younger brother got all the fanfare.

Jesus was trying to communicate one important point in the story: life is not an agreement but a gift. The story underscores the gift of God's grace. Even if the irresponsible brother did not earn a party, the father wanted to give him one out of love. If we were to know more of the details, we would probably discover that the older brother had received far more from the father than he deserved, even if it was not a party. In fact, the father told the older son that all that he had would be his. Life is a gift, not an agreement. In moments of jealousy today, just remember that all we enjoy is a gift, party or not.

"About that time no little disturbance broke out concerning the Way." (Acts 19:23)

Somewhere I read this statement: "If one tenth of the things we say we believe as Christians are true, then we ought to be ten times as excited as we are." This is true, but what has happened to the excitement of many of us? Real Christianity can and does cause excitement; it also challenges ideas and customs. The verse for today speaks of Paul and the stir he caused in Ephesus. He was willing to place the claims of Christianity squarely against the cult of Diana. This was no small event, requiring a fair amount of courage.

Could it be that our own Christian witness often causes little excitement because it is weak and undirected? We might discover that our fundamental beliefs are so close to those of the world that very little challenge is offered. Perhaps we need to go deeper before we can cause even a small agitation. No one is suggesting that a stir be caused today for the sake of upsetting anyone or "just for the sake of it." Yet, do we carry anything with us today that challenges evil or injustice or apathy? Excitement concerning our faith is like some other things; we cannot give away what we do not have!

June 26

> **"For truly I tell you, if you have faith the size of a mustard seed, you will say to this mountain, 'Move . . . ' "** (Matt 17:20a)

Our world is so complicated. We seem to have a need to add complication to simplicity. We take some of the most simple things and turn them into complicated nightmares. Yet, a desire for simplicity also forces us to give attention to the smaller details.

Try to find a statement anywhere that does a better job of summarizing the basics of what God expects from us than today's verse. In life small, simple things are vital to human well-being. Simple human consideration is basic to human brotherhood. Mutual respect is more important to peace than large armies. Faithfulness to small duties makes for happiness. Simple things can also be destructive. The small deceit, the harsh word, or the closed mind can destroy personality and endanger success.

In matters of personal belief it is not so much the great faith we lack, but the failure to translate this faith into the common ways of each day. A faith that is triumphant does not spring full blown in the heart. It grows from such smaller, simpler things as daily prayer, acts of love, and the honoring of God. Meeting the expectation of our Lord does not require a majority vote in a church conference but the submission to a small, yet powerful faith—even that of a mustard seed.

June 27

> **"Blessed are the poor in spirit, for theirs is the kingdom of heaven."** (Matt 5:3)

This verse has often been misunderstood. It is not a case for a "backboneless" way of living out our days but represents an attitude toward ourselves, others, and the world. Someone has said that many of our headaches come from halos that do not fit. In other words, the image we have of ourselves does not always correspond with reality. Jesus taught that halos do not fit because people feel they have arrived and there is no room to grow.

When Jesus referred to those who are "poor in spirit," he was referring to those who are not arrogant and guilty of false pride. One of the most admirable qualities in life is to remain teachable. The "poor in spirit" are persons who do not let their false pride and egos get in the way of their relationships with others. Pride can lock the heart like nothing else can, causing barriers in our relationships. The "poor in spirit" recognize how much they need each other, not letting little things become big things that terminate a relationship. More than anything else, the "poor in spirit" recognize their dependency upon God. The only poverty that is ever commended by God is the poverty of arrogance. The height of arrogance is the assumption that we can do life alone, a condition known as foolishness.

"Build up each other, as indeed you are doing." (1 Thess 5:11b)   *June* 28

I continually feel a sense of indebtedness to those persons around me who always are a source of encouragement. Some people just seem to have that gift. Victor Hugo once said, "We live by affirmations more than bread." How could anyone disagree? Some of the most memorable moments in our lives have been those when we received encouragement at a very critical time. One of the most important gifts we have to give to each other is the gift of encouragement. Through this gift we have the power to lift others up and make a difference or possibly let someone fall down when it might be avoided.

In his letter to the Thessalonians, Paul told some struggling Christians of the importance of encouraging and building up one another. Encouragement may come as a simple word, a smile, a note, or a pat on the back at just the right time. So much in this world tears down, and many of our friends and family are close to defeat. We need to remember that frequently we hold in our hands the difference between despair and hope. So, today, be mindful of the gifts of encouragement that come your way. Don't take them for granted. Also remember that you hold the same opportunity and gift. Encouragement is one of the few gifts we have that does not diminish by giving it away.

"Blessed are those who are persecuted for righteousness'   *June* 29
sake, for theirs is the kingdom of heaven." (Matt 5:10)

The words of Jesus in this verse could just as easily have been left out as far as I am concerned. I would much prefer hearing that following Jesus would bring about success, plenty, and good fortune. I always cringe just a bit when I hear that following the way of the Kingdom might cause a touch of persecution. After all, Roman prisons have been gone for centuries, and we live in a country that allows the expression of our faith.

Jesus clearly stated that following him would sometimes involve a cross. Our crosses may be a little different than those of the early church. Given the competing value struggle of our society, our cross may come at the point of standing up for our convictions in what could be some inevitable persecution. Jesus also told his disciples that from these commitments would come blessings. The payoff may be as simple as the satisfaction that comes from involvement in something meaningful.

Dietrich Bonhoeffer once said, "Life has to involve commitment, for we are made to give ourselves to higher causes; never pity the man who is persecuted because of his commitment, but feel sorry for the man whose life was never worth persecuting." When standing for our convictions in the midst of unpleasant circumstances, we discover a part of our character that little else in life will bring out. Today may be the day for a little test.

June 30   **"Blessed are those who mourn, for they will be comforted."** (Matt 5:4)

The chances are that today we may ask the familiar question, "Why?" The query may come because we hear, read, or experience some kind of sad or tragic event. Questioning does not reflect a pessimistic attitude, just reality. There are no easy answers to the "whys" of life. The explanations for many of these events are far beyond us and our limited ability. The challenge for us may not be understanding but the challenge of mourning.

Jesus said, "Blessed are those who mourn." He knew that from some of our common grief can come the awareness of life's truest values. Grief has a tempering and refining effect on the personality. The sharing of grief requires us to reach back into our own experience and remember what we thought, felt, and even believed.

Today we may encounter some truly struggling souls. Their greatest need is not an explanation, even if they ask for reason. They need for someone to mourn with them, to be sensitive, to care, to listen, and to embrace them even when no answers are available. Don't be a theologian; be a shepherd. There is nothing wrong with an explanation, but a hug may go a whole lot further.

July 1   **"Then Jesus laid his hands on his eyes again; and he looked intently and his sight was restored, and he saw everything clearly."** (Mark 8:25)

I am quite envious of the blind man in this verse who was touched by Jesus and then saw things clearly. I realize that he was referring to his actual vision, but the verse is quite symbolic of another type of seeing. I wish Jesus would touch me and give me the ability to see more clearly. Scripture indicates that Jesus laid his hands on the blind man's eyes and asked him if he saw anything. The man said, "I see people, but they look like trees, walking." Jesus laid his hands on his eyes a second time, and he saw everything clearly.

Many times we see people as things to be manipulated to our own ends rather than seeing real people who are of value in and of themselves. We need that clear view, the view that enables us to see things more clearly. Along with many other changes in our lives, Jesus can help us to see people in the correct way.

We are living in a time of great deal depersonalization. How desperately the personal touch is needed! Jesus saw through crowds of individual faces. He saw and treated people as individuals of infinite worth. If we are truly faithful, then we must strive to see people as our Lord did. If you seek that as a goal today, you will probably have to make some changes. What are those changes? You will have to figure that out for yourself.

"So teach us to count our days that we may gain a wise heart." (Ps 90:12)   *July 2*

The Psalmist was suggesting far more than just learning how to count. He was encouraging a certain attitude about life rather than a mathematical process. Life is so short. We should fill every minute with a certain appreciation of our days. After all, they pass so quickly.

The artist William Hunt was teaching a class. The students were outside painting a landscape. The artist looked up at the sky and told his class, "We will now paint the glorious sunset." He noticed one student gazing at some decaying shingles on a nearby house. He said to the student, "Son, it's not going to be light very long; you must choose between the sunset and the shingles."

Time moves by so swiftly. We don't have light forever. We have to make choices as to how we will use this limited resource called time. I don't know exactly what circumstances caused the Psalmist to offer these words, but I do know there was a sense of urgency in his voice. Wisdom comes when we learn to appreciate every day as a gift from God.

Regardless of our age, young or old, we should learn to value every day as a gift. Our days really are numbered. That is not pessimism but reality. Today is one day. It is only one number. Appreciate this one day, and then take the same approach to tomorrow.

"For freedom Christ has set us free. Stand firm, therefore,   *July 3*
and do not submit again to a yoke of slavery." (Gal 5:1)

At first reading, this verse might sound a little repetitious, but it is not repetitious at all. Paul was talking about the way we use our freedom, the very special freedom that Christ gives. Paul encouraged people to use this freedom responsibly, not just to follow every personal whim but to help and serve one another.

The July fourth celebration is only a few hours away, a time of offering thanks for our freedom as a nation. This freedom serves its highest purpose when we fulfill a will larger than our own and serve a purpose greater than our individual purposes. This larger sense of destiny is an important part of our national heritage. When we use our freedom to serve others and follow the will of God, our lives become full and abundant. Through apathy and the pursuit of false values, we forget or ignore our heritage.

Paul's words remind us that freedom means choices. To be free means we must decide how we are to use this freedom. What kinds of choices will we make today? Will our concerns deal only with our own personal needs? Will we commit to a destiny that exceeds our own concerns? Will we be responsible in all of our dealings with others? Freedom may at the same time be the best way of life and the hardest way of life. How will you exercise your freedom today?

July 4

"Blessed are those who wash their robes, so that they will have the right to the tree of life and may enter the city by the gates." (Rev 22:14)

A part of our July fourth celebration is recognizing and giving thanks for the heroes of the past. The history of our nation is a litany of names who gave far more than was required and through courage forged a nation that has stood well the test of time. These individuals not only believed in our founding principles but stood up for them. We are the beneficiaries of their commitment to these principles. For the heroes of the past we are grateful.

I remember reading a magazine article in which the author was bemoaning the absence of heroes today. Yet, he concluded the article having found some heroes. They are nameless, but they can start your mind thinking of your own list. Consider that person who, though in actual pain, continues to look to the needs of others. Consider the one who, although facing a difficult decision, refuses to decide merely on the basis of prudence or to rationalize his or her qualms. Consider another who, in spite of bitter disappointments, still praises God as the giver of all good gifts. Consider all those who stand by promises and commitments made in good faith, who remain loyal to friends, who are truthful in conversation, who are alert to opportunities for helping others.

This holiday is a time of remembering heroes. Along with those of the past, consider many who are close to you. They may never make a history book, but they have made it a more important "book."

July 5

"For to me, living is Christ and dying is gain." (Phil 1:21)

A news editor recently concluded that Americans are more unhappy than ever before, even though a vast number of persons have made it their goal to seek happiness. The problem is that happiness is not an end but a result. It is a by-product.

Seeking after your own happiness will result in disaster. According to most people, to make yourself happy, you must direct most of your thoughts inward. When our happiness is our goal, we become preoccupied with ourselves rather than others. Their happiness is secondary. Our search for happiness can cause us to be quite selfish in the end. This is not to say that people who are selfish never do nice things for others; they frequently do. The motivation is seldom to please the other person, however, but usually to receive some type of payoff. It is niceness for self-centered reasons. Thinking about yourself is not the way to happiness.

God has placed within our hearts the desire for happiness and given us a way to secure it. Happiness is always just outside our reach. The homing beacon in our hearts points to the true sources of deep, contented happiness. As Paul said, "Living is Christ and dying is gain."

"The Lord is a great God, and a great King above all gods." (Ps 95:3) *July* 6

When I think about all that stands before me this day, I realize how inadequate I am. My strength is so limited. My vision is so short-sighted. My wisdom is insufficient for my daily struggles. I desperately need something beyond myself.

Last night before I turned in for the night, I stepped outside and looked up into the heavens. Whenever I see that vast array of stars, I am reminded of what a great God we worship. No small God could create the heavens that stretch out above me. Yet, even though our God is high and lifted up, our God also knows us by name and is as close to us as the air within our lungs.

Following a trip through the lake region and mountain ranges of New Hampshire, Fred Engelhardt, the late president of that state's university, was heard to say, "I hope I will never get used to it." I hope we never get used to the majesty of God. We need somebody bigger than ourselves. Our God is no small God and is capable of meeting any need that falls before us each day. God is a great God, and all we have to do is just reach out with confidence. We have nothing to lose and everything to gain as we recognize the divine as not just a god but a great, great God.

"If we love one another, God lives in us, and his love is perfected in us." (1 John 4:12b) *July* 7

Recently I heard someone say that the greatest business of our life here on this earth is to more and more submit our hearts to God's great grace of love, yielding ourselves daily and giving ourselves continuously. We are to let God's love enter more fully and freely into us, so that it may even fill our whole heart and life. Day after day we must drive back the sin that causes us to resist the very presence of God in our lives. Prayer will win and keep God's presence; work will strengthen and exercise it; the Bible will teach us how to know and value it; and the Holy Spirit will ever quicken its power in our hearts. This yielding of ourselves to God's grace will give us peace and joy beyond all that we can ask or think.

Through love, God will forgive our faults and failures and bring us at last into the fullness of that life that even here God has suffered us to know. This yielding brings us even closer to an eternal home where love is perfect, unwearied, and unending, and where nothing can ever separate us from one another or from God. Let our task today be one of yielding, a yielding of strength and control to the one who gives totally for us. In our yielding, may we discover strength at its very best.

July 8

"The fruit of the Spirit is love, joy, peace, patience, kindness, generosity, faithfulness, gentleness, and self-control." (Gal 5:22)

Whenever I read this verse, I always feel a little uneasy. You see, patience is not my best trait. In fact, I have been accused of being absent from the line-up when patience was distributed—not bragging, just a fact. Patience is far more than just a willingness to stand in line without snorting and complaining, however. It is more than a toleration of the kid's stereo next door. Patience is a discipline, a very important one.

An incident from Lucas Malet's story "The Wages of Sin" has a helpful word for all of us. The heroine asks her uncle, "What does one do when the sun of one's happiness has set?" He answers, "After a time . . . one lights a candle called patience and guides one's footsteps by that. Try to light your candle of patience, my dear, in faith, remembering that you are not alone. More than half the noblest men and women you meet carry such candles likewise."

I want patience right now! On second thought, maybe I should just pray for it and wait. But I don't like waiting. Maybe God can help me, and I want that help right now!

July 9

"Bless the Lord, O my soul, and all that is within me, bless his holy name." (Ps 103:1)

Someone has appropriately reworded this psalm to read, "Bless the Lord by not forgetting all His benefits." Not a bad thought, but can we afford to slow down long enough to be mindful of anything? We are too busy just trying to survive.

Recently I saw a sign in an office recently that read: "Blessed are those who run around in circles for they shall be called wheels." The sign seemed to reflect the kind of hectic lifestyle most of us live. We all need moments in our lives when we can gain a sense of perspective of what life is all about. We should occasionally take a longer look. The psalmist was taking that longer look. To praise God and to be in touch with all we have been given is so vital to life, but we have to take just a moment to think about it. A little humility also helps.

An old adage says, "Show me a self-made man, and I'll show you an example of unskilled labor." Whenever we have the attitude that we have fully earned and deserve all that we have, our lives are getting out of focus and we should get in touch with how much we have been given. In other words, "Bless the Lord by not forgetting all His benefits." Right now would be a good time.

"Therefore, take up the whole armor of God, so that you
may be able to withstand on that evil day." (Eph 6:13a)

Recently someone suggested to me that a certain type of stubbornness could be a positive thing. I have to be honest and say that I always thought of stubbornness as a negative trait. Truly, much that is called stubbornness is bad. When a person is stubborn for trivial reasons or for no reason, the harm can be great. Yet, often a strong loyalty needs a trace, at least, of stubbornness. The ability to be stubborn can become "I shall not be moved" for the highest and best of reasons. We can fulfill the injunction in Ephesians, "Having done all, to stand," if we have a touch of "I won't" for the best of reasons.

The issue for us today may not a question of stubbornness but rather stubbornness for the right things. We will be faced with choices today. Some of them will be subtle, so subtle that we hardly know we have made them. Others will require hard thinking. A little stubbornness for the right reasons can go a long way in helping us to be faithful. Are you stubborn? That trait could be okay if you exercise it for the right reasons.

"Then Jesus, crying with a loud voice, said, 'Father,
into your hands I commend my spirit.' " (Luke 23:46a)

The victory of Christ in our lives should be evident both to ourselves and others. This victory is first evident in our minds. Where anxiety and worry once dwelt, trust and peace now abide. In the Sermon on the Mount, Christ bids us to be free from the slavery of things. He advises us to take a lesson from nature, even from a bird and the lily, which accept God's care as a matter of course. Strange that only man, of all God's creatures, doubts this loving care.

Christ said that if we will put God's kingdom first and trust God, we will have clothes, food, drink, and all other things in sufficiency. He did not say, "Trust me and I will make you rich, successful, and worldly wise." Rather he promised to supply all of our needs. Christ not only taught by word of mouth concerning this matter, but he practiced it. Faced with a horrible death on a Roman cross and burdened with the world's sin, he said, "My peace I give to you. I do not give to you as the world gives." Not without the struggle in the garden or the pain on the cross did he triumph, but at last he said, "Into your hands I commend my spirit."

The last word of Christ is the key word that frees us from anxiety. How much difference it would make in our world if we could only say to our Lord, "Into thy hands I commend my spirit." The victory of Christ in our lives is first evident in our minds, the place where worry and anxiety find their home—then again, maybe not.

July 12

The victory of Christ is evident also in the body. The religiously inclined of all peoples and faiths have recognized the body as a barrier to spiritual attainment. All sorts of methods have been used to overcome the flesh: chastisement, fasting, and outright self-punishment. The cruder the religion, the more blood-curdling the torture. Christendom has not been without such mystical rites, although most of them were man-conceived and without foundation in the scripture.

The Christian system teaches that the flesh and all it is heir to must be disciplined and brought under control and held captive to Christ. Once Christ comes to dwell in us by the Spirit, the process of that control begins. The body is a very important part of the submission of the total self. From scripture we are instructed to mind the things of the Spirit; to ignore the "will of the flesh"; to be cleansed from the way of the world. The follower of Christ, like Paul, can keep the body under control. The goal is to know and believe that life is much more than just the "flesh," but the "flesh" is one way of expressing this total commitment to Christ.

The submitting of the body involves patience and courage, as well as knowledge. We cannot make ourselves disappear. God does not expect that. A victory evidenced in the mind finds its way to the body, which becomes an expression of commitment—or at least it could.

July 13   **"God, who is rich in mercy, out of the great love with which he loved us." (Eph 2:4a)**

For the last three days we have been talking about the way the victory of Christ is evidenced in our lives. This victory is most supremely evident in our spiritual nature, something beyond the mind and body. Its hallmark is love. If a Christian can truly say in the language of the popular chorus, "I have the love of Jesus down in my heart," he or she has the power necessary to overcome evil.

The love of God for mankind caused Him to send His only begotten son to earth. The love of Christ caused him to suffer and die for us. The love of Christ constrained the heroes of the first-century church to throw themselves with such abandon into the Christian life and program. Indeed, the Christian heroes and martyrs of all ages have been men and women in whose hearts burned the holy passion for the Master.

The victorious life is often not so much our victory over the world as the victory of Christ's love in us. How different people would be if Christ's love was their ruling passion! We would be personally patient, kind, generous, humble, courteous, unselfish, sincere, faithful, and true. In life, in death, and in the life to come, love abides. Faith and hope are lost in love. The victory of Christ is evident in the mind, body, and spirit, all reflecting this victory in the life of a believer.

"But I say to you, do not resist an evildoer. But if anyone strikes you on the cheek, turn the other also." (Matt 5:39)

I have just heard the report of the execution of a man in North Carolina for the murder of a college student. The execution was the end of many years of trials and appeals and enormous expense. One part of the report described the impact of this man's actions on both his family and the victim's family—so much brokenness and heartache. What could have prevented it?

Broken relationships, hostility, and violence blight our world and reduce the meaning of life for everyone involved. When communication falters, we end up misunderstanding, hurting, and frustrating one another. Resentment turns into anger, and we do and say things that separate us farther from each other. These are reasons for the major emphasis of Jesus' teaching on forgiveness. He knew there is no love, friendship, or society without it. The last word of verbal abuse finally becomes only an echo. Revenge may be sweet on our lips, but it ultimately becomes a sour stomach and a bitter memory; and violence breeds more violence.

We build bridges over troubled waters when we ask for forgiveness. In saying it, feeling it, and acting on it, we indicate how we want the relationship to be restored. We build bridges when we offer forgiveness and provide a chance for healing. We are not alone as God's spirit strengthens and guides us.

"Blessed is that slave whom his master will find at work when he arrives." (Luke 12:43)

The last half of the summer has a way of putting us in a series of mad scrambles. We push to get in all the things we promised ourselves that we would do this summer; but as of yet, we have not gotten around to them. Now we realize that the summer is passing very quickly and if we are to do those things, we had better gear up and get with it.

The result is a mad scramble. We face the usual problem of much to do and not enough time to do it. We focus upon a problem that is much larger than summer: the problem of "too little time." We sometimes forget that time is like any other resource. It is not endless, and we are charged with being good stewards of our time. It is not unlimited. The challenge, therefore, for each one of us becomes the wise use of our time.

Most all of us have faced the fact that, since our money is not endless, we must make decisions as to where it goes, preferring some things over others. Our time must be approached the same way. Most of us find time to do the things we really want to do. Therefore, the real issue is not our limited time but our priorities in using it. We all have twenty-four hours in each day; the challenge is to use if wisely. Like many other things, it is a matter of what is important.

July 16

"But we do not want you to be uninformed, brothers and sisters, about those who have died." (1 Thess 4:13)

One day I drove by a little country church that was surrounded by a cemetery on three sides. A graveside funeral service was just concluding, and people were walking from the tent to their cars. I did not know the people and obviously could not hear their comments, but I have relived the scene countless thousands of times.

The service was over, and the preacher had said his words. I couldn't help but wonder if the person's death was due to a long illness or if it was sudden. Was it cancer or a heart attack? Was the death due to an automobile accident? Was the person prepared for this event? Given that it was in a church cemetery, I assume that spiritual preparations were made.

As I drove past, I could see the open grave. Another question came to me as I picked up the scene and carried it with me in my mind. An open grave, the service concluded, family and friends walking away—was this the end or the beginning? The secular world would say it was the end, and to many persons it could be. Yet, our faith shouts back in response that death is only the beginning. What we experience here is only a momentary prelude to that which lies on the other side of the door. Was this the end or the beginning? I'm staking my life on the belief that it is unquestionably the beginning! "Do not grieve as others who have no hope."

July 17

"He subdues the ancient gods, shatters the forces of old; he drove out the enemy before you." (Deut 33:27)

The story is told of a man who, while hiking late in the day along a high cliff, accidentally slipped and fell over the edge. Somehow he managed to grasp the very edge and break his fall, but he was left hanging over a vast gorge. To fall would mean certain death. His grip began to slip and, in spite of his efforts to hold on, his hands slipped away and he fell. Instead of falling to his death, however, he fell only about a foot to where his feet found a ledge hidden in the dark. He would never have known the ledge was there had he not let go, intentionally or unavoidably.

This story becomes a parable for all of us in our unwillingness to let go and trust God in our lives. We try to hold on. We will give pieces of our lives to God. Yet, we struggle to hold on and resist with all the fear we can muster in our hearts the possibility of granting God full control of our lives. We discover that when we let go, the fall is quite short. The exact distance between our feet and the ledge is not the issue, but rather that underneath are the everlasting arms of our Lord who awaits our fall. So relax and let yourself drop, not off a ledge but into the loving arms of a God who has promised to always be there. Let go and see what happens.

"A perverse person spreads strife; a whisperer separates close friends." (Prov 16:28) *July* 18

Few things can damage our own spirit and the spirit of a group more than malicious gossip. I should just leave it as gossip since most gossip is malicious. It would be a pleasant change if we used gossip to build up, but most of us spend gossip activity in a less-than-positive manner. An empty brain and a tattling tongue are very apt to go together. The most silly and trivial items of news or scandal fill the empty brain and are readily distributed by the tattling tongue. Narrow-minded and ignorant people talk about persons and not things. The sages of old equated gossip with moral leprosy.

The sadness of the whole enterprise is that gossip selects the effortless way of building up one's weak ego. By tearing another down, one builds himself or herself up. Truthfully, gossip comes from a foul-mouthed, foul-tongued slanderer who is suffering from a serious affliction. The following lines from an unknown author should cause us to think carefully before we use hurtful words.

> There is so much good in the worse of us,
> And so much bad in the best of us,
> That it ill behooves any of us
> To find fault with the rest of us.

"In the days of his flesh, Jesus offered up prayers and supplications, with loud cries and tears, to the one who was able to save him from death." (Heb 5:7a) *July* 19

I cannot help but think of so many people who are struggling today. Suffering is a part of life. I think of a friend of mine who died recently, and now his family grieves so much for him. I think of a member of my church who lost his job and is having real difficulty in finding new work. I think of a lady whose purse was stolen, including her money and credit cards, while she was helping hungry people.

The verse from Hebrews speaks of Christ being made obedient through suffering. Because he suffered, we can make certain assumptions. Pain is an inevitable part of life. Christ could not avoid pain; neither can we. Some pain may even be essential for our emotional and spiritual growth. To will for us fullness and growth, God weaves into the tapestry of our lives both pain and joy. Some pain may even turn out to be beneficial. Notice, I said some pain, not all. Pain is not necessarily a sign of God's will. Yet, God knows far more than we do, and God's ways are not always clearly known and understood by us. As in the life of our Lord, our struggles might be preparing us for service yet unknown. God, give us grace to face the inevitable struggles of life with courage.

July 20

"So we do not lose heart. Even though our outer nature is wasting away, our inner nature is being renewed day by day." (2 Cor 4:16)

Outwardly wasting away, inwardly being renewed. This phrase sounds rather dark and foreboding, but not if you read the rest of it. "Don't lose heart," Paul said. There is more to existence than just the exterior. When life is doing a number to us on the outside, something positive can still be happening to us on the inside. I remember a Peanuts cartoon years ago in which Lucy said, "Adversity is preparing us for that which comes later in life." "What's that?" Charlie asked. Lucy said, "More adversity."

Based on Paul's letter, allow me to suggest three ways that we can grow stronger, even when life is taking its toll. First, believe in the future. Paul wrote, "For this slight momentary affliction is preparing us for an eternal weight of glory beyond all measure." The second step is to focus on the task at hand. Let go of the regrets of the past and anxieties of the future, and concentrate on those things that you must do today. Third, and most important, is a little trust of the heavenly father. Worry and trust cannot live in the same house. When worry is allowed to come in the door, trust walks out the door.

We cannot do away with stress. We don't even want to. Stress keeps us on track and directed. The key is management, and the key to management is not attitude but faith. It is a faith and a belief that God cares and is involved right this very moment.

July 21

"So no one stayed with him when Joseph made himself known to his brothers." (Gen 45:1b)

Have you ever noticed how much space is given in the Book of Genesis to the experiences of Joseph, especially his encounter with his brothers? If you are familiar with his story, you are aware that life was not always fair. His brothers did a number on him, and others also took advantage of him. Yet, what intrigues me most about Joseph's story is that he did not blow up in rage, but always dealt with people in a forgiving fashion, even when he had every right to do otherwise. He was a big dreamer but became a very successful man. The key to his success was his ability to forgive. Read history and you will discover the same.

I cannot help but wonder how many of our dreams go unrealized because we hold to resentment. How many of our plans are short cut into disarray? How many relationships are scarred and destroyed? How many bottles of Pepto-Bismol are consumed to put out the fires that burn from resentment? All because we refuse to make forgiveness a way of life. The beauty of forgiveness is that it frees both the giver and the receiver.

Only strong men and women can move beyond resentment to rekindled love, but it can be done. Consider the examples of Joseph in Egypt and Jesus on the cross. There is no honor in being a small person, particularly if we claim to follow the one who was and is the epitomy of forgiveness.

"God did not send the Son into the world to condemn the world." (John 3:17a)
July 22

The verses that precede and follow this verse have to be the best summary statements of the gospel I have ever read. In just a matter of a very few words, we have a description of the heart of God and God's forgiveness and what we should do in response to that act. We can create some terribly complicated systems of theology. We can devise explanations of the gospel that only a scholar can understand. Yet, these verses are so simple that even a child can understand them. If we would just accept them and claim them, what a difference they would make in our lives.

Our generation has been dubbed by some persons as the age of anxiety. When we feel unloved, our lives are filled with anxiety. According to one psychologist, this is because we have failed in the ability to trust, the most elementary stage of our development. How can we trust unless we know ourselves to be loved?

Many of us are a bundle of anxieties. Therefore, we accomplish little. We need to relax in the knowledge that we are loved. "God so loved the world that He gave His only son, so that everyone who believes in him . . ." Do you believe in Christ? Then what in the world are you worried about? Accept his love. Lay your deepest concerns at the foot of the cross. Sounds so simple, so unbelievably simple!

"Jesus went through one town and village after another,
teaching as he made his way to Jerusalem." (Luke 13:22)
July 23

Luke 13 is filled with words from Christ that are as strong and hard as any you will find in the Gospel. Jesus had just finished a discourse on "repent or perish." He talked about the fig tree and how it would be cut down if it did not bear fruit. Then he discussed the narrow gate and the feast in heaven where the first will be last and the last will be first. His questioner was talking about salvation and pointing to a time in the future, but Jesus essentially said, "What you do now will determine what happens out there." There is no passive waiting in the kingdom of God. The choices we make now are of eternal significance.

Many of us are uncomfortable with this passage because we are closet universalists at heart. After all, God is loving and merciful. Would God really close the door on anyone? The Bible teaches that the open door will not always be open. There comes a point in time when you simply have to seize the moment and make it work. This particular text should cause us to stop and think about our own salvation and also encourage us in our reaching out to others. Most likely, this very day each of us will have a chance to encourage someone to walk through that door. In an intriguing way, choices today are hooked up to tomorrow's outcome.

July 24

"But when he noticed the strong wind, he became frightened, and beginning to sink, he cried out, 'Lord save me.' " (Matt 14:30)

In this particular story Jesus shared the spotlight with a man who has been debated more than any other New Testament character. Peter has been esteemed and criticized, commended and ridiculed, reverenced and made fun of. Why does Peter trap our attention and emotion? He was real, very involved, and impassioned, but more than anything else his character reminds us of our own behavior. Whatever was going on, Peter was in the middle of it. Every time he stumped his toe, he got up and brushed himself off, ready to go again.

Nearly everyone who accomplishes anything in this world stubs a toe somewhere along the way. If you hide in the boat and hold your toe, however, that is where you are likely to remain. People who never go anywhere do not have to worry about stumbling. The person who never makes a mistake will not make anything else either.

Christ wants us to be people of action. He means for us to make a difference in the world. Therefore, he calls us light and salt. It is not enough just to be nice in a cruel world. I offer some questions for you today: When you look at the scene of the disciples in that boat long ago, where do you see yourself? Are you in the bottom holding on? Or are you willing to let go and get out on the water where there is risk and challenge? Maybe today is a good day to get out of the boat and into the water.

July 25

"But the Lord provided a large fish to swallow up Jonah." (Jonah 1:17a)

I have always enjoyed reading short stories. One would be hard pressed to find a more intriguing short story than that of Jonah who was told by God to go to Nineveh. He objected, said he had rather die than go, and then headed toward Tarshish by way of boat. God hurled a storm, which frightened those on the boat, and they threw Jonah overboard to appease an angry God. God caused a great fish to swallow Jonah as he reluctantly agreed to go along with God's plan.

Jonah did everything he could to avoid doing what God had instructed. Yet, he discovered what many of us learn: there is no easy way to escape from God. Some of us may have even gone to sleep and are no longer aware of God's call. Such a dilemma is cause for concern. Then some of us, like Jonah, simply ignore the call of God in our lives.

I wonder how many of us today are refusing God's call. After spending three days in the belly of a whale, Jonah decided that it was time for him to do what God instructed. The most amazing thing happened. The people in Ninevah heard the message and repented. They all witnessed a revival. Maybe it is time to get out the old spiritual compass and determine if we are heading north or south. Even more so, are we running to or from a persistent God?

"I tell you, unless your righteousness exceeds that of the scribes and Pharisees, you will never enter the kingdom of heaven." (Matt 5:20)

July 26

Not all change is necessarily good. One change that causes me great concern has to do with our society's attitude about right and wrong, more specifically the vagueness of our culture on just exactly what is right and wrong. Thirty years ago we could make some assumptions about ethical issues that we cannot make today. I am convinced that a moral fiber existed at one time that now seems to have disappeared from our society today.

The verse for today deals with righteousness or, in contemporary language, doing what is right. Our culture needs to hear these words. Whether we realize it or not, we have a major crisis in our land, a crisis of honesty, integrity, and morality—of just doing right. Is this really a big deal? Does it really matter?

On a practical level, society suffers when we cheat. Everybody loses. Everybody pays more. Nothing is free. The bill has to be paid. Our economy is built on a foundation of trust. The system crumbles without it. On a personal level, people of integrity are usually more successful in their lives. There are exceptions to the rule, but in the long run it pays to do the right thing. Many large corporations are enrolling their employees in business ethics courses. Their success depends upon the integrity of their employees. Oh, for what it's worth, integrity pleases God!

"When they came to the crowd, a man came to him, knelt before him, and said, 'Lord, have mercy on my son.' " (Matt 17:14-15a)

July 27

Today's verse is about the healing of a young boy but, if there is a spotlight, it is really shining on two characters, Jesus and the disciples. The disciples had tried unsuccessfully to heal a young boy. They could not understand why they failed. In actuality, the disciples' failure was charged to their little faith, not to their unbelief. There is an enormous difference between belief and faith.

The kind of faith our Lord was talking about in this text is more than an intellectual nod. It is not saying that I know all about God or that I believe that God exists somewhere. That sort of believing costs nothing; it is easy. The Christian faith means that we have come to know God in such a way that we are willing to stake our lives upon Him.

Once Harry Emerson Fosdick preached a classic sermon on the importance of doubting your doubts. Faith isn't easy. True faith is the end of a struggle. Faith is not just believing God exists. Faith is believing in God and putting your life in God's hands.

The disciples could not heal the boy. The problem at first glance might appear to be a matter of faith. It was more than just saying, "I believe I can, I believe I can." It was the difference between believing that God exists and giving one's life to God.

July 28

"From one ancestor he made all nations to inhabit the whole earth." (Acts 17:26a)

If only we could claim and grasp the common nature of mankind. We are so close in proximity but at times galaxies apart in spirit. In *There Is a Spirit*, Kenneth Boulding makes reference to "a burning oneness binding everything together." To what is he referring? Could it be the same thing Paul was talking about when he wrote the verse for today? Whether we like it or not, this burning oneness is becoming more of a reality everyday. We are no longer an isolated people living in one corner of the world. We are part of the complex of nations that is one big neighborhood. The world of today is radically different than a century ago.

We must come to see ourselves as a part of the whole family of God. Our concerns must be as broad as the love of God whom we worship. Because of our proximity to each other, we have obligations to each other that we dare not ignore. We are in the wrong if we let children starve who could eat with our help, allow youngsters to die when medical skill can save them, leave men and women without shelter, accept—in the midst of our own abundance—the iron pains of degrading want. Our walk with Christ will give us opportunities to embrace the people we encounter. Remember that we all are all neighbors.

July 29

"So then, brothers and sisters, stand firm and hold fast to the traditions that you were taught by us, either by word of mouth or by our letter." (2 Thess 2:15)

This verse always catches my attention. Its words are not only a natural description of Paul but also his exhortation to us. If these words could describe us, how much better equipped we would be to face each day. Although Paul faced many problems, he seemed to always stand strong and confident. How can we have that same confidence?

Confidence and assurance begin when we truly understand the nature of God. God is not a divine policeman, an angry judge, or impassionate executioner. There is a vestige of fear and resentment toward God that stands as an obstacle to a saving faith in the one who would be our redeemer. Confidence and assurance come when we are aware that God is at work in our lives and in our world. We are surrounded by an unseen presence. We have a friend who is with us as we face life's most difficult moments.

Wouldn't it be nice if we could live with that kind of confidence and assurance? I am convinced that so much of this boldness and certainty is determined by whether or not we believe God really loves us more than anything else in the world. Have you experienced the inner witness of the Holy Spirit dwelling within your life? Such is the best avenue you will ever find for positive and reliable living of your days.

"In the morning, . . . he got up and went out to a deserted place, and there he prayed." (Mark 1:35)

July 30

Mark has a rather unique style of relating the gospel. As one writer said, "Mark hits the ground running." The Book of Mark introduces Jesus by way of John the Baptist, and then you fasten your seat belt and hold on. The first few chapters of Mark are filled with constant activity of Jesus. One demand after another is described, but couched right in the middle of those early chapters is a description of Jesus doing something that was the key to his vitality. What may sound at first like an incidental statement was really the source of Jesus' energy: he went to a deserted place and prayed.

The incident took place on the morning after an extremely hectic day. Jesus had been teaching in the synagogue, was interrupted by a man with an unclean spirit, healed Simon's mother-in-law, and at sundown all who were physically and spiritually sick were brought to him. Even though Jesus obviously was not afraid of silence and longed to share with us by his own example, when morning came, he withdrew to a lonely place. Why do we have such a hard time accepting the necessity of solitude and prayer? We have time for everything else but push our quiet time aside. If Jesus needed it, are we any different?

"If you do not stand firm in faith, you shall not stand at all." (Isa 7:9b)

July 31

Praying involves more than just routinely stringing some words together and going through an exercise. Praying is not an external activity but one that proceeds from the depths of our soul. No matter how long and earnestly we pray, no matter how many tears we may shed or the depths of our suffering, unless we have an active faith in the one to whom we are praying, we are just going through the motions of religion.

Unless we believe that God hears and answers, we have no assurance that we will receive that for which we pray. We must remember that faith in God is the substance of the things we hope for. We must believe that God sees our present situation and is able to bring good into our lives.

I like what the Psalmist said when he described God as having thoughts toward us that number more than the sands of the sea. Jesus talked about abiding in him and letting him abide in us so that we may ask what we will and it will be granted. The bottom line is that the issue of belief is far more important in our prayer life than whether or not we offer our prayers on bended knee. Ultimately, the posture of the body is not the concern, but rather the posture of the heart.

August 1

"I am the Lord, and there is no other; besides me there is no god." (Isa 45:5a)

In the text from which this verse is taken, Isaiah describes God as saying to Cyrus, king of Persia, "I go before you to open doors for you, to make the rough places smooth. I strengthen and support you, Cyrus, even though you do not know I am doing it." Imagine that; someone not being aware of the blessings of God. How could Cyrus be so insensitive? Before we answer that question, we might want to take a look at our own lives. We are just as guilty of ignoring blessings that surround us everyday.

So many of life's blessings travel incognito, and we are not aware of them. How many times have we been saved from some kind of serious dilemma by a friend, work associate, or family member, and we were not even aware of it? Even more so, how many times has God stepped in and changed some kind of situation without our even realizing it?

Long ago this old prayer was repeated in worship services: "For all thy blessings, known and unknown, remembered and forgotten, we give thee thanks." Such a prayer might be appropriate for many of us. As we move through this day, we would do well to be especially alert to blessings unknown and make them known and to remember those forgotten, offering our thanks to the author of all good.

August 2

"And even the hairs of your head are all counted." (Matt 10:30)

Since I have been losing my hair for many years, I always feel I am making God's job easier, at least in keeping count of the hairs on my head. The Bible says God knows, but it surely does not take as long to count them now as twenty years ago. Yet, this verse will continue to intrigue me. It was not designed to impress us with God's mathematical skills. God's ability to count hairs, many or few, is not the point of the verse. The good news of the verse is that God cares enough to give so much attention to the details of our lives. Knowing the number of hairs on our head is not an indication of divine boredom, but a symbol of indescribable love for people like ourselves.

In a Peanuts cartoon strip, Lucy says to Charlie Brown, "I love humanity; it's people that I can't stand!" While this may be the attitude of Lucy and many of us, it certainly is not the case with our heavenly Father. The story is told about a deaf girl whose illness could be traced back to hearing her father say of her "We could well have done without that one." In good or bad times, we can be sure that God would never feel that way about us. God is reaching out to us in love beyond measure.

108

"The hour is coming, and is now here, when the dead will hear the voice of the Son of God, and those who hear will live." (John 5:25)

Many of us prayed the childhood prayer, "If I should die before I wake, I pray the Lord my soul to take." I never really thought much about the prayer as a child. As I grew older, I developed a rather ominous feeling whenever I repeated the prayer that possibly it might be my last, that I might not wake in the morning. An even more appropriate question is not whether I will die before I wake, but if I will die before I live. I can be physically alive according to my vital signs, but be spiritually dead.

People die before they really live when they have no sense of direction nor chosen and commanding goal. Jesus came that we might find a compelling purpose and direction for our lives rather than just drifting from one whim to another. As ominous as it might feel to question if I might die before I wake, as an adult I am now considerably more concerned about dying before I live.

I want to be alive to the presence of God that not only wants to surround me but seeks to actually enter my life. Yes, I want to be alive in the morning. Yes, I want to be alive to life. "Lord, until you decide to take my soul, make me alive to you in every way!"

"Whoever is faithful in a very little is faithful also in much; and whoever is dishonest in a very little is dishonest also in much." (Luke 16:10)

The story is told about a boy who came home from school one afternoon with his report card. The father looked at the boy's card and shook his head with disappointment. The boy quickly asked the father, "What do you think the problem is, Dad: heredity or environment?" Not a bad response on the part of the boy. I wish I had thought of that question a few times in my own life. Yet, that boy's response is quite symnbolic of how many people go through life looking for excuses for their mistakes and failures. The Bible teaches us to be faithful and responsible. Jesus' words in this verse are very clear and direct. We must make decisions and be responsible for the choices we make.

We cannot blame someone else for our own failings, and we are to be faithful even in the small ways. Our faithfulness in small things prepares us for larger things. Stewardship and faithfulness are required throughout all our days. Each of us determines whatever significance life has for us by the attitudes we adopt, the goals we seek, the decisions we make, and the loyalties to which we give our energies and attention. Let's pray today that God will give us wisdom and courage to be faithful in all things, big or small, known or unknown.

August 5

This verse is found right in the middle of a parable Jesus was telling about a king who was preparing a feast. All of the preparations were made, and he issued invitations to the feast. In fact, he sent the invitations on several occasions, but they were not taken seriously by those persons who were invited. Two of the invited guests paid no attention and left; one went to his field, and the other returned to his business. What a shame! An opportunity to attend a feast by a king, and the invitation was given no consideration at all.

Before we throw too many rocks at the ignorant souls in Jesus' story, let's remember that he was talking to people just like us. There are many ways of applying the metaphor of the banquet to our lives. The bottom line is that we ignore so much of God's invitation to join in the festivities of life. The range of possibilities for those festivities is endless: to receive the redemption of our souls to the abundant life God freely offers, to see the beauties and wonders of nature, to share the thoughts of great minds in reading, and above all to hold communion and become partners in life with God. Yet, like the men in the parable, we make light of God's offers and go on our way. The parable has a hint of sadness to it. If it has application to our lives, the result is worse than sad.

August 6

"This is the day that the Lord has made; let us rejoice and be glad in it." (Ps 118:24)

Several years ago I wrote a book entitled *Hurry Up and Rest*. The book dealt with an issue that has been a struggle for me for a long, long time: the assumption that if I hurry and get everything in order, I will be rewarded with rest. After all, can we not rest better when everything is in order? But when is everything finally in order? Something is almost always left undone or hanging over our heads; rest seldom comes. The same dilemma occurs with our desire to be joyful in life. Many people go through life "getting fixed to enjoy it," but then life passes. Each day God's world is before us to see and enjoy. Pity the person who is too busy getting ready for the future and never sees the wonders of the present.

A fussy traveler was having trouble placing her belongings in the railroad coach. She put bundles first on the seat, then on the floor. She opened and closed windows, adjusted shades, and fidgeted like a nervous hen. When her husband protested, she said, "I want to get fixed so I can see the scenery in comfort." He shook his head and said, "Susan, we ain't goin' far, and the scenery will be all over before you get fixed to enjoy it!" The man was right. The journey ain't real long!

"To ourselves we seemed like grasshoppers, and so we seemed to them." (Num 13:33)

One of the best sermons I have ever heard was preached by a former pastor of mine, John Claypool. It was entitled, "Grasshoppers in a Land of Giants." The verse for today is a part of the text for that sermon. Moses had led the children of Israel out of Egypt to the edge of the promised land of Canaan. He chose some spies to cross over the border and get a glimpse of what they might expect. They returned with mixed reports.

The spies said the land was great and fertile, but it was inhabited by giants. "The inhabitants are so big," they said, "that we feel like grasshoppers." Two spies said that the Israelites should take the land immediately. The other eight said, "We'll never do it." The sad part of the story is that God had already given them the land, but they were too afraid to take it. As a result, they went wandering back into the wilderness. The opportunity did not come again for forty more years.

Although this story is ancient history, it is relived everyday in our own lives. The story is a classic example of what fear and a lack of confidence can do to people. The children of Israel allowed their fear of the unknown to play games with their imagination. They not only underestimated their own abilities but also underestimated the resource that had promised them the land long ago. Everyone lost in the process; so do we when we do not trust God to supply our needs.

"Let the words of my mouth and the meditation of my heart be acceptable to you, O Lord, my rock and my redeemer." (Ps 19:14)

Have you ever thought about how much time we spend talking? The number of words we use in chatting with friends, transacting business, discussing the weather, criticizing the President—just to mention a few uses—is phenomenal. We spend so much time talking but give very little thought to its proper use. Words have an amazing power, and once we release them, they are out of our control. We would do well to try to give them a positive reason for their existence. It was said of Job, "Your words have kept men on their feet." Can that be said of the words that will come from our mouths today? Consider a couple of thoughts as guidelines.

First, don't talk so much. Most of us say a lot more than we need to, particularly in moments when we ought to be listening. We should always seek to communicate well, but much of what we say is little more than nervous chatter. When we are chattering, we are not listening. Most of us should listen more. Second, make a conscious effort to be more positive in what you say. Will your words build up or tear down? Some words have to be strong and constructively critical, but not all of them. We develop certain habits in our talking; make them positive. Words have power. Once out of the mouth, we no longer control them.

August 9

A recurring problem for me in my Christian walk has to do with my inability to let go. I want to respond and do "right," but sometimes it means letting go of the old in order to take hold of the new. Jesus often encouraged people to let go. In his healing, forgiving, and teaching, he frequently told people they must let go of the old in order to grasp the new.

The more I think about it, the more I am convinced that letting go is woven into the fabric of life; and the older we get, the more difficult it becomes. Yet, we never outgrow the need to occasionally let go. As we accumulate more and more experiences, relationships, and memories, we find ourselves working even harder to hold things in place. Deep down, however, we know that we really can't prevent change.

Our faith requires letting go. Following the daily call of Christ in our lives requires leaving some things behind. Growing into the person God called us to be requires that we let go of the familiar and grasp the unknown. Letting go has never been easy and never will be. Some things are meant to be held onto forever; some things must change. Deciding when and where to let go may be a question you face today.

August 10

Jesus was speaking to believers such as you and me when he described us as salt. His words are both a compliment and an exhortation. We are to function as salt. In our day of artificial preservatives and concern for heart disease, do we really appreciate the role of salt? Recently I heard this interesting description of salt: "what you notice when somebody forgets to put it in." That phrase gave me a whole new perspective on the role of salt. I was reminded of not only the need for my life to be salt, but of many other people who function as salt for me. I do not notice many things and persons until they are absent. Our lives are constantly enriched by essentials without which our life would be stale and flat.

While we could make a case for those things we take for granted, I am even more concerned that I develop increased sensitivity to persons around me who enrich my life. Who are they for you? Once you become sensitive to these persons, you will begin to notice a whole host of persons who make life better for you. Jesus' words about salt have new meaning for me. Not only are they words of affirmation and exhortation, but they encourage me to be more sensitive to the salt of other people in my own life.

"Do not think that I have come to bring peace to the earth;
I have not come to bring peace, but a sword." (Matt 10:34)

These words of our Lord sound very harsh. There was no hesitation in his voice. What are we to make of all this talk about a sword? What about these words about his not coming to bring peace? What about setting man against father and daughter against mother? These words from Jesus may sound strange, like the gospel of Christ could be an interruption of the normal flow of things. No one likes an interruption and even moreso a disruption. We want to do things our way, and we dislike anything that changes our direction.

There is no question that Christ brings us comfort. He tells us to cast our burden on him. All who labor and are heavy laden are to come to him. Yet, we must also remember that he confronts us. Jesus is both a shelter from the stormy blast, but sometimes he is the stormy blast himself. Christ comforts, nourishes, and shelters; but he also confronts, challenges, and disturbs. Our acceptance of Christ is not an either/or question or a multiple choice. You either take Christ or you don't.

Today as we go through our daily duties, we should be mindful of Christ's comforting presence and his constant invitation to join us under our load. Yet, because of his presence, we will also be confronted by a radical gospel that may cause a disruption in our normal activities. The gospel can be very, very hard.

"All of these died in faith without having received the promises,
but from a distance they saw and greeted them. " (Heb 11:13a)

A *New York Times* article asked, "Where have all the heroes gone?" I am afraid that we have substituted celebrities for heroes, "Lifestyles of the Rich and Famous" for epics of the good and the courageous. Hebrews 11 represents the Bible's gallery of heroes: Enoch, Noah, Abraham, Isaac, Jacob, Joseph, Moses, Rahab, and Gideon, as well as many who are unnamed but not forgotten. God is still in the business of making heroes. While many ingredients go together to make a hero, consider these three.

First, heroes are people of great courage. Courage is the resource God gives us when we are fighting giants. If we never go out to fight giants, we have no need for courage. Second, heroes are people of great character. Many of us can remember the story of Sir Galahad and his search for the "Holy Grail." Remember how this gallant knight was described? His strength was as the strength of ten because his heart was pure. I don't know very many celebrities today who would be described as having "pure hearts."

Most of all, heroes have a great confidence. The amazing thing about the men listed in Hebrews 11 is not how heroic they were but how human, ordinary, and very much like us they were. Their courage and character were not their own. To the writer of Hebrews, these men were the essence of what faith is all about. There will be a need for a hero in your world today. Anticipate it. Be ready. Go for it!

August 13

"I went after it and struck it down, rescuing the lamb from its mouth." (1 Sam 17:35a)

Regardless of who we are, life has a way of bringing to our doorstep more than a few problems, some large and some small. Yet, they are always a part of our agenda. David can teach us some lessons about problems. In this case his problem was a giant named Goliath. We also face giants, not necessarily human, but giants nonetheless. The way he dealt with this giant can be a model for us as we encounter some of our giants. Consider several principles.

First, David did something. You say, "Big deal!" but taking action is important. The talk only lasted a short while, then he got busy. David identified the enemy and took action to defeat him. Very few giants have ever been talked to death. There is a place for discussion and planning, but there comes a time when doing something is the right thing.

Not only did David take action, but he attacked the first giant that he met. He could have made plans to approach a number of other enemies and then return to this ugly foe, but Goliath was causing the immediate problem. David looked at him and said, "Make my day!" David also assaulted the giant with the weapons at hand. He did not want Saul's armor. He used the weapons he already knew, those God had given him. As for your giants today, do something!

August 14

"The Lord, who saved me from . . . the paw of the bear, will save me from the hand of this Philistine." (1 Sam 17:37)

Yesterday we talked about the lessons we can learn from David in his dealing with the giant. We mentioned his using the weapons at hand, but he had more than just five smooth stones. First, he had already spent some time in preparing: "Your servant has killed both lions and bears." David had faced other giants and learned from them. The smaller battles prepared him for the battle with Goliath. David was also prepared spiritually. Taking one's problems to the Lord is always a weapon against the evils of the day. At times we take our problems to God as a last resort rather than the first remedy, however.

Most important, David was willing to recognize the need for God's power in his life. He said, "The Lord will save me." We are occasionally defeated by our giants because we choose to walk into the battle alone and unarmed. We should follow David's example. His true power came not from his sling nor the ability to use it, but from following the power and authority of God.

"So Naomi returned together with Ruth the Moabite, her daughter-in-law." (Ruth 1:22a)

The lady in our verse today is no stranger. She was even a distant great, great (and on) grandmother of Jesus. She is remembered most of all for unselfishly following Naomi, her mother-in-law. The story is too long to repeat here, but it celebrates her love as put into action. I am upholding the belief that love has to be more than words. It has to be put to work in life, or its effect is of little consequence. Love is definitely a feeling; but if it stops there, as with many of us, little has changed. When we love someone, we had better find ways to show it. The same principle applies to all areas of life.

Do you love God? You say, "Of course, I do." But what does your love do? Our love for God must be broken into small spendable change. It might be beneficial for us to count the ways. The same is true in our relationships with others. Talk is cheap. What are we willing to do to give support to our words? Our love for others must also be broken into spendable change. We may not have to follow someone into a foreign country, but our love should require more than just words. Love is more than just a feeling; love is something you do. It was in Ruth's day, our Lord's day, and our day as well.

"Where there is forgiveness of these, there is no longer any offering for sin." (Heb 10:18)

The light of God has been offered to us, though many of us have essentially refused the offer. We are enormously frustrated because we know in our hearts that we were made for God's community, but we have frustrated that intention. Because we have turned our backs to the light, and because there is sin in our life, we all carry around a great burden of guilt—and guilt has a bid price. A guilty conscience will cause us to do some strange things, even destructive things. Most people will not feel so much guilt that they physically punish themselves, but you have to wonder how many people drink themselves into a stupor, or fix themselves with a chemical high, or deliberately sabotage themselves to fail in order to keep coping with a guilty conscience.

The answer to our human plight is a spotlight focused on the cross. God takes the action and connects that which was separated. The writer of Hebrews said, "I will remember their sins and their lawless deeds no more." To whom was this writer referring? You and me. The writer went on to say that we have been forgiven, and there is no longer any sacrifice needed for sin. If we will only allow, the cross will do its work completely for each of us. Most likely, you and I will sin today in one way or another, either by an act of omission or commission. We do not have to climb up on the cross. That act has already been done. Forgiveness is for the asking.

August 17

> *"Making a whip of cords, he drove all of them out of the temple, both the sheep and the cattle."* (John 2:15a)

The secession of hostilities does not always guarantee tranquility. The absence of arms can frequently be accompanied by clenched teeth. Anger is so prevalent and obvious in our society. Recently an elderly lady driving a 1963 Plymouth in front of me changed lanes to my right just as we approached a traffic light. The person to my immediate right had to slow and let her into the lane. When he did, he absolutely exploded in rage, waving his fist and shouting insults at the lady who was oblivious to everything. I couldn't help but ask myself, "What causes a man to explode that easily over something so insignificant?" The answer is more than a little frightening. He obviously was carrying much repressed anger, and very little was needed to release the volcano.

I am reminded whenever I read of the life of Jesus that some things in life are worth getting angry about, but not everything. We must always remember that we live in an imperfect world. The world is filled with its share of evil. We cannot stick our heads in the sand, but our anger should empower us to do the positive thing and not explode in rage and make everything worse. Anger can be a great energizer, but it must be controlled. Put the anger to work. Ask God for guidance. Let anger force us to make things better. In other words, bitter or better, we must decide.

August 18

> *"But Peter, standing with the eleven, raised his voice and addressed them, 'Men of Judea and all who live in Jerusalem.' "* (Acts 2:14)

Every pastor would like to have the kind of response to a sermon that Peter had. Three thousand people were added to the church. Not long ago a friend of mine raised the question in regard to his ministry, "Does all this preaching really make any difference?" A part of the issue today is that preaching is so easily confused with entertainment. We can become just a glorified after dinner speaker. The goal, however, should be to point us to a vital faith. Preaching should point toward repentance.

One-time baseball manager Dave Bristol once said, "There will be two buses leaving the hotel from the ball park today. The two o'clock bus will be for those who need a little extra work. The empty bus will leave at five o'clock." In other words, everybody needed a little work. Preaching, like that of Peter, reminds us that repentance is for everyone. Anything less is just entertainment.

Preaching should point to the source of forgiveness, a man by the name of Jesus. For those who have already experienced that name, Peter might say that our great need is to reaffirm that faith. Preaching also calls for change. Peter boldly called persons to change, and they responded. Perhaps we could say that the preached message in the form of a sermon is a bunch of words that separate Sunday School from lunch. Those words point to the one who separates life from death.

"Jesus, full of the Holy Spirit, returned from the Jordan and was led by the Spirit in the wilderness." (Luke 4:1)

The verse today is taken from the experience of Jesus retreating into an obscure corner of the desert in Israel where he fasted for forty days. Physically he was alone; spiritually he was not. The experience can be summed up in one word: temptation—something we all know about first-hand. Satan appealed to Jesus. He approached him on three levels, all with powerful temptation. Notice that Jesus did not argue with Satan. He did not rationalize or blame God. He just recognized the bait and in each case faced the enemy with a statement of faith.

That is all it takes to silence Satan. Don't grab the bait, no matter how hungry you are. Don't get into an argument with Satan, because his ability to deceive you with your own mind is stronger than any intelligence you may use. James said, "Resist the devil, and he will flee from you." I should add, not for good but for awhile.

Remember, however, that if one kind of bait does not succeed, Satan will seek an alternative. You may have no difficulty resisting temptations of the flesh, but the enemy will try other kinds of baits to lure you into sin. Be warned that you will be tempted today. Even though no one since our Lord has been totally successful in resisting temptation, we do possess the ability to turn back a lot more than most of us realize. Scripture also reminds us that when we fail, our Lord understands. He's been there. That's why this verse is shared.

"She had a sister named Mary, who sat at the Lord's feet and listened to what he was saying." (Luke 10:39)

A young man was applying for a job. As a part of the increasingly more complicated application process, he had to take a series of psychological and aptitude tests. As the test began, the young man's attention focused on surrounding things such as the sharpened pencils and their number-two lead. He checked out the special erasers and straightened the papers countless times. Then, suddenly to his surprise, the testing time was over. The poor fellow had been so engrossed in the inconsequential that he never took the test.

Today's verse is taken from the experience of Jesus with Mary and Martha. Mary and Martha had differing ideas as to how they should use their time with Jesus. Martha was busy doing all kinds of housekeeping things, which in most cases would have been very appropriate. Yet, Jesus made it very clear that on this occasion Mary was the one who was addressing the real needs of the moment, both hers and those of Jesus. She had her priorities in the right order. Priorities are not a once-in-a-lifetime choice. They must constantly be reviewed, even daily. Are we focusing our attention on that which really matters, or are we being sidetracked by what appeals to us at the moment?

August 21

"The promise that he would inherit the world did not come to Abraham or to his descendants through the law but through the righteousness of faith." (Rom 4:13)

A young lady on a cruise ship kept glancing at an attractive young man. He could not help but notice her attention and was flattered. Finally he mustered up the courage to approach her. "Pardon me," he said with a gentle smile. "It may be my imagination, but I could not help noticing that you keep looking in my direction. Is there anything wrong?" She blushed and said very shyly, "Oh no. It's just that I can't help but notice how much you resemble my first husband." The young man looked puzzled and asked, "How many times have you been married?" She gave a mysterious smile and answered, "None, yet."

I like this lady's attitude. Faith is something like that. It is more than just strength for the present moment. It also has something to do with a positive attitude toward the future, not just some vague hope but a hope grounded in a power beyond ourselves. Faith is not grounded in a religious system or institution, but in a relationship. It is not accepting a handful of propositions and saying, "Yes, I believe. Now I am saved." Faith is not an intellectual exercise that takes place within our heads. The power of faith is found in a dynamic relationship that grows a little every day. Is there a need for power in our lives? Where does it come from? Most of us are not willing to run the risk of finding out. How unfortunate!

August 22

"The kingdom of heaven is like a landowner who went out early in the morning to hire laborers for his vineyard." (Matt 20:1)

A man who had been a real rascal most of his life was in the hospital for surgery. Coming out from under the anesthetic, he found the blinds in his room were drawn. He complained to the nurse that he could not see out and asked who had drawn the shades in the first place. The nurse said, "Calm down now; there is a big fire burning across the street, and we did not want you to wake up and think that you had gone to hell."

One of the more popular questions that people ask concerning faith in Christ is: "Can you really live a terrible life, wait right up to the last minute before you die, then ask for forgiveness for your sins, make a confession of faith in Christ, and still be received into the kingdom of God as if you had been the greatest saint who ever lived?" From the reading of the verse for today, we would have to answer in one word: "yes."

Relying upon a death bed confession has a hint of sadness. It is risky because the crises that fall upon us do not always go according to our schedule. A late night cram for an exam can sometimes have unexpected distractions. Also an earlier decision could have brought blessing in this life. Fortunately, God is in love with humanity so the door to salvation is always open—at least to a point.

"All of them were filled with the Holy Spirit and began to speak in other languages, as the Spirit gave them ability." (Act 2:4)

Jesus promised his disciples that he would give them power. He told them that they would be his witnesses and to wait patiently for this power. "Stay in the city until you have been clothed with power from on high," he said. That power came at Pentecost. The winds of change had come, and the church became empowered for its life and ministry in the name of Christ. The winds of the Holy Spirit had blown.

The question has been raised, "Can those winds ever blow again? Is that kind of empowerment just a memory of the past?" The answer to the first question is an emphatic "yes." So, if the wind can still blow, why do we not experience that power? In other words, "What is standing in the way of our power?" Two problems seem obvious.

First, we are satisfied with the familiar and have contempt for the new. The winds of the Holy Spirit bring change—change in personal outlooks, change in institutions, change in relationships, and change in priorities. Change can be frightening. The second problem is practical atheism. This is not a lack of belief in God. One may believe in God and yet have little belief in God's power. One's belief can become a memorial to the past rather than promise of the future. The winds of change are blowing right now. You can swing the door open or keep it shut.

"Beware of the dogs, beware of the evil workers." (Phil 3:2a)

When I lived in Augusta, Georgia, and needed to give directions to my house, I could name a few simple turns and describe a fairly direct route from most any side of town. If you came from one direction, I would always encourage you to be alert to one particular curve that is extremely dangerous. The curve is on a hill and known for its accidents. Cars on both sides have a way of taking the middle of the road. So you have to be alert to the danger.

The verse for today is taken from a text where Paul warned his readers to be aware of dangers ahead. In this particular case, the danger was false teachers, of which he said, "Beware." The new Christians were being misled and pulled away from paths to which they had made commitments. Paul warned them against anything that pulled them away from faith in Christ.

Most of us are not newcomers to the faith. Long ago we made commitments to the path of faith. Yet, many forces seek to sidetrack us from our faith. Paul would say, "Be careful. The risks were real then, and they are real now. If something pulls you away from your committed pathway, leave it alone. Watch out for the curve." Some serious curves await you this day. Danger lies ahead. Ignore those curves, and harm is sure to follow. Watch out for the one on the way to the "house." It's a killer!

August 25

Whether in sports, business, or even matters of faith, at times we must return to the basics. We always run the risk that we will forget the basics that have made us what we are. This is especially true in matters of faith. We must never become so sophisticated in our religious pursuits that we program out of our faith the whole issue of salvation. Religion involves so much: moral conduct, social concerns, ethical decisions. Most of all, we must remember that salvation is not just religious jargon. It is an event, something real, something that really happens. It forever changes our life and destiny. We can ignore it as a trivial issue if we choose, but the Bible reminds us that the payment for sin is death. That particular truth is carved in stone for all time.

We talk a lot about the cross. Crosses are on our steeples. We wear them around our necks, use them as bookmarks in our Bibles, and even decorate with them. The cross stands for the way our salvation was provided. When we get so sophisticated that we move beyond the role of the cross, we begin to ignore something called judgment. A price was paid for you and me. A way was planned, prepared, and carried out. The cross will always be the basic of our faith. Our lives today will be lived under the shadow of the cross.

August 26

Paul's words find a place in our lives regardless of the circumstances. They are good advice when we find ourselves down and out and are beginning to question the future. They are just as appropriate when times are good. His words have to do with pressing on and offer one of the keys to success in the Christian life. Paul suggested that we forget the things that are behind. In other words, we should never glory in the past, the good or the bad. In effect, Paul was saying that Christians must forget all they have done and look to what lies ahead. We cannot rest upon our laurels nor hold on to past failures.

Paul went on to say that one should reach out for the things that are in front. He used a very vivid Greek word that meant a racer going hard for the tape. Use your mind and imagination to visualize a runner straining with all his or her might to reach the goal line. Remember, however, the goal is not just any goal, but the calling of Christ in our lives. Paul was saying, "Press on. Move forward. Forget the past. Strive for that to which Christ has called you. Don't look back. Look forward. The race is on. Don't give up. Strain forward."

"Do not give what is holy to dogs; and do not throw your pearls before swine." (Matt 7:6a)

At a very practical, down-to-earth level, we human beings do an important task in determining the value of various things that we encounter in life. The value I attach to something in my life will shape my relationship to that thing. It is not always a conscious process, but everyday we attach a value to things around us. Deciding the price tag I place on this or that is very crucial. Yet, most of us need help at this point. We can be very insensitive and unknowing about certain realities. Jesus' image of the pearls before swine is an apt one at times.

I remember several years ago when I decided that I would buy my wife a ring for our anniversary. I took the several hundred dollars that I had saved into a very nice jewelry store. It was one of those stores where the price tags are not clearly shown, which should have been my first clue to go elsewhere. I pointed to one ring that I knew would excite her. I was nearly shocked into a coma when the salesman turned over the price tag. The ring cost many thousands of dollars. I very quickly left the store. There was nothing wrong with the ring. I just did not know how to value it. The experience reminded me that many times I do not attach the right value to something. Part of my task today will be assigning values. Lord, help me to do it right.

". . . Let us also lay aside every weight and the sin that clings so closely, and let us run with perseverance the race that is set before us." (Heb 12:1)

One of the most important traits that is found in the Christian lifestyle is persistence. We do not talk much about persistence as a virtue, but I am convinced that it may be one of the most highly valued of our virtues. If it isn't in the Bible, it should be—like the verse that should also be in there: "Grin and bear it." Often we must decide whether to stick with something or call it quits. All of us experience times when the only logical thing to do is to back out, but that choice should not be made every time nor always at the first sign of trouble.

To persist means to continue in the cause, to remain, to endure, to not quit. Too soon many Christians grow weary in well-doing and seem ill-prepared for the grind of the long haul. We must develop the ability to keep on keeping on even in the midst of adversity. A good beginning is great, the big splash is great, the spectacular plunge is exciting, but in the end the battle is won by those with persistence to continue. Almost anyone can start something, but not everyone has the faith to see it through. Persistence is the secret behind the great achievements of life. The electric light bulb was not made in a flash. Edison worked on it, gave up on it, and experimented with it for months. The idea may have come in a flash, but the reality required persistence. Persistence means that when we fall, we just get up again, and again, and again.

August 29

"About midnight Paul and Silas were praying and singing hymns to God, and the prisoners were listening to them." (Acts 16:25)

Today's verse is taken from the experience of Paul and Silas in prison, but only after they had been dragged to the marketplace, whipped, and then thrown into prison. Yet, look at their response. They were praying and singing hymns. What a powerful witness to those who were observing them! I continue to be intrigued by this description. Amazing strength, phenomenal spirit—they were praying and singing hymns in spite of all that was happening.

Did this strength come from a sound theology? After all, no one could ever accuse Paul of not being orthodox in his faith. Paul's theology was very sound. Did it account for this unusual strength and hope, the obvious feeling that pervaded all he did? It certainly did not come from having all his theological t's crossed! You can read every book ever written and know every word that Christ spoke, but has he invaded your soul? Have you felt his presence? In the final analysis, head knowledge alone will not be enough. Faith involves more than just knowing the facts.

The primary reason for Paul's spirit was a faith that not only made sense but one that he felt. Faith is not just a matter of knowing the facts. It is a matter of the heart as well as a matter of the head. Hopefully you will not have to sing hymns in prison this week like Paul and Silas did, but those hymns may be needed somewhere else.

August 30

"Jesus said to them, 'Peace be with you. As the Father has sent me, so I send you.' " (John 20:21)

Consider the setting of this verse. Most likely the disciples continued to meet in the upper room where the last supper was observed. They were afraid. They knew of the bitterness of the Jews as was demonstrated in what they had done to Jesus. The religious and political leaders could be planning the very same fate for each of the disciples. As they met in terror, listening fearfully for every step on the stairs, Jesus suddenly appeared in the midst of them. He said, "Peace be with you."

Notice that Thomas was not there. This whole thing, the cross and all, had turned out just as he had expected. So, when the news came to Thomas that Jesus was alive, it was just too good to be true; he refused to believe it. For this incident and other reasons we call him "Doubting Thomas." But was Thomas any different than the majority of us? Do we also at times struggle with our doubts? We all have doubted. We have had curious and serious reservations about our faith.

Allow me to go out on a limb and suggest that doubts can even be sources of growth. There is far more hope for the honest doubter than those who never struggle with either the meaning or misery of life. Frederick Buechner once said, "Doubts are the ants in the pants of faith, that keep faith alive and moving." Yet, the true joy that God intends for us comes when we begin to doubt our doubts.

"In all toil there is profit, but mere talk leads only to poverty." (Prov 14:23) *August 31*

My grandfather was a shoe cobbler. He repaired shoes for his living and was quite good at it. People would bring worn and torn shoes to him, and he would skillfully make them into comfortable, wearable shoes again. His shop also provided me with an after school and weekend job. In retrospect, I appreciate that job a lot more now than I did then. He taught me a lot, not just about shoes but about life and hard work.

I remember one Saturday evening as we were closing the shop that I became somewhat upset about my hands being so stained. The materials and the work itself were really tough on my hands. I had a big date that night and felt somewhat embarrassed. I made the mistake, or so it seemed then, of voicing my disgust to my grandfather. He walked up beside me, reached out for my hands, and said with enormous confidence, "Don't ever, never, be ashamed of hands that are stained from hard work." He walked over and locked the door.

The incident was not a mistake but a memorable moment for me. I have recounted my grandfather's words hundreds of times and appreciate them today even more. Never feel any shame in being guilty of hard work. If your hands are stained, wear them like a badge. Sometimes we can get a little too sophisticated for our own good. When we have too much pride to get our hands dirty, we had better be careful. Thank God for the health, opportunity, privilege, and stains of hard work.

"Your word is a lamp to my feet and a light to my path." (Ps 119:105) *September 1*

Several years ago Katherine Crosby, widow of Bing Crosby, auctioned her entire collection of Bing-a-Brac for charity. Some of the items sold were Bing's platinum record for "Silent Night," a plastic cup to "The World's Greatest Dad" from his son, all of Bing's fishing gear, and the Crosby family Bible. Of all the items, the last one caught my attention most. The auctioning of a Bible is certainly not unique. Through the years, Bibles that belonged to famous personalities have become valuable.

I am sure that only good intentions were in the offering of Bing's Bible. The person who bought it was very fortunate. I wonder if that person even realized what treasure he or she had. The value I am thinking of has nothing to do with Bing Crosby. Instead, I am referring to anyone as fortunate who has before them a copy of this treasured document. The ownership of this one by Bing neither adds to nor takes away from its value.

One of life's most important possessions is so close to us and so taken for granted that we can easily trade it off for things that pass with the night. The Bible is a special gift. Do we take it for granted? Do we really appreciate how easily accessible this book is? Whether it belonged to Bing or anyone else has nothing to do with its value. Its value comes from the author, not the owner.

September 2

"But strive first for the kingdom of God and his righteousness, and all these things will be given to you as well." (Matt 6:33)

A boy from a remote Appalachian valley finally had the chance to see a circus. When he learned the circus was coming to town, his father gave him the price of admission. The boy arrived at noon on the day of the circus and saw coming down the street a spectacle beyond his wildest imagination. There were camels, horses, acrobats, elephants, and more. Clowns were walking from one side of the street to the other. As one clown extended his hand to the spectators, the little boy thought this was the time to pay his money, so he placed it in the hand of the clown. When the parade ended, the boy went home thinking the circus was over. A few days later, after talking to a friend who saw the whole circus, the little boy realized that he missed the main show. He had missed what the circus was really all about.

This story is a parable of the lives of too many people. Endless parades call for our attention, and we will leave those parades like the little boy, thinking there is nothing more. Jesus encourages us to do otherwise. He warns us about seeking security in the parades that pass so quickly we miss the main attraction. Seeking the will of God for our lives is the main attraction; anything else is just a passing parade. What we miss is far more than a circus.

September 3

"Its priests have done violence to my teaching and have profaned my holy things." (Ezek 22:26a)

Even a superficial observation of our society indicates that we have lost our sense of the holy. As one author stated, "We have confused our priorities and have surrendered treasures for trinkets." We lose so much of the great wonder of life when we lose the sense of what is beyond ourselves. Our society has allowed our pursuit of immediate pleasures to dull our sense of wonder and awe. A sense of the holy, a sense of something beyond ourselves is so important in keeping our lives in focus and proper perspective. Our vision is at stake, and vision is important to every generation.

In his work "The Rock," T. S. Eliot wrote these words about people who have lost their sense of the holy.

There is no beginning, no movement, no peace, and no end. Only noise without speech, food without taste. And the wind shall say: "Here were decent godless people; their only monument the asphalt road and a thousand lost golf balls."

If all we are seeking is found within our own senses, we will find nothing more. But life at its best is so much more, so much more that is holy. The holy will be all around you today. Will you notice? Will you care? Will it reflect to you the majesty of a holy God? I hope so. Just notice.

"It was now about noon, and darkness came over the *September 4*
whole land until three in the afternoon." (Luke 23:44)

Possibly 550 years before Jesus was born, Isaiah said, "He was wounded for our transgressions, crushed for our iniquities; upon him was the punishment that made us whole, and by his bruises we are healed." Is this why the people who executed Jesus had to torture him so much before they killed him? Even though so much of this event was predicted long before it happened, we cannot write off the behavior of those around the cross by saying it was predestined.

I am reminded whenever I read of the cross that too many of us have a mean and cruel streak when we are faced with love and forgiveness. Sometimes we seem to have a need to humiliate and hurt those who have sought to help us before we can accept their healing and care. God knows it, Isaiah discovered it, Jesus experienced it, and the world lives by it.

The Book of Mark describes this treatment plainly. They put a purple robe on Jesus and placed a crude crown of thorns on his head, pushing it down until blood sprinkled from his brow. They beat his head with a stick, spat on him, and bowed before him in mockery. Then they crucified him. Why the cruelty? Why the humiliation? We can point our fingers at the persons who crucified Jesus and condemn them with the sound of righteousness in our voice, but we must be careful. Can we guarantee that we would not have been in that group? Would we have been so blind to the holiness of God? We might be in for a surprise.

"Then he began to speak to them in parables. 'A man planted *September 5*
a vineyard, put a fence around it.' " (Mark 12:1a)

Our verse today is taken from Jesus' well-known parable of the tenants. This parable must have been important to Jesus and the recorders of the Gospels because it is found not only in Mark's recording but also in Matthew and Luke—exactly the same story. The parable is so full of truths about God that we can only note them in the briefest way.

- God is generous. The vineyard was equipped with everything that was necessary to make the work of the cultivators easy and profitable. God also gives us all that we need.
- God trusts us. The owner left the cultivators to run the vineyard themselves. God trusts us enough to give us freedom to run much of life as we choose.

125

- God is patient. Not once or twice, but many times the master gave the cultivators the chance to pay the debt they owed. He treated them in a way they did not deserve. God gives us more chances than we deserve.
- God's justice will ultimately triumph. People might take advantage of the patience of God, but in the end come judgment and justice. God may bear long with disobedience and rebellion, but in the end God acts.
- God gives us the freedom of rejection. Forced love is never love at all.

September 6

"For it is a credit to you if, being aware of God, you endure pain while suffering unjustly." (1 Pet 2:19)

Two sportscasters on television were discussing the great running backs in professional football. They came to Walter Payton, one of the all-time leading ground gainers in NFL history. "What a runner!" said the first commentator. "Do you realize that altogether Walter Payton has gained over 9 miles rushing in his career?" The second sportscaster thought a moment and then responded. "And to think that every 4.6 yards of the way, someone was knocking him down."

Do you feel that same statistic sometimes describes your life? The writer of 1 Peter was dealing with persons who were getting knocked down and finding difficulty in getting back up. He advised them to "suffer with patience." Many of those Christians were knocked down because of their faith. They were suffering not because they were doing wrong, but because they were doing right.

The writer of 1 Peter implied that one should seek to turn defeats into victories of the spirit. We all have met people who have done just that. People all around us face giant adversaries, but they do not give in. Patient suffering, more than anything else, is simply refusing to give up and quit. It means holding on, even when nothing makes a lot of sense. It's not easy to get knocked every 4.6 yards. Being patient does not mean being passive. Even our despair can be used redemptively.

September 7

"The word of the Lord came to me." (Ezek 22:23a)

God appeared to Ezekiel with a call. Judah's sin cried out for judgment. The leaders, prophets, priests, and princes had given themselves to evil. A very few bold leaders, among them Jeremiah and Baruch, had taken a stand, however. God needed someone to step forward and draw the nation back from ruin. God had a gracious purpose in wanting someone to stand in the gap. Unless the gap closed, God would judge. God preferred to bless rather than blast and yearned to find someone who would turn aside judgment. With no one to intervene in the hour of need, no one to rise to the challenge, no one to answer the call, no one to stand up and be counted, and no one to lead out in the fight for the right, long-delayed judgment became reality. The Babylonians broke down the wall, robbed and destroyed the temple, and burned the city to the ground.

Under similar conditions in any century, God's need is the same. Even now this nation teeters on the brink of self-destruction and spiritual disaster. God is still looking for men and women who will take a stand. Today, in this time and place, the need still exists. Judgment is not necessarily a thing of the past. It is not a remote issue from the present or from this generation. Could it be that you will have an opportunity to stand in the gap today? The need exists just as in days of long ago.

"If I ascend to heaven, you are there; if I make   *September 8*

my bed in Sheol, you are there." (Ps 139:8)

One theologian has suggested that many of us suffer from a God that is too small. The problem is not with the size of God but with our perception of God. Many people have not found a God big enough for their modern needs. We may be carrying around a nine-year-old child's concept of God along with our adult understanding of history and science and even ourselves. If you and I are going to live in the modern world with a strong relevant faith, we will need an adequate concept of God. We must discover a God who can demand and capture our minds, hearts, and lives.

Many men and women are living without a faith in God. This is not because they are wicked or selfish or even arrogant, but because they have not discovered an adult God with whom they can live. We work hard to acquire an education, find a job, and keep the family together; but for some reason, we naively expect a casual yet adequate pilgrimage with God. It does not work that way.

Some people seek a God who is a help in trouble. Others want a way to heaven. Some seek God as a bridge to moral responsibility. Many are just satisfied with the "God of their fathers and mothers." The secret is found in discovering a God who is bigger than any concept we can construct. Take your best attempt at defining God, and then realize that God is a million times bigger!

"See, I have set before you today life and   *September 9*

prosperity, death and adversity." (Deut 30:15)

Most of us can remember lectures from our parents when we were younger about the importance of making the right kinds of choices. Sit up at the table, and you can have the rest of your meal. Clean up your room, and you will be allowed back into the family again. Take out the trash, or plan to eat it for breakfast tomorrow. Cut the grass, and you will be allowed to live for a while longer. Making choices is very much a part of our lives.

Our verse for today is taken from Moses' farewell address in which he recounted God's acts. He reminded the children of Israel that God had freed them from Egypt and journeyed with them through the wilderness. He told them that in response they should stand before God in order to enter into the covenant. Obedience to this covenant would mean crossing the river and going into the promised land. Disobedience meant that they would be rooted out of their land, however. Moses literally placed before them the decision of life or death. He knew the people well enough to know that they would need some help in making the right kinds of choices.

Even today, making choices is never easy. It always involves struggle. Discipleship is a long series of making right choices. Love the Lord. Walk in God's ways. Hear the divine voice. Be faithful over the long haul. The promised land becomes ours one day at a time.

September 10

"Be merciful to me, O God, be merciful to me, for in you my soul takes refuge." (Ps 57:1a)

This verse is taken from one of the psalms that is seldom read but so adequately describes the cry of the human heart. The writer of Proverbs came very close to the same words when he said that whoever trusts in the Lord shall be safe. The issue placed before us by this verse is one of trust.

God has brought us into this time and, not ourselves or some dark demon, is providing us with each day of our journey. If we are not fit to cope with that which God has prepared for us, we would also be unfit for any condition that we imagine for ourselves. In this time we live and wrestle. If we are to find meaning and joy, it will be in this moment. Let us not wish that the sun go back ten degrees. This is the moment and the place; now is the only moment we can use.

If easy times are departed, difficult times may make us more earnest; they may teach us not to depend upon ourselves. If easy belief is impossible, we may learn what belief really is and in whom it is to be placed. Trust is a word easily spelled but considerably more difficult to live out in the long stretches of life. Yet, trust is the only thing that provides joy during daylight hours and sleep for the night. Trusting in the Lord is indeed the way of safety.

September 11

"Happy are those who observe justice, who do righteousness at all times." (Ps 106:3)

The Psalmist suggested that doing the right thing should be characteristic of our lives whether or not judgment is the issue. In other words, do right for the sake of judgment, and do right for the sake of doing right. In the darkest hour through which a human soul can pass, whatever else is doubtful, this truth is certain. Regardless of whether we are judged for our acts or not, it is better to be generous than selfish, better to be chaste than licentious, better to be true than false, and better to be brave than to be a coward.

The man or woman will find blessing who, in the darkest hour of the soul, has dared to hold fast to what is good and seemingly right for no other reason than the fact that it is right. As one anonymous writer of the nineteenth century said,

> Thrice blessed is he, who, when all is drear and cheerless within and without, when his teachers terrify him, and his friends shrink from him, has obstinately clung to moral good. Thrice blessed, because his night shall pass into clear, bright day.

When in doubt, just do right. Doing so may require a lot of discipline now, but the outcome has to be better than doing otherwise. If that is not the case, the whole system falls apart. Nevertheless, "Time will tell."

"Then a servant-girl, seeing him in the firelight, stared at him and said, 'This man also was with him.' " (Luke 22:56)

September 12

Two older ladies were at a worship service. They were cheering on the preacher as the Word of God was proclaimed. When the preacher lambasted adultery, they offered a hearty "Amen." When he denounced drunkenness, they said, "That's right!" When he attacked stealing and lying, they audibly agreed. Then the preacher began to decry the sin of gossip. Suddenly the two women were silent. Then one turned to the other and said in a disturbed voice, "That preacher done quit preaching and gone to meddlin' now."

The scribes, Pharisees, and Sadducees thought of Christ as a meddlesome troublemaker. Were they right? Sometimes, when we turn from the will of God and Christ challenges our consciences, we may think of him as bothersome too. If we take Christ seriously, he can become quite disturbing. He does not affirm our dark side. He does not give his blessing to our living just any old way. However much we may neglect Christ, we still should be willing, as were the apostles, to give our all for him. The gospel is a radical gospel. Our culture and sometimes even our churches are simply not ready for the radical nature of obedience.

"Examine yourselves to see whether you are living in the faith. Test yourselves." (2 Cor 13:5a)

September 13

Paul also wrote to the Corinthian Christians, "Do you not realize that Jesus Christ is in you?—unless, indeed, you fail to meet the test?" His advice is appropriate for us too. Occasionally we need to take a look at ourselves. We need to examine the condition of our spirit and test the strength of our faith. We need to consider how we are living according to Christ's standards. We may discover when we examine our spirit that we don't like what we find. There may be sins and an ugliness we have been trying to hide or ignore. Even so, we must not despair.

We can learn another lesson here. Paul reminded the Corinthians that Christ lived in them and they should focus on that goodness within. We would do well to examine ourselves and look beyond all our failures to the goodness and power of God who is within. Paul had a motive. Frankly, he knew that the Corinthian Christians, by and large, were definitely not living the Christian life in a serious way. In fact, he believed that they were falling quite short of the example of our Lord.

Sin is a very serious matter. It is separation from God with all of the resulting raging guilt and inner torment and disintegration. Yet, precisely at that point of our utter despair, Christ's salvation is most meaningful. The instruction to examine ourselves is always balanced by the promise of God's grace.

September 14

"As he went ashore, he saw a great crowd; and he had compassion for them." (Mark 6:34a)

What groups of people in our society would you judge to be like a sheep without a shepherd? Would they be the thousands of homeless persons wandering about our city streets with no address to call home? Perhaps another logical group might be the prison population that is lost in immorality and crime. What about the hundreds of responsible, hardworking, bill-paying folks who work in your office building? What about all the students who attend the schools that surround you? What about the children who play on your children's athletic teams? Could the group even include members of your own household?

Not all sheep are outwardly lost. Many of us are sheep in our hearts and spirits—wandering, confused, and hurting on the inside. The good news of the gospel is that our Lord looks at all of us as sheep without a shepherd. Have you fallen over the cliff of some type of abuse? Are you wandering around due to some kind of unhealthy relationship? Do you have a heart that is fractured because of some tragedy in your life? Then, our Lord sees you as the one lost sheep. If he has to, Christ will put you on his shoulders and carry you back to the fold. He looks upon us as sheep without a shepherd for he is the Good Shepherd who willingly lays down his life for his sheep.

September 15

"For the Son of Man came not to be served but to serve, and to give his life a ransom for many." (Mark 10:45)

The request that James and John had just made of Jesus was no different than the requests of many of us. They were seeking places of power and were just bold enough to ask for such. I have often thought that perhaps the other disciples became angry because James and John had the courage to ask for what they too wanted.

How tempting it is to have power—the power to shape history, to change lives, to have people at our beckon call! Deep down inside, many people think this is what life should be. They long for power. Jesus presented a radically different alternative when, in settling this argument with James and John, he spoke about becoming servants and even slaves to others. In his statement about powerlessness, Jesus was actually saying a great deal about power. In effect, we do not always need to kick sand in the face of the bully on the beach. Rather, by living near him and ministering to him, we can turn the bully into a friend. Sometimes you can love him enough that he stops being a bully.

You say, "Na, won't work." Granted, sometimes such treatment will not produce any change, but sometimes it does. Jesus said that if we err, we should err on the side of giving it a chance. That sense of being a servant, of helping and caring, makes the gospel message so strong. How ironic that powerlessness can be so powerful! Try a little of it today. You will be surprised.

"But in those days, after that suffering, the sun will be **September 16**
darkened, and the moon will not give its light." (Mark 13:24)

This particular verse is not normally included in daily devotional books. Who wants to read about the chaos of the end of time? Yet, there is a valuable lesson here even for daily thought. The text in Mark 13 is strange and somewhat upsetting. It speaks of persecutions, believers being delivered to councils, brother against brother and father against son, and wars and earthquakes. At first sight, one finds little comfort in such a passage.

The text applies to our world today, however. As we confront such events, we are able to enter more fully into the mood and spirit of the New Testament, which was written when the end of the world was imminently expected. It affirmed a trust and faith in God that enabled early believers to be confident in the midst of chaos. When applied to our day, this text from Mark reminds us of the reality of judgment, the limitations of human wisdom, and the assurance of always being held in God's love and care, even in the midst of chaotic events. In the end God will gather the elect, those who have opened themselves to God's grace and live with assurance of the present and the time to come. The invitation is open.

"Six days later, Jesus took with him Peter and James and John, **September 17**
and led them up a high mountain apart." (Mark 9:2a)

Although I still claim to be a semi-young man, I can remember when most of the railroad crossings were not protected with electric gates. Usually there were signs with the words: "Stop, look, listen."

Unfortunately, through the years many persons did not heed the warning and lost their lives as a result. In a way, this was the experience some of the disciples had on the Mount of Transfiguration. They went up to the mountain and were mesmerized by what they saw and heard, but then they were commanded to listen and go out and act on what they heard from Jesus.

We must not keep our faith experiences to ourselves. We have to reach out and come down from our own mountaintop times to the real world below where people need to hear about and come to know more fully Jesus Christ. We must stop and listen to what scripture tells us about Jesus, both what God tells us about His son and what Jesus tells us about himself. Then, we have to move out into the world and tell others about Christ based on what we have listened to and heard from him through scripture, prayer, and the living out of our faith. With the old railroad crossings, our lives were in danger when we did not "stop, look, and listen." In matters of faith, the lives of others could be lost if we don't "stop, look, and listen."

September 18

"When Jesus heard this he was amazed at him." (Luke 7:9a)

Parenting is often a frustrating experience. Some of the lessons of life we try so hard to teach our children seem to go in one ear and out the other. Sometimes we wonder if they will ever develop the traits we desire for them. Then there are those occasional moments, when we are least expecting it, when children will say or do something that indicates they really were listening after all. Who would have thought it?

Occasionally, Jesus too was pleasantly surprised to find someone in whom his message had unexpectedly taken root. The verse for today is a part of a larger story in which a Roman centurion, a person who was not among those to whom Jesus usually preached, demonstrated such a genuine faith that Jesus marveled at him. Jesus even said that he had not seen so great a faith among the people.

Many persons in Jesus' audience thought that faith was a matter of accomplishment. Those who carefully followed the Old Testament laws and performed good works believed they most deserved God's blessings. These same people believed that the Roman centurion who built their synagogue and treated them with respect also deserved Christ's attention. The centurion sent word to Jesus saying, "I am not worthy." He could only ask for help based on Jesus' mercy. We need to be careful in assuming anything about ourselves. We become ready only when we claim "unworthy."

September 19

". . . He asked them, 'Who do the crowds say that I am?' " (Luke 9:18)

According to the New Testament, Jesus was the long-awaited messiah. At Caesarea Philippi, when Peter confessed that Jesus was the Christ, Jesus acknowledged that Peter was right but asked his friends not to tell anyone. Jesus wanted to finish his work of proclaiming the kingdom for God before the knowledge of his uniqueness as the anointed one was known. Furthermore, Jesus had a different concept of the role of the messiah than most Jews had. He came not as a powerful general but a humble, loving, sacrificing teacher. After the resurrection and Pentecost, the time came for the news of his messiahship to spread. Indeed, the resurrection proved conclusively that he was both Lord and Christ.

Our task today is to tell dispirited and confused souls that Christ the Lord has come to stand with them against all of the negatives of life—and life certainly has its negatives. Just listen and take notice. The negatives may not be in your own life but in the lives of people you encounter today. Some people are waiting for your word of encouragement. Jesus can meet needs today just as he did long ago, and people are all around us whose needs are so apparent. Be alert; be sensitive. The good news is still good news. People are waiting.

"He said to the woman, 'Your faith has saved you; go in peace.' " (Luke 7:50) *September* 20

Jesus had been invited to dine with a certain Pharisee, and during the meal something very interesting happened. A woman known for her sin entered and covered the feet of Jesus with perfume and wiped them with her hair. She was weeping because of her sin. The Pharisee was somewhat taken back that Jesus would associate with this woman. He was even more surprised when Jesus pronounced that her sins were forgiven. She discovered first-hand what millions of people since have discovered: a contrite and sin-sorry heart and the grace of Jesus are always a match.

Someone said, "If the best of men had his innermost thoughts written on his forehead, he would wear a large hat and never take it off." Jesus said, "There is nothing covered that will not be revealed, and hidden that will not be known." In fact, our hidden thoughts and guilts from past sins often keep us from fully loving Christ, ourselves, and others. Too many of us are mistakenly convinced that our past sins make us unlovable. That assumption could not be farther from the truth. We have difficulty believing that anyone could ever forgive and forget, especially if we live with a lot of memories of past sins. Through our Lord's loving response to a promiscuous woman, however, we can catch a glimpse of Christ's complete and sweet forgiveness.

"My sheep hear my voice. I know them, and they follow me." (John 10:27) *September* 21

A little boy rushed up to his mother in the kitchen, exclaiming, "Look at me, Mommy. I am as big as Goliath. I am nine feet tall." His mother asked him, "What makes you think you are nine feet high?" He answered by saying, "Well, I made a ruler for myself and measured myself, and it says I am nine feet high."

Sound familiar? We all tend to measure ourselves against the standards of the world or the standards we create for ourselves. If we make up the criterion, then we can proclaim ourselves Goliaths, or successes by misleading norms. Our only measure should be our Lord, although following his requirements is difficult, not necessarily because we think we cannot, but because we do not really listen to him.

Today's verse reminds us that the sheep hear the shepherd's voice. They listen to him. We are the sheep, and we should listen to our Lord. He speaks about following him, being motivated by him, and finally about receiving from him the gift of eternal life. No one can take that gift away from us. We must listen to Christ and not worry so much about listening to what the world says. When we no longer measure ourselves against the world, we find ourselves open to the leadings of the Good Shepherd. Listening, following, loving—these are the only measures that matter. Against what measure will you place your life today? Listen to the right voice today, the one voice.

September 22

> "My Father is glorified by this, that you bear much fruit and become my disciples." (John 15:8)

An ancient fable tells of three merchants crossing the Arabian desert. Traveling in darkness to avoid the intense heat one starless night, they were passing over a dry creek bed when a voice from the blackness commanded them to halt. They were instructed to stop, pick up pebbles from the creek bed, and put them in their pockets. After obeying the strange command, they were told to leave that place, camping nowhere near. The mysterious voice then told them that in the morning they would be happy and sad. Shaken and confused, and obeying the mysterious intruder, they traveled through the night. When morning came, the men anxiously looked into their pockets; and rather than finding the pebbles as expected, there were precious jewels. Indeed they were happy and sad. They were happy they had picked up the jewels, but sad because they had not picked up any more while they had the opportunity.

We are charged to gather pebbles also. One such pebble is the command to abide in Christ and therefore produce fruit. When we attempt to produce spiritual fruit with our human nature, we will always meet with failure. Our Lord asks us to dwell in him and allow him to dwell in us and produce the fruits of our lives. The day will come when, like the three merchants in the fable, we will wonder why we did not let him do for us what he said he would do. We are in the creek bed. Pick up the pebble. Abide in Christ; let him abide in you. What a jewel you could easily miss!

"No one has greater love than this, to lay down one's life . . . " (John 15:13)   *September 23*

What is the greatest love you can imagine? We love in all sorts of ways, but occasionally we hear of persons who are willing to love by placing their life in jeopardy even if it means death.

Two soldiers were the best of friends during World War II. While they were in battle one day and several yards apart, one of them was severely wounded. Immediately his friend started for him, but was held back by others. Nevertheless, the soldier tore himself loose and crawled to his bleeding friend. He was able to return with him, but his friend was dead. When the rescuer's sergeant tore into him for risking his life in such circumstances, the soldier said, "Sarge, he wasn't dead when I got to him; and he said to me, 'I knew you'd come.' "

A good question for today might be, "Can my friends count on me?" Jesus commanded us to love one another as he loved us, which ultimately means giving up our lives for our friends. Each of us as Christians face this challenge. The chances are that we will not have to sacrifice our lives for anyone today, but our Lord says that we should be willing. Are you willing? Keep that thought in mind as you encounter your friends today. Ask for God's help to meet the challenge with faith and courage.

"It is not for you to know the times and period that   *September 24*

the Father has set by his own authority." (Acts 1:7)

Jesus told his disciples that for the moment they should not leave Jerusalem. He instructed them to do something that has always been very difficult: "Wait." For some reason, this word strikes a note of anxiety with me. Patience has never been my long suit. I do not like to wait on anything. That's not bragging, just a fact. Waiting is a discipline with which I must struggle everyday. Yet, the Lord said, "Go to Jerusalem and wait."

Such tests as waiting in lines, waiting on traffic lights, and waiting on my family to get ready have always stressed me. Waiting seems like such a poor use of time, but it is a part of our routine whether we like it or not. Perhaps the most difficult waiting is a much more profound problem. I am thinking of waiting on God. We pray for guidance and direction, but we are forced to wait. We pray for others to understand or change; we are made to wait. We ask for relief, yet suffering continues. We pray for assurance, but uncertainty abounds. We pray for deliverance from nagging problems, but we have to wait.

Waiting can present some of God's best opportunities to establish direction for our lives. As we step back from the regular pace, we often gain a perspective that is totally impossible while we are running in little circles. The disciples were told to go to Jerusalem and wait. They did, and God was faithful. Their waiting, like ours, paid off.

135

September 25   **"We look not at what can be seen but at what cannot be seen." (2 Cor 4:18a)**

We are faced with the task of determining those things in life that are of lasting value for us. We have to separate and distinguish between that which is passing and that which is eternal. We experience and encounter much each day that is misleading. We get our values all confused and pursue the temporary in lieu of the permanent. Seeking after material things captures most of our time. We so often count material things as the most important in life and lose our sense of the eternal.

We live in a culture that, generally speaking, has lost its belief in the invisible and believes, hopes, and works only in the visible. That which is infinite has been cast aside for that which is finite and conditional. We live as if we believe that if we cannot touch it or see it, it really does not have much value. A growing edge in our faith is to understand the true values of life, realizing that the spiritual dimensions of life are what nourish our spirits and give depth and meaning to our lives. Another growing edge for us is to pay closer attention to the dimensions of our day that are permanent, giving less of ourselves to that which is only temporary. May God give us grace to be able to distinguish between the two.

September 26   **"He answered, 'It is written, one does not live by bread alone.' " (Matt 4:4a)**

Walk into any bookstore and you will notice as many books on the shelf about diet as any other subject. There are about as many diet plans as there are people to invent them. A simple definition of the diet is "the habitual food of a person." The word is derived from the Greek word *diaita*, which means "manner of living." We know that the food we eat affects the nerves, tissues, and organs of our bodies, so naturally we are concerned about what we take in.

Another form of diet, however, has a far more important effect on our general well-being. This is the material we daily feed our minds and spirits; this spiritual food determines how we react to life's joys, sorrows, and problems. It is also our way of life. We are free to choose this type of food just as we select our physical food. How do we go about selecting this spiritual food, that which is true, pure, and lovely?

We must use the discipline of prayer. Nothing else will work. Prayer for guidance is both talking and listening. We forget that prayer is more than just our making certain petitions known. Prayer is also listening to God's voice as we make choices about our diet. Remember, diet is a way of life. We must concern ourselves about far more than just the physical food that occupies much of our concern. Another type of food is even more important.

"Even though I walk through the darkest valley, I fear no evil." (Ps 23:4a) September 27

The valley of the shadow is an interesting image. Think of the deep, narrow gorges of the mountains. Think of the travelers as they pass through these narrow paths slowly. The opportunities are unlimited for bandits and thieves to hide among the shadows. Travelers are easy prey for wild animals who wait. This pathway is anything but safe as the shepherd leads the sheep.

As sheep we want to get through to the other side, the place where green pastures are found. Before we find those pastures, however, we must make our way through the valley of shadows. The shepherd has the rod and the staff, the rod to direct and the staff to protect.

Do not forget that the Psalmist adds, "I fear no evil." Imagine that, walking through shadows with no fear. The courage comes from the one doing the leading: the shepherd. "For you are with me," are the words of encouragement. The shepherd hears my voice and hastens to help me. The shepherd is both powerful and tender and carries a stout club to beat off the enemies. Going before the sheep, the herder beats the grass with the staff and, if these reptiles do not scamper away quickly, strikes them with the club.

Just remember that these words are more than just beautiful imagery. They are a description of the way Christ leads us every day: through the mountains, through the valleys, even the shadows in the valley. When we realize the role of Christ, fear melts away.

"The time is fulfilled, and the kingdom of God has come September 28

near; repent, and believe in the good news." (Mark 1:14b)

John Claypool once preached a sermon in which he said people could be divided up into three basic lifestyles: coping, choosing, and changing.

- The copers possess little or no power and spend more of their energy just trying to get by. They lead a reactionary type of existence and settle for responding to the circumstances that surround them. Life is a matter of surviving. Survival is the goal.
- The choosers have reconciled themselves to the fact that humankind must make certain choices in life. At least they have come to the conclusion that life is more than just getting by.
- The changers take the process a step further and seek to make if different, even better. They make a difference for people other than themselves. They are not satisfied to leave the world as they found it. Their motivation may not always be pure and benevolent, but they make a difference.

Where do you fall in these three categories? Granted, at times we just want to survive, and sometimes the best we can do is claim a few choices. If we are true to the call of our Lord, however, we should make a difference. We are to be salt and light. Our surroundings are to be influenced by our presence. How about it? Today will you cope, choose, or change?

September 29   **"It does not rejoice in wrongdoing, but rejoices in the truth." (1 Cor 13:6)**

As a minister I have many opportunities to officiate at wedding ceremonies. Unless the couple selects some other scripture, I almost always use this text from 1 Corinthians as a part of the wedding. The words are far more than just nice sounding phrases for the setting, however. They describe the epitome of a loving relationship. Consider the part of the verse included for today. The New English Bible has a rather intriguing translation: "Love keeps no score of wrongs." What a superb word of advice! And oh so hard to live up to! But what a difference it would make in all of our relationships —including marriage, family, and friends.

In Polynesia, where the natives spend much of their time fighting, all men keep reminders of their hatred. They suspend articles from the roofs of their huts to keep alive the memory of wrongs that were done to them. When reminders are intentionally kept before them, there is little chance for new beginnings. Paul urged just the opposite. He strongly suggested that we do not keep reminders, that we do not keep a score. At its best, love has a short memory, and a short memory is the best friend a relationship has. So, you decide. You can hang reminders all around you and nurse your hatred, or you can forget to make the entries in your ledger and create all kinds of new possibilities.

September 30   **"You shall love the Lord your God with all your heart, and with all your soul, and with all your mind." (Matt 22:37)**

No one can ever accuse Jesus of soft peddling his words. He had the ability to cut right through to the heart of the matter. In one of his many encounters with the Pharisees, he moved right to the essence of religion when he quoted the first great commandment. As one writer stated, "A fully functioning faith that gives us the strength we need is a combination of using our heart and mind and strength." All are a part of the way we love God.

The heart was considered by the Hebrews as the source of human emotions. To love God with our heart means that we love with all the emotion that is found within us. Emotions are the driving force for so much of what we do. Why shouldn't those same emotions drive us to express our love for God? Loving God with our mind keeps our heart and emotions in balance. Feelings may motivate and drive, but the mind is necessary to keep our emotions focused and integrated. Our mind is a gift from God and a part of our response to God. God does not want blind emotion. Commitment without the mind is short-lived.

Loving God with our strength implies resolve and commitment. Our faith must be more than blind emotion and good intention. Sooner or later it must find expression in how we live day by day. Our head and heart must have the help of the body to make our response of love to God find long-lasting, permanent, enduring expression.

"God said, 'Let there be lights in the dome of the sky to separate the day from the night; and let them be for signs and seasons and days and years.' " (Gen 1:14)

October 1

In a world of plastic and artificial ingredients, we can easily become insensitive to the natural change of the seasons. We have done ourselves a real injustice if we become too busy to notice the beauty of the changing seasons. In an urban world of concrete and air conditioned-rooms, it can easily happen.

I have always enjoyed visiting my wife's parents. One reason is because they make a very obvious but regular response to each season of the year. As each season moves in, they make some simple changes such as moving certain flowers inside and moving the yard swing to the basement at the presence of autumn and the coming of winter. Now, such activity may not sound like such a big thing but, at least, it causes one to notice that something in God's nature is happening. Otherwise, those changes take place without any observance on the part of most of us, which seems like such a loss.

Autumn is a beautiful time. The colors of the leaves, the brisk cool air, and the excitement of special holidays ahead create a very unique climate. The change of the seasons is a beautiful process, although most of us hardly notice. God has produced a fascinating cycle of life in the world of nature. We cheat ourselves when we do not take note of the beauty and change all around us.

"Immediately something like scales fell from his eyes, and his sight was restored. Then he got up and was baptized." (Acts 9:18)

October 2

Something is wrong at the very heart of humanity—something sick, something twisted, something perverted. The Bible calls it sin. Where is the solution? Conversion is the answer to man's dilemma.

A Sunday School class of first graders was being quizzed by the pastor on the meaning of certain religious words such as baptism and repentance. The pastor asked one of the little boys, "What is conversion?" The little boy thought for a moment and gave the only definition that he knew: "It's the extra point that's kicked after a touchdown."

Conversion is a biblical word that means change of direction. Conversion is about change. There need be no blinding light or visitation by angels, but there must be change. Our verse today is taken from the experience of Paul's conversion. For him it was a radical change, from one who persecuted the followers of Christ to one who was an advocate of Christ.

Are you an advocate of Christ? There is no neutral position; we are either for him or against him. We do not have to experience a blinding light on the Damascus road, but at some point in time we must totally and completely give ourselves to Christ. To make that commitment to him is the essence of conversion. To do so is to kick the extra point that wins the game.

October 3

"After taking some food, he regained his strength. For several days he was with the disciples in Damascus." (Acts 9:19)

A psychologist suggested that persons fit one of four distinct styles of behavior. Dominant folks like to be in control. For "people" persons, life is a party. A third group is marked by steadiness and predictability. Detail people make up the fourth group; they like to do things right. While I would love to take off and have some fun with these personality types, I mention them to you now only to make a point of how Christ can change a person's natural behavior.

No one would question that Paul was a dominant person. He liked to be in control. He was a take-charge person. Nobody had to ask him what he thought. Blunt, direct, and fast to make judgments—that was Paul. Then he met the risen Lord on the Damascus road. Saul, the dominant, became Paul, the committed. Even the way Paul submitted to Christ, such as his willingness to go to prison for his faith, caught the attention of people. Many of them did not understand. They probably looked at him and called him crazy. "He was so eccentric about this man Jesus. Crazy." Wouldn't we be better if we were a little crazy too?

October 4

"Because it is the Lord your God who goes with you; he will not fail you or forsake you." (Deut 31:6b)

You might remember a man several years ago by the name of Terry Fox, a one-legged runner who became a symbol of courage to his nation as he raised more than $24 million for cancer research with his Marathon of Hope. In 1977, Terry lost his leg as a result of cancer. When his former basketball coach gave him an article about a one-legged man who ran in the New York Marathon, he began to build his body for what was to become his Marathon of Hope. Before death claimed him at the age of 22, Terry had run 3,300 miles, in constant pain. He never made it to the Pacific Ocean, but he made an impression upon the world and taught a lesson about courage.

Jesus said that in this world we will experience tribulation. His words were not a threat but rather a warning about life. The one factor that enables us to face life's difficulties is courage. Courage is the silent resignation that God will never give us more than we can endure and also the belief that God will be "in there" with us. All of us have our troubles in differing degrees, but we must face disappointments with courage and go on living. Persons who do not have that courage will give up and quit, cry and moan, become full of despair and bitterness. In the meantime, life goes on; and it is still a life with meaning and possibility for those who face it with courage.

"But a Samaritan while traveling came near him; and when he saw him, he was moved with pity." (Luke 10:33)

Jesus told a number of parables during his earthly ministry. One of the most well-known is that of the good Samaritan. The parable focuses upon a man who was beaten and left for dead. Three people passed by him, but only one offered help in his time of need. A priest came by first and offered no help. Next came a Levite who also ignored the man's plight. The sharp edge of the story is the obvious background of these two men. They were religious men, community leaders.

The spotlight shines on the Samaritan. At first, he seemed to be the most unlikely to offer help. Maybe because he was considered a racial half-breed, ceremonially unclean, and excluded from all self-respecting people, he knew what it was like to be forgotten and ignored. Nevertheless, he offered help when the other did not. Possibly the Samaritan's own suffering made him sensitive to the plight of others. So, it is not surprising that he stopped and gave aid to the hurting man.

Possibly our own suffering can make us more sensitive to people around us. If you have known pain or possibly are experiencing it now, then the experience has given you the ability to empathize with the suffering around you. Like the Samaritan, your experience with suffering makes you sensitive to the struggles of people you encounter. You can give of yourself because you have been there.

"Every tree therefore that does not bear good fruit is cut down and thrown into the fire." (Matt 3:10b)

In an effort to ease our guilt we frequently say to ourselves, "You're a good person; you don't steal, you don't swear, and you wouldn't think of killing—at least only occasionally. We are telling only half of the story when we evaluate our life performance in terms of what we do not do. In this story about the barren tree, the tree was committing no crime. Yet, it was to be cut down because it bore no fruit. It was simply existing, using space and air, putting back very little in return. Unfortunately, many of us are guilty of the same problem. We are content to exist and give little concern to the fruit we should produce. We are satisfied to compare ourselves with the thieves and murderers. We feel that since we are not guilty of those crimes, we pass the test.

Are we giving, or are we content to see life in terms of what we can take? Our form of taking is not necessarily illegal. We can never break a law and still be a "taker" in God's eye. We all have opportunities of influence and input. We can seek to make a contribution, or we can just sit back and criticize the efforts of those who want to help. There are enough takers in this world, people who are content to watch a world of suffering and see it as someone else's responsibility. Jesus said that if the tree does not bear fruit, it will be cut down. Our world desperately needs fruit.

October 7   **"Since, then, we have such a hope, we act with great boldness." (2 Cor 3:12)**

Most things in life worth having require some kind of risk. With a little effort I could offer a number of examples, but one certain area of living is as risky as any I know: relating to people. To reach out to anyone—whether a friend, parent, or spouse—means opening ourselves to the possibility of being hurt. In reaching out to other people we make ourselves vulnerable. We could be rejected, belittled, or betrayed. Even worse we could simply be ignored, which may be the most painful hurt of all.

To relate to anyone requires risk. Most of us have at some point opened ourselves to someone only to be hurt. After a bad experience the temptation is to close ourselves off from the world and build an emotional wall. If we don't get close to anyone again, we think there will be no more risk or pain. Yet, isolation is a very high price to pay for safety.

A song by Simon and Garfunkel states, "I am a rock, I am an island. And a rock feels no pain." To become a rock is to feel no pain. Cutting one's self off from the world is safe but terribly lonely. As a rock feels no pain, neither can we experience joy and warmth when we are alone. What a high price!

October 8   **"Every generous act of giving, with every perfect gift, is from above, . . . from the Father of lights, with whom there is no variation or shadow due to change." (Jas 1:17)**

Today is my daughter's birthday, which brings to my mind change—the one predictable characteristic of life. This date reminds me of the day I took Melody to get her driver's license. She got in the car with the examiner and proceeded with her driving test. When she returned, she got out of the car with a smile that exposed every tooth in her mouth. Matter of factly she said, "I passed." I was thrilled for her, but more than just a minor change had occurred in my life. The examiner didn't even realize that by passing Melody, she cut loose my unprotected, helpless child. My daughter would no longer need me to be her chauffeur, a job I strangely enjoyed. In that moment of her unforgettable smile, I aged twenty years. Then, Saturday night arrived, and she drove out of the driveway without me.

The following Sunday morning at church I was sitting on the platform and noticed the oak tree outside the window, a scene that through the years has become symbolic. You guessed it. The leaves were beginning to turn. The seasons had changed again. What happened to summer? Yet, the view has become symbolic to me of the unchanging nature of a God who supervises all these changes. In the midst of seasons and children who change overnight, I need something to grasp that is solid. Our God never changes.

"Love is patient; love is kind; love is not envious or boastful or arrogant." (1 Cor 13:4) *October* 9

A certain little thing exists in relationships that weakens and distorts them. In fact, it can eat away and consume a marriage. It is called jealousy. What is jealousy? Why does it exist? We might understand jealousy better if we realize that it is a natural, protective emotion like fear. In normal amounts jealousy can be helpful and beneficial, but when it grows too big, it becomes destructive. It makes us watchful over the relationships upon which our security and happiness depend. The problem comes when our protective emotions get out of hand and trigger us into a state of disturbance that has no real justification.

At times jealousy has a valid reason for existing. Perhaps we have not dealt with an experience of the past and fear that we will relive it. Sometimes, though, jealousy is irrational. This insecurity may be due to something that happened long ago and has nothing to do with the present relationship, but the threat may have a bleed-over effect on today's situation. The actions of an irrationally jealous spouse or friend can produce in the other person the same behavior, irritation, impatience, or resentment—the very thing jealousy suspects.

"By the grace given to me I say to everyone among you not to think of yourself *October* 10
more highly than you ought to think, but think with sober judgment." (Rom 12:3a)

How do you feel about yourself? This is a very crucial question. In fact, practically every other area of your life will be affected by your attitude about yourself. In regard to the question there are two extremes. One extreme is to think too highly of one's self. This happens when we begin to have an unrealistic attitude about ourselves and when we do not recognize our limits as human beings. We develop an impression of our appearance, talents, time, place, and possessions.

The other extreme is to think too little of one's self. This attitude involves an unrealistic attitude about ourselves. It undercuts reality. While recognizing our limitations, we should claim the gifts that God has given to us. Unfortunately, we get caught up in the gifts of others and become defensive and fail to recognize our own. Unless we believe in ourselves, how can we expect anyone else to?

To have some degree of pride in one's self as a person is not sinful. The Bible reminds us that we are created in God's image. This fact alone should be a source of pride for us. At one point God even looked at the new creation and said, "It's good; it's very good." We cannot grow and become anything better until we first accept who and what we are right now. We must accept ourselves, not without blindness to our faults, but claiming God's gifts.

143

October 11

"Truly I tell you, just as you did it to one of the least of these who are members of my family, you did it to me." (Matt 25:40b)

A friend of my father decided to take a vacation for a month. During that time he decided that he would not shave or cut his hair. Upon returning home he decided to do something that would become an eye-opening experience for him and his church. With his long hair and beard, he dressed in some old clothes and entered his own church. Appearing as a homeless person, he walked with a cane as he awaited the response of his people.

Not realizing who the man was, the ushers essentially ignored him. He intentionally sat in someone else's pre-ordained spot and watched those seated next to him slide further down the pew. During the service he got a first-hand view of how an unkept stranger would be treated. During the invitation hymn he went forward; the pastor's anxiety became obvious. The stranger asked to speak. Upon his first word, the congregation recognized who he really was. He told them that he knew then how strangers really felt and how they were treated. The experience became a turning point for the congregation. The people became sensitive to the discrepancy between pious words and actual behavior.

The chance is good that we will meet a stranger along the way today. We will have an opportunity to reach out or pull back. Our treatment of strangers is more than a social issue. It is deeply rooted in the teachings of our Lord.

October 12

"And what is the immeasurable greatness of his power for us who believe, according to the working of his great power." (Eph 1:19)

God has so much to give and share. Could it be that God created the world and the human race to provide an avenue for the divine need to give? We can never exhaust God's ability to give. Paul reminds us of that fact in his words to the people of Ephesus.

A root set in the finest soil and the best climate, and blessed with all that sun and air and rain can do for it, is not as sure of its growth to perfection as every person may be. The sun does not meet the springing bud that stretches toward God with half the certainty that God, the source of all good, communicates to longing souls.

Many years ago T. C. Upham wrote: "If we stand in the openings of the present moment, with all the length and breadth of our faculties unselfishly adjusted to what it reveals, we are in the best condition to receive what God is always ready to communicate."

God has so much to give to you today. The real issue is whether or not you will give God the chance. Open your soul to the source of all goodness.

"I have sworn an oath and confirmed it, to observe your righteous ordinances." (Ps 119:106)

My wife purchased an ant farm for her classroom. The kit came equipped with everything, that is everything but ants. A book provided great details on the facts of the ant world. There was also a form to order the ants for the farm. Suzanne asked me to put the kit together. I was glad to help, but I had better things to do than read the book; and I couldn't see ordering ants through the mail when the yard was full of them. So I put a cup outside with a little sugar and water in it, and in a matter of minutes the cup was crawling in ants. Am I sharp or what? We transferred the ants to the farm and watched with interest during the evening.

Early the next morning I walked into the kitchen and noticed there were no ants in the ant farm. They were all over the kitchen. The ants had evidently crawled through the air holes and were having a ball, everywhere. I then read the book and realized why it was called a giant ant farm. The ants needed were a different type than yard ants. The order blank also mentioned that the ants were free. I ordered the proper ants, which arrived quickly in the mail. In the meantime I learned some other interesting facts from the book.

We frequently ignore another book that offers a free gift. Due to haste of the insane belief that we already know enough, however, we go ahead on our own and suffer the consequences of our independent actions.

"And you, my son Solomon, know the God of your father, and serve him with single mind and willing heart." (1 Chron 28:9a)

This short verse from 1 Chronicles carries far more wisdom than at first meets the ear. The word that attracts my attention is "willing," an unqualified willing. I'm all for a perfect heart, which I assume to mean undivided or unhindered, but a willing mind is something of a challenge for me. Consider how a willing mind should be used in daily life.

Little things come daily, hourly within our reach. They are not less calculated to set forward our growth in holiness than are the greater occasions that occur, even though rarely. Moreover, faithfulness in little things, even little frustrations, and an earnest seeking to please God in little matters is a test of real devotion and love. Let our aim be to please our Lord perfectly in little things and attain a spirit of childlike simplicity and dependence.

In proportion as self-love and self-interest are weakened and our will is wed to that of God, so will many hindrances disappear. Many of the internal struggles that harass the soul will vanish, and in their place will come peace and tranquility.

October 15   "Let us kneel before the Lord, our Maker!" (Ps 95:6b)

The memoirs of Edward Burne-Junes relate the story of a young artist of considerable talent who one day visited the studio of the great painter. With his customary courtesy, Burne-Junes showed her his pictures. The two artists lingered for a time in delightful talk over the part they both so dearly loved. When they returned to the drawing room, the painter asked the young artist what she intended to do with her art. "I mean to begin again," she replied very simply.

The great moments in our lives are the moments of inspiration when we can gain a new vision of who we are and what we can become. For us the vision of excellence is Jesus Christ. Through his life we see what real life ought to be. Not only does he give us the vision of excellence, but the resources to move our lives forward, to begin again. Alfred North Whitehead once said: "Moral education is impossible apart from an habitual vision of greatness." Christians find that vision in Christ.

It is most likely to come in our busy routine through the process of worship. Worship, on Sunday or otherwise, is the lifting up of that vision of excellence. I cannot imagine my life without regular worship. It meets a need that cannot be satisfied in any other way. Whether as worship leader or participant, I have discovered that my life is directly influenced in and through worship.

October 16   "For my yoke is easy, and my burden is light." (Matt 11:30)

One of the best friends I have ever had is a black Lab dog named Dooly. He is loyal, faithful, and requires very little from anyone. In recent days Dooly has had a lot of medical problems, the worst of which is a hip problem that often plagues large dogs. Because of the problem we try to walk him as often as possible. He loves the attention and exercise, plus he knows he will get out of his usual area. Pick up the blue leash, and he really gets excited. What intrigues me most is that he has come to associate freedom with a restraining leash.

How can something that, on the surface, restrains become a source of excitement? I have an idea. The leash means contact with people Dooly loves and who love him. It is a connection. It means freedom beyond the regular boundaries of his normal world. It means new experiences, new faces, and a walk into the yet unseen. A leash that seems to restrain has become a symbol of freedom. What a paradox! Yet, you and I are confronted with a similar paradox.

Christ said, "Take my yoke upon you." Sounds heavy at first. He also said we are to make him our master. Sounds enslaving at first. It is precisely in our enslaving ourselves to the Master that we, too, make life's most vital connection. We discover freedom beyond the normal boundaries of our usual world—new faces, new experiences, and a walk into the yet unseen. That which at first seems to restrain becomes a symbol of freedom, much like Dooly's leash.

146

"For whoever has despised the day of small things shall rejoice, *October 17*

and shall see the plummet in the hand of Zerubbabel." (Zech 4:10a)

This interesting verse frequently goes unnoticed in the rush and demands of the big world. The prophet was talking about some enormous changes that God's people could anticipate, and then he asked who could despise the day of small things. That is an intriguing statement.

Most of us measure ourselves in terms of great acts, noticeable and obvious to everyone. Perhaps because we read and hear of those who are lifted to notoriety due to their highly publicized deeds, we might desire to be so recognized. Yet, occasional efforts of ordinary holiness may accomplish great things. Constant discipline in unnoticed ways and the spirit's silent unselfishness give to life unmistakable beauty.

There is enormous power in little acts of love. Great acts take time and planning that is not always available. Little acts become a way of life and are available to us at any given moment. True maturity is attained most readily by faithfulness in the minor details of life, through self-forgetting love. Love's secret is to be always doing things for God and not to mind because they are such very little ones. Remember that holiness does not consist in doing uncommon things, but in doing everything with purity of heart.

"God saw everything that he had made, and indeed, it was very good. *October 18*

And there was evening and there was morning, the sixth day." (Gen 1:31)

We were recently traveling in North Carolina on Interstate-77 south of Charlotte. The most memorable part of the trip for me occurred late in the day. We were on a stretch of highway that was relatively unknown to me. The sun was very low and beginning to create beautiful colors against the horizon. To my right was a large body of water with sailboats returning to a marina. To my left were the foothills of the mountains with leaves so full of color they could have been on fire. It was one of those scenic moments you want to remember but, as usual, the camera was at home. Sailboats against the setting sun on one side and the fiery colors of autumn on the other—one would be hard-pressed to find a more majestic display of God's creativity.

I must be honest and confess, however, that one part of creation amazes me even more. The hills and waters would be meaningless without our eyes. Sight becomes our bridge to God's creation. I don't understand how sight works. I have friends who are physicians who try to explain it, but I still have trouble comprehending how God's autumn becomes an image in my mind. This I do know: I am grateful for my eyes. Much more than the excitement of the seasons depends upon their proper functioning. I also know that I take my eyes for granted. Today I plan to be more alert to everything around me and give thanks for my eyes.

October 19

> "Be strong and courageous; do not be frightened or dismayed, for the Lord your God is with you wherever you go." (Josh 1:9)

The mountains are a popular place this time of the year. They are beautiful at any time of year but, filled with the colors of autumn, they take on a majestic presence that only God can create. When I drive through the mountains, I frequently try to imagine how the mountains appeared to the early settlers. The mountains are awesome enough when we are traveling on smooth, well-planned roads in powerful automobiles. Can you imagine what the settlers thought when they came in their horse-drawn wagons to the first view of the peaks?

The settlers must have been overwhelmed with fear and apprehension. The saving factor for them was that they did not have to make it over the peaks in a single journey. They would travel as best they could one day at a time. What other choice did they have? In fact, their traveling philosophy is not bad advice for other times and places as well.

Mary Ann Kelty lived during the days of wagons in the eighteenth century. Listen to her words:

> Watch your way then, as a cautious traveler, and don't be gazing at the mountains or river in the distance and saying, "How shall I ever get over them?" But keep to the present little inch that is before you. The mountains and the river can be passed in the same way. When you come to them, you will find light and strength as well.

October 20

> "As for mortals, their days are like grass; they flourish like a flower of the field." (Ps 103:15)

Several years ago I took a trip to the North Carolina mountains with the senior adults of our church. One of the experiences I remember most on this trip was during the bus ride home. We were traveling on Interstate-20, riding into the sun. I was quite interested in a book I was reading. Everyone in the bus began to talk about the beautiful sunset. From the back of the bus I did not have a good view, but I was determined to finish the chapter I was reading. When I finished the chapter, I quickly moved to the front of the bus. The sunset was breathtaking. The bus driver said that it was even prettier a few minutes before. As pretty as it was, I had come close to missing the entire scene. The colors lasted for only a few more minutes, and darkness came quickly.

Many of our experiences in life are like that. They come quickly and then are gone. We must be in a position to receive them and take advantage of the moment, or we may miss the whole opportunity. Consider the experiences that have no price tag: the smile of a loved one, the laughter of a child, a beautiful sunset. Think of God's leading in our daily walk. We have many opportunities for service, but they too do not remain static. A door is open today and closed tomorrow.

"Now faith, hope, and love abide, these three;
and the greatest of these is love." (1 Cor 13:13)

Every good mate in a marriage knows that once in a while we need to break down and say "I love you." These words have a mysterious power. Most of us don't say them enough, but the partner may hear them in another way. For example, our mate may see love in the faces and hear it in the voices of loving couples with whom we associate.

Practically everything we say and do concerning our spouse returns to that person. Whatever joy or frustration we may feel will communicate itself to our friends and sooner or later will reflect back to our mate. The wife who shares the nice things her husband does and speaks of him with joy is building a picture of him as a success in the most interpersonal relationship of all. The same is true of a husband who speaks to others of his wife with deep affection and tenderness. When he speaks tenderly of her he is telegraphing "I love you" to her through every person he meets.

We also publish our love or distaste for our mate by the stories and jokes we tell. Others hear our message loud and clear, and sooner or later it returns to our mate. Whenever our friends are around our mate, their attitude will hopefully be a message from us to our partner of "I love you."

"Are any among you suffering? They should pray. Are any
cheerful? They should sing songs of praise." (Jas 5:13)

George Gershwin's masterpiece *Porgy and Bess* is beautiful but profound. Take, for example, the old gentleman who sings, "I got plenty of nothing, and nothing's plenty for me." As he sings there seems to be a hint of contentment. He obviously does not have much materially speaking, but what he does have seems to satisfy him. As he concludes his song, he becomes a little more specific when he says, "I got my gal, I got my Lord, and I got my song." He has a right to be happy. He has a wife who cares about him, a Lord who loves him, and a song in his heart. He seems to have discovered a secret, whether he realizes it or not. He is very close to what happiness is all about.

Happiness is such an illusive rascal. We all want it, but we just don't know how to find it. It is not something we seek directly. It tends to be a by-product of one's commitment to the "basics" of life. The old gentleman in the song seems to have found it in his gal, his Lord, and his song. Most of the other things are simply decorations for the basics of life. Somehow we get side-tracked, and the things that are a means to an end become an end in themselves. The man in *Porgy and Bess* found it because he knew where to look. I am afraid most of us are looking in the wrong places.

October 23   **"And all who touched it were healed." (Matt 14:36b)**

A number of years ago Neil Diamond and Barbara Streisand recorded a popular song entitled, "You Don't Send Me Flowers Anymore." In the song they lament back and forth to each other, "You don't say you need me; you don't sing me love songs; you don't say you love me; you don't send me flowers anymore." They have grown so far apart that they have neither the courage nor the knowledge of each other to be able to say goodbye. As they look back, they miss most of all the small things, the little things, the little niceties that came so naturally in times past.

The song is a reminder of the importance of little things in relationships. While big problems sever relationships, many more relationships have been weakened or destroyed by the little things. On the other hand, many relationships have withstood the "big" problems because of the presence of the nice "little things." Just as little problems eat away and erode a relationship, the little remembrances, the impulsive "I love you," and the silent hugs nourish a relationship. The little things are not expensive and do not require long-range plans. They do require effort. Never underestimate the power of a simple touch, an unexpected gift, or a "how are you feeling?" that waits for an answer. The little things are super important. Read the Gospels and learn from the Master of the simple touch.

October 24   **"A glad heart makes a cheerful countenance, but by sorrow of heart the spirit is broken." (Prov 15:13)**

We live in a free world and have the right to be unhappy if we choose. Therefore, you may want to consider the following four easy steps if you desire to be unhappy.

* Develop a negative attitude, a great guarantee of misery. The negative attitude of the people of Israel was revealed in the early chapters of Genesis when Moses led them out Egypt. It was demonstrated in the crises of the Red Sea and their food, water, and meat. Every time we sow negatives, we reap a harvest of negatives.
* Develop the "I" personality. How many times do we use "I" in a two-minute conversation? When we constantly think only of ourselves, we are preparing for unhappiness.
* Develop the unforgiving spirit. We are to forgive not once nor twice but an indefinite number of times. An unforgiving heart guarantees unhappiness.
* Gossip about other people. A gossiping person is a very insecure person. Puritan Christians in early American tarred and feathered the two gossips.

By kicking the addiction of a negative attitude, the "I" personality, the unforgiving spirit, and the gossip habit, and remembering that we who have been "born again" are a new creation, the Holy Spirit will lead us into divine new relationships. Happiness is the by-product of doing what God suggests we ought to do.

"Knock, and the door will be opened for you." (Matt 7:7b)

Through the teachings of Jesus we are given the freedom to pray for our needs. "Ask and it will be given," we are told. We are given unqualified freedom to offer our prayers. If we have any trial that seems intolerable, we may pray that it be relieved or changed. We may pray for anything, with perfect freedom, if we do not pray selfishly. One disabled from duty may pray for health that he may do his work. One who is burdened by some particular sin may pray for God's help and forgiveness so that she may serve better.

The possibilities for our prayers are endless. Yet, the answer to our prayers may be, as it was to Paul, not the removal of the thorn but, instead, a growing insight into its meaning and value. The voice of God in our soul may show us that divine strength is enough to enable us to bear it. The best approach to prayer is to feel complete freedom to pray for any concern or need, but to also grant God the freedom to respond to those prayers with divine wisdom. Freedom here, freedom there—that is praying at its best!

"Now may our Lord Jesus Christ himself and God our Father, who loved us
and through grace gave us eternal comfort and good hope." (2 Thess 2:16)

Have you ever had the kind of morning, even a whole day or week, when you just wanted to be left alone? Possibly there was some major stress in your life, a problem that needed to be solved, a dilemma that seemingly had no resolution. When we have clouds of varying sorts hanging over our heads, the last thing we want is something else with which to deal. Yet, the real question for us is whether or not it is best for us in the long run to turn a deaf ear to the new need. When we turn away from some duty or some fellow-creature, saying that our hearts are too sick and sore with some great yearning of our own, we may sever the line on which a divine message was coming to us. We shut out the person and the messenger.

God has a divine plan for our lives and, if we keep our hearts quiet and our eyes open, it will be revealed to us. If we don't, fighting results. Does this mean that we should never say no to a need that places itself before us? Absolutely not. At times "no" is the right response, but not every time. The key is to keep an open eye, an open mind, and an open heart. Subtle angels are always at work.

October 27

The world that surrounds us is filled with great mysteries, many of which have stumped the wisest minds of the ages. Yet, the greatest mystery may not be found in the world beyond but in the world within. In fact, the one person I have the most difficulty in understanding is the one I should know the best: myself.

I find great comfort in knowing that God understands us even when we don't understand ourselves. God knows us through and through. Not even the most secret thought that we hide from ourselves is hidden from God. As we come to know ourselves more, we come to see ourselves more as God sees us; and then we catch some little glimpse of God's designs with us, how each ordering of divine providence, each check to our desires, and each failure of our hopes is fitted for us and for something in our own spiritual state.

Such a perception of ourselves is, indeed, an act of faith. So much of the mystery of ourselves remains unknown. Until we come to this knowledge, we must take all in faith, believing—though we know not—the goodness of God toward us. As we know ourselves thus far, we know God.

> Nay, all by Thee is ordered, chosen, planned;
> Each drop that fills my daily cup Thy hand
> Prescribes, for ills none else can understand:
> All, all is known to Thee.
>   —A. L. Newton

October 28

A wise friend suggested to me recently that I learn to accept frustrations and aggravations as opportunities for growth. I have to be honest and admit that in the midst of trouble, growth is not always my foremost desire. Yet, what a difference it would make in my own spiritual maturing if I could develop that approach to life.

The challenge is to receive every inward and outward trouble—every disappointment, pain, uneasiness, temptation, darkness, and desolation—as a true opportunity and blessed occasion of dying also to self and entering into a fuller fellowship with our self-denying, suffering savior. The challenge is to reject negative thoughts about every kind of trial and distress so that our days become those of prosperity. That state is best that exercises the highest faith in and fullest resignation to God.

The thought of such an aspiration sounds so noble. Living it out is a different matter. It is so much easier, so much more human to pitch a fit, feel sorry for myself, and bemoan my very existence. I realize, however, that growth is seldom the result of doing the natural thing.

"Relieve the troubles of my heart, and bring me out of my distress." (Ps 25:17) *October 29*

Life's greatest difficulties are not necessarily the most obvious ones, and some of life's greatest tasks are those that are found within our hearts. For example, the greatest burden we have to carry in life is life itself. The most difficult thing we have to manage is self. Our own daily living, our frames and feelings, our particular weaknesses and temptations, and our peculiar temperament are the very things that perplex and bother us most and often leave us in personal darkness.

In an honest attempt to deal with our burdens, we must first get rid of the self. We must hand all of our inward experiences, temptations, temperament, and feelings over to the care and keeping of our God and leave them there. The real enticement is to take our burdens to God and then reclaim them, which makes about as much sense as taking out the trash and then bringing it back to the house. If we could only remind ourselves hourly that God made us, knows us, and knows how to manage us if we will only give God the chance.

"Therefore keep the commandments of the Lord your God, *October 30*

by walking in his ways and by fearing him." (Deut 8:6)

Moses spoke these words to the children of Israel long ago, and the chances are good that some of the demands did not set well. Many words of instructions both precede and follow this verse. Many of the instructions involved a whole new way of life for these people. Yet, the instructions were clear. Whether or not the people obeyed was still to be determined.

What do we do when God calls and we are not sure we really want to obey? Like the children of Israel, the truth may not set well with us. If God calls us to duty, however, the only correct response is obedience. If it can be a glad response, fine. If it cannot be, then obedience is still in order. Our pleasure or enjoyment from our acts of obedience is not the issue. The secret is in discovering that the will of God must be done for the sake of God, not for the sake of ourselves. If we undertake the duty, step by step God will provide the disposition.

When God calls, we just obey. If we cannot respond with the whole heart in obedience, then we must begin with what we have. As an old wise man said, "It is better to obey blunderingly than not to obey at all."

October 31

"Those who are unspiritual do not receive the gifts of God's Spirit, for they are foolishness to them." (1 Cor 2:14a)

This is the day and night when many persons in our communities raise the possibility of the world of the spirit. Granted, Halloween may not be the best way to introduce us and our children to the spirit world, but it does cause us to raise some questions. For example, is there a world of the spirit? Is this a real world or something we have created to make us feel better about the limited physical world as we know it? The answer to the first question is an emphatic yes. There is a world of the spirit. It is real and not a creation of our minds.

We frequently forget that if we truly subscribe to a faith in the Jesus of the New Testament, we have no choice but to recognize an unseen world. Constantly Jesus acknowledged the presence of the Holy Spirit. When he made ready to leave the disciples, he assured them that he would not leave them comfortless; the Holy Spirit would be their advocate. Recognizing the reality of the Holy Spirit is only scratching the surface.

The world of the spirit is not a world of Casper the ghost and Halloween horror houses. I sincerely think a day will come for each of us when we discover that the unseen world is the most real world of all. To believe otherwise is to operate with a handicapped faith. It is a shame that we will play Halloween games with the world of the spirit and then question the very presence of God in the most real world of all.

November 1

"Wait for the Lord, and keep to his way, and he will exalt you to inherit the land." (Ps 37:34a)

We frequently make crosses for ourselves by our restless anxiety toward the future. Many of these crosses come more from our own doing than from God, and much of our anxiety comes from our lack of faith in God. Through our false wisdom, we frequently try to forestall God's arrangements and supplement divine providence by our own need to control.

A future accepted in faith is recognizing a future we cannot control. The future is not yet ours. In one sense it may never be. When the future comes, it may be totally different than we anticipated. Wise persons will shut their eyes to that which God hides from them and keep in reserve the wealth of spiritual strength that is available for the future.

Faith is more than a way of perceiving life. Sometimes it means following without seeing. Faith is also accepting in silence what we cannot change. That silence is more than just a lack of noise. The end result is peace, sweet peace. Care for a little peace today? Take a deep breath, and leave the future in the hands of the one who owns it. Just remember, we cannot control everything, especially the future.

"The nations are in an uproar, the kingdoms totter; *November 2*
he utters his voice, the earth melts." (Ps 46:6)

Psalm 46 is truly one of the most powerful portions of scripture in all of the Bible. One reason for its power is found in the vivid description of a changing world. From trembling mountains to roaring waters to the breaking of the bow, changes are occurring all around us. Some are as conspicuous as earthquakes, while others take place tenuously within us, known only by ourselves. Yet, change is unavoidable. We can ignore and deny it, but it will take its course regardless. Life is filled with "hellos" and "goodbyes." As the Psalmist described life, our days flourish like grass and flowers until the wind passes over and all is gone.

Change is an inevitable part of God's creation. It is neither good nor evil; it just is. God made it that way. A certain resignation to God's plan is the only option that makes sense. Wisdom is to be found in the way we respond to the inevitable. We might choose to fight it, which is as ludicrous as trying to keep the sun from rising. We can deny reality and spend life in a closet. We can become angry and thrash the ground, even though the ground feels no pain. Or, as the Psalmist offered, we can stop in the midst of roaring waters and trembling mountains and be still and know that God is still God.

"If you truly amend your ways and your doings, *November 3*
if you truly act justly one with another." (Jer 7:5)

A friend of mine had an interesting experience while attending a conference out of town. He needed to catch a cab. As he approached an awaiting, but occupied cab, everyone in the car—including the driver—seemed to be bowing their heads. After a period of time, they all started to get out of the cab. My friend discovered that they were, indeed, praying. The driver had been led to make a profession of faith in Christ.

Many of us tend to doubt the validity of such experiences. We may try to write off such conversions as being purely emotion and short-lived. The fact of the matter is that God can touch lives anywhere and at any time, and many of these experiences are very genuine. If the power of the gospel is restricted to our ordering, the work of the Holy Spirit is seriously limited.

God not only touches lives anywhere and at any time but also through you and me. God does not work in a vacuum. We are God's hands and feet. In our desire to meet our own inner spiritual needs, let us not forget that the beauty of the gospel is to be found in its ability to change lives. God forbid that our religion becomes so sophisticated and "watered down" that we strip the gospel of its power. God always has been and forever will be in the business of changing lives.

November 4

"Do not wear yourself out to get rich; be wise enough to desist." (Prov 23:4)

I recently read a paragraph in a personal devotional book that I think is worth passing along. This particular book has a little age; it was published in 1884. The only inscription for this piece was "A Poor Methodist Woman, 18th Century." Listen to her wisdom:

> I do not know when I have had happier times in my soul, than when I have been sitting at work, with nothing before me but a candle and a white cloth, and hearing no sound but that of my own breath, with God in my soul and heaven in my eye . . . I rejoice in being exactly what I am, a creature capable of loving God and who, as long as God lives, must be happy. I get up and look for a while out of the window and gaze at the moon and stars, the work of an almighty hand. I think of the grandeur of the universe, and then sit down, and think myself one of the happiest beings in it.

The inscription may have said a poor Methodist woman, but this woman was rich and did not know it. Then again, she probably did know it!

November 5

"And he said to them, 'Take care! Be on your guard against all kinds of greed; for one's life does not consist in the abundance of possessions.' " (Luke 12:15)

Several years ago a television documentary filmed a method for trapping monkeys. In the film, the natives made a big hole in a log and put bait inside, bait most tempting to monkeys. The monkey reached his hand in to get the bait, but when his fingers closed on it, his fist enlarged his hand so much that he could not get it back through the hole. The poor creature was so determined to hang on to what he had that he would not let go. Even while being captured, frightened to death by the possibility, he still could not let go.

We may think to ourselves, "Poor, silly monkey." But consider what God must think when we reach out and become possessed by what we are supposed to possess. What must our Lord think as our hands cling to things, whether large or small, that we cannot let go? To let go of things we possess and let God possess us is faith. To find the courage to let go and return a portion to the giver, joyfully, is the essence of Christian stewardship.

Stewardship is a personal and a corporate matter, an individual and a church matter. We would do ourselves a big favor to periodically stop and take a look at what we have in our fist. We may prevent ourselves from being caught in a trap, and our traps can be much more serious and deadly than a log.

"Anyone who resolves to do the will of God will know whether the teaching is from God or whether I am speaking on my own." (John 7:17)

There are a number of things that I am always "going to do" but, for some reason, I never get around to them. Take, for example, the dash pocket of my car. Every time I open it, the contents fall onto the floor. Confidentially, I believe the automakers play a trick on the consumer by making the dash pocket tilt forward and, therefore, guarantee that everything will fall out. I cannot count the times I have promised to clean it out, but I never do. Another project I am always "going to do" is to clean out my sock drawer. Our washer and dryer play games with me. They eat up one sock at a time. I do not know where the socks go, but they disappear. Someday I know the dryer will cough up a basketful of socks.

What are some things that you are always "going to do" but never get around to? They may be as simple as cleaning the car dash pocket or the sock drawer, or they may have considerably more importance. The very thing you are putting off may be blocking your spiritual growth, a very personal issue, or it may have to do with something you need to do for someone else. Regardless, you have been putting it off and you know you shouldn't. Messy dash pockets and frustrating sock drawers have little significance in life, but other things have everything to do with life. Maybe they should be addressed today.

"People who speak in this way make it clear that they are seeking a homeland. (Heb 11:14)

Whenever I read this verse, I remember from my boyhood something my dad would say occasionally when he was having a hard day. In flat, distraught tones, he would mutter, "It's not my world; I'm just passing through." I also knew these words meant I should exercise caution in whatever request I might make. It was not the right time to ask for a new baseball glove or some special favor.

Yet, my dad's words were more than just a bemoaning of a hard day. There was great truth as well. He was right in that it really isn't our world and we are just passing through. In today's verse, the writer of Hebrews was speaking of many past great figures of our faith. He was paying them great tribute as he described them as having eyes on more than just immediate times and places. They were on a journey, making their way to a homeland. So are we!

I like Paul's phrase "for our citizenship is in heaven" (Phil 3). We would do well to remember daily the end for which we were made. We were not created for just this time and place but for eternity. We are in the world to seek God and employ ourselves with God. If we could ever truly accept this fact in our heart and believe it with our head, it would have an enormous influence on our joy and peace. We are so tied down, yet we are just on a journey. "We are just passing through."

November 8   **"Now there are varieties of gifts, but the same Spirit." (1 Cor 12:4)**

Like many well-known people, Nathaniel Hawthorne kept a journal. In it he made this entry: "Subject for a story: a story in which the main character never appears." Evidently he never wrote the story on that theme, but unfortunately many people have lived it in their own lives. Their lives become sad stories because the main character never appears. Oliver Wendell Holmes described their situation as, "They die with all their music in them." All God ever expects of us is simply to be ourselves at our best.

Saint Paul encouraged the Corinthians to play out the music within them: "To each is given the manifestation of the spirit for the common good." While we are all created in God's image, we are given different gifts and abilities that God expects us to use. Today we will make an entry in our journal, whether written by us or not. As you make that entry, remember that we are never called to be carbon copies of our colleagues. We are called to be ourselves, at our best. We have our music within us.

November 9   **"The law of the Lord is perfect, reviving the soul; the decrees of the Lord are sure, making wise the simple." (Ps 19:7)**

A pastor friend in North Georgia recently wrote in his weekly bulletin some suggestions for turning from our own wisdom to reliance on God's wisdom:

- Look in the right place; listen for the right voice. The Bible admonishes us to be still and know God. When faced with a problem, we usually dash about looking for quick solutions. All too often our last instinct is to be quiet and wait on God.
- Learn from wilderness experiences. Most of us fear dry times, but after we have been emptied of our good ideas, we're in a prime position to receive a fresh revelation from God.
- Learn in a squeeze. When the walls seem to be closing in around us and there is no way out, we have a unique opportunity to see things from God's perspective. When everything around us seems small and cramped, we often receive from God a revelation of bigger things to come.
- Press into God. When nobody believes in us, when everyone seems to misjudge our motives, when all we hear is criticism, it is time to press into God and let God fill us with new ideas.

A little wisdom goes a long way. We can pray for an increase of our own. The backup plan ain't bad either.

"But grow in the grace and knowledge of our
Lord and Savior Jesus Christ." (2 Peter 3:18a)

Little things come daily, sometimes hourly, within our reach that are just as important for our growth as the greater occasions that periodically occur. Small trifles are a part of human experience; no one is immune to them. They present real opportunities to please God, and an earnest seeking to please God in little things is a test of real devotion and love. Our aim should be to please our Lord perfectly in little things as well as the big ones and, in the process, attain a spirit of childlike simplicity and dependence.

We will discover that as we think less of ourselves and bow our wills to God, many of our hindrances and trifles will disappear. In the end, many of the internal struggles that harass the soul will vanish, and we will be filled with peace. Growth is not limited to those who make great triumphs over enormous obstacles. Notoriety and celebration by great numbers of people do not measure real growth. Growth for most of us goes unnoticed by all except us.

"I do not run aimlessly, nor do I box as though beating the air." (1 Cor 9:26)

I love Paul's image in this verse, "beating the air." Have you ever boxed the air? Does a lot of good, doesn't it? If you choose, you can put great energy into it. I remember a boy I went to high school with who really imagined himself as a soon-to-be boxer. He was always going around shadow boxing. He would really get into it—really dramatic. Then one day he picked a fight with a kid about half his size, and the little guy nearly beat him to death. After that day on the playground, I don't remember the soon-to-be boxer doing any more shadow boxing.

Paul used this image of beating the air to convey a truth to the people of Corinth. Evidently, people were running about with great vigor but going nowhere in particular, losing energy and influence. They were arguing about which person they should claim as leader. Paul criticized them for quarreling over this matter and likened it to boxing the air. Consider the energy and resources the Christian community wastes in quarrelling among itself. Paul was saying to the Christians at Corinth that some issues are more important than quarreling among yourselves. Deal with issues that count. Our world needs more than our shadow boxing.

"A fool gives full vent to anger, but the wise quietly holds it back." (Prov 29:11)

Our attitudes are so important and underlie the way we respond to our circumstances each day. Consider how often some of us become angry. When we do so, all kinds of changes take place in our bodies. Arteries tighten, blood pressure elevates, and serious problems can result At times we should become angry and get upset, but some selectivity is in order. Acknowledging a direct relationship between one's health and state of mind, the American Medical Association makes these suggestions:

- Quit looking for a knock in your motor.
- Learn to like your work.
- Have at least one hobby.
- Learn to like people.
- Learn to be satisfied when you cannot change your situation.
- Learn to accept adversity.
- Learn to say the cheerful, helpful, and humorous thing.
- Learn to face challenges and problems with confidence and decision.

Does all of this sound too theoretical or impossible? Ask God to help you. God is waiting for you.

November 13

"Give us this day our daily bread." (Matt 6:11)

Depending on the particular word that is emphasized, this verse can take several different meanings. For example, focus on the word "give." In other words, provide for me—"hand it over." Consider the word "bread." We certainly need sustenance in order to continue. Think about the word "daily." Bread only satisfies us for a short while.

In recent days I have come to appreciate the importance of the phrase "this day." In the economy of God we are given strength one day at a time. So often when we face difficult situations, the problems of the moment do not get us down as much as projecting our anxieties into the future. We have so many anxieties about tomorrow or the more distant future. When we become so concerned about the distant future, we lose the power and resources we have in the present moment.

The wording of this sentence in the Lord's Prayer is not incidental. "Give us this day our daily bread" should be a reminder that God's resources are given each day. The prayer asks for only one day's worth. We should keep that in mind as we extend ourselves into the future. The early Romans used to build sundials to help them tell time. On some dials they inscribed, "In this hour dwells eternity." Every moment is very valuable, and we should live each to the fullest and not let an unknown future become a thief.

November 14

"With all humility and gentleness, with patience, bearing with one another in love." (Eph 4:2)

I had an interesting experience on my way to the church the other day. I had been rather busy at home trying to finish a few duties and, as a result, was running late. Entering the road, I pulled in behind a gray Ford that was obviously not in the rush that some of us were. Cars behind me were blowing horns, and several made a rather risky pass in front of us all. I could see only two people in the Ford. The big guy who was driving was pointing to various things along the street. Every now and then he would reach over and pat the other person. The world was in no hurry for them.

As I moved closer, I noticed the head of the passenger who remained perfectly still and facing forward. I thought to myself, "That woman has the longest and most pointed ears I've ever seen." In fact, I wanted to take a closer look at this lady. She just might keep me from being the ugliest person around. When the street changed to a double lane, I pulled around. Sitting straight up in the seat next to this man was an enormous bulldog. The man once again reached over and gave his friend a pat. The dog nodded in approval. I felt guilty that I had thought the creature was ugly.

What is the lesson here? When we are in a rush, we tend to jump to conclusions. Hasty assumptions are often wrong. Paul stated the idea much better: "Bear with one another in love."

"The Lord is the everlasting God, the Creator of the ends of the earth. He does not faint or grow weary. His understanding is unsearchable." (Isa 40:28b)

November 15

> Because I spent the strength Thou gavest me
> In struggle which Thou never didst ordain,
> And have but dregs of life to offer—
> O Lord, I do repent.
> —Sarah Williams

We should never forget that God wants our best work, not the dregs of our exhaustion. Without a doubt, God is interested in quantity, but I am convinced God has greater interest in quality. If people all around you are carrying on their business at a pace that drains the life out of you, resolutely take a slower pace. Even at the risk of accomplishing less or making less money, be what you were meant to be and can do.

Our body and spirit is like a well-tuned engine in that we have natural limits of power. Even the most expensive of engines, if run hard enough and long enough, will sooner or later fail. We fool ourselves by thinking otherwise. In all our doings we should possess our soul in peace. There is little wisdom in performing a deed in haste just so that we might get it done sooner. We should do whatever we have to do with tranquility. In so doing, we retain the peace of the soul.

November 16

"When he is quiet, who can condemn? When he hides his face, who can behold him? . . ." (Job 34:29)

Did you really pay attention to the words of this verse? They touch me because many times I long for and truly need a sense of quietness. Most of the noise, however, does not come at me from outer sources but from within. To be quite candid, most of it comes from anxiety about the future.

Why are we so busy with the future? It is not our province. Is our business with the future not an interference with the one to whom it belongs, particularly as we try to feverishly fill it according to our imagination? Life would be so much more peaceful if we would only seek to do God's will as it is made known to us.

If only we would do what God requires of us and leave ourselves, our friends, and every interest to divine control, and do so with a cheerful trust that the path God marks will be for our happiness.

> As God leads me, will I go,
> Nor choose my way;
> Let him choose the joy or woe
> Of every day
> They cannot hurt my soul,
> Because in his control:
> I leave to him the whole.
> —Anonymous

November 17

"Present your bodies as a living sacrifice, holy and acceptable to God, which is your spiritual worship." (Rom 12:1b)

In his letter to the Romans, Paul also said, "Do not be conformed to this world, but be transformed by the renewing of your minds." At times I am really awed by the mental or spiritual powers of some people. In fact, sometimes I am almost intimidated by these people because I do not possess the same abilities. By comparison I feel inadequate.

Would it not be a comfort to those of us who feel that we do not have those powers to notice that the living sacrifice mentioned by Paul is our body? Of course, that includes the mental power, but does it not also include the loving, sympathizing glance; the kind, encouraging work; the ready errand for another; or the work of our hands? Such opportunities come for all of us more often in a day than for the mental power we are often tempted to envy. We would be wise to simply offer willingly whatever we have. God will surely bless it.

"Say to those who are of a fearful heart, 'Be strong, do not fear!' " (Isa 35:4a) *November* 18

Isaiah's words of long ago continue to have meaning for us today. We create some crosses for ourselves; they do not come from God. Consider those crosses that come as a result of our restless anxiety for the future. Our struggling with the future may even take on the appearance of a poor witness. A compulsive need to forestall or rearrange God's providence by our own providence may be an indication of our lack of faith.

When the future arrives, it is usually different than we expected, but usually we have resources that are equally unexpected. Faith may mean that we shut our eyes to that which God hides from us and then trust in the depth of divine treasures to provide for us when the time is upon us.

> Why should thou fill today with sorrow
> About tomorrow
> My heart?
> One watches all with care most true,
> Doubt not that He will give thee too
> My part.
> —Paul Flemming

"As long as I am in the world, I am the light of the world." (John 9:5) *November* 19

Our Lord said, "We must work the works of him who sent me while it is day; night is coming when no one can work." By putting things beyond their proper times, one duty treads upon the heels of another, and all duties are felt as irksome obligations, a yoke beneath which we fret and lose our peace. Consequently, we usually have no time to do the work as it ought to be done. Therefore, it is done with eagerness and a greater desire to get it done than to do it well, and certainly with very little thought of God throughout.

> He who intermits
> The appointed task and duties of the day
> Untunes full oft the pleasures of the day
> Checking the finer spirits that refuse
> To flow, when purposes are lightly changed.
> —Anonymous

November 20

Most of us have never fully comprehended this seldom-read verse. Job came close to understanding this truth when he said, "He knows the way I take." The bottom line is that while we may not understand the pattern of our life, God does. For example, we may complain of the life we are forced to lead. Our life may appear to move slowly, moving neither in the direction nor with the speed we would desire. Our position in the scale of society may be far from what we desire. At times we may feel locked into a routine or circumstances we would not dare choose for ourselves.

Do we say that God is not directing our lives? Has God forgotten us? By our complaints, do we forfeit the strength of our inner spirit? In this moment our faith is tested. Because we are not sent into the labors we would choose otherwise, has God ceased to remember us? Certainly not. Because we may be forced to be active inwardly instead of outwardly, do we have no place in the heavenly father's business? Certainly we do. Could it be a period given to us to mature ourselves for the work that God will give us to do? God is no external bystander to our lives; neither are our lives the victim of chance. As with other times, trust of our creator may be the critical issue of life.

November 21

Not long ago my dad spent a weekend with his sister and four brothers. As a part of the weekend, they took a side trip to Cuthbert, Georgia, where they as a family lived for a brief period of time. They visited the old farmhouse that has been abandoned for many years. All that remains is the source of bittersweet memories. My dad commented that he could not help but think of all the changes that have occurred since that time. The years have brought joy and pain, good times and bad.

In front of the house still stands the old tree that was there when they were children. My dad has a picture taken of the family under that tree when they lived there. As you might expect, another picture was made of them on this trip under the same tree. Even though the old house has fallen in, the tree is still there, healthy and producing shade. There is a certain sense of comfort in such a thought. How we need something steadfast in a world of change!

An old tree that seems to withstand the storms of time is only a symbol of the true, unchanging source of security. According to today's verse, Isaiah knew that source. He was thinking of the same truth when he referred to "the shade of a great rock in a weary land."

"Do not worry about anything, but in everything by prayer and supplication with thanksgiving let your requests be made known to God." (Phil 4:6)

Saint Paul was a master of the fine art of appreciation. He said to give thanks in everything. This exhortation, which was sent to a group of his fellow Christians, has a tone of the impossible. To think in terms of giving thanks for everything seems a bit much, quite difficult. As a result, most of us do not take very seriously these words. We think that this kind of attitude toward life would be nice but feel it is asking just a bit too much. The apostle himself was perfectly serious and genuinely sincere in giving this exhortation, however. Based upon his own life, he believed it. His words were not only a command for his day, but good advice for us.

First, we should cultivate the habit of looking at what we have instead of what we have missed. Second, if we are to be grateful, we must look with eyes that see. Thus, we will realize with Paul that everything we have comes primarily as a gift and will conduct ourselves as if we have earned and deserve all that we have. We must give expression to our gratitude, to our family and friends as well as to God. You may say, "God knows of my gratitude." How does God know if you do not express your feelings? Right this very minute is a good time to say thank you.

"As you sing psalms and hymns and spiritual songs among yourselves, singing and making melody . . ." (Eph 5:19)

According to a presidential proclamation, the fourth Thursday in November shall be declared a day of national Thanksgiving, commemorating the first such observance. Thanksgiving Day is a fine custom because, for many of us, gratitude does not come easily. We can learn a valuable lesson from our Pilgrim ancestors.

Remember that thanksgiving was not their only choice. Some of the Pilgrims suggested that they set aside a day of mourning, and they had every right to mourn. So many of that original group had died due to all the hardships. Of the eighteen wives on the *Mayflower*, only five remained alive for the first Thanksgiving Day. Only one half of the ship's original roster survived to eat the first Thanksgiving meal. For a little bread instead of none, for a slim hold on life in place of death, for a glimmer of hope in an otherwise uncertain future—in those circumstances the Pilgrims gathered, by an act of discipline of the will, to sing and make music in their heart to God for their blessings.

Our Thanksgiving celebrations set in the midst of festive tables surrounded by beautifully decorated homes and landscaped surroundings provide a rather interesting comparison with that first Thanksgiving. In our celebration, our gratitude should reflect the abundance of our blessings. We have so much, not just on this day but every day. Too bad we need a presidential proclamation to make us say thank you!

November 24

"They called out, saying, 'Jesus, Master, have mercy on us!' " (Luke 17:13)

Leprosy has always been a dreaded disease. In the time of Jesus, the disease carried with it more suffering than we can possibly imagine. A leper had to deal with more than just the physical suffering. There were mental and, especially, social implications. A leper was considered unclean and was forced to live with persons who had the same dreaded disease. In the life of a leper, we can envision one who had a most intense need.

Jesus had an encounter with a group of ten lepers. They said, "Master, have mercy on us." Jesus said to them, "Go and show yourselves to the priest." As they proceeded to do this, they all realized they were cleansed. As they left, one of them—a Samaritan—when seeing that he was healed, turned back and with a loud voice praised God. He fell on his face at Jesus' feet and gave thanks for what had happened to him. Some of the joy of the moment was dampened when Jesus asked him, "Were not ten made clean?" Only one had returned. Then Jesus said to him, "Get up and go your way; your faith has made you well."

A big part of the leper's faith was to acknowledge the source of the great gift. Yet, only one out of ten returned to say thank you. What a sad commentary on the human spirit! Before we get too judgmental, let's ask if we are not guilty of the same oversight. But we are so busy and just don't think about all the gifts God sends. That makes it okay, right?

November 25

"Let us come into his presence with thanksgiving." (Ps 95:2a)

Can any of us not think back to those times when a friend or relative gave us a gift and our parents gave us the familiar refrain: "Now, what do you say?" Then we said with reluctance, "Thank you." Sometimes the words would almost not come out, especially when the gift was some ugly shirt that Aunt Sally gave you and you wanted something to play with. Yet, saying thank you is more than just a social amenity. If we could ever develop the habit, we would discover that such a spirit makes more of a difference in our lives than we could imagine.

A spirit of continual gratitude positions us for so much more that God has prepared for us. Sounds selfish? Maybe so, but it is still the truth. A comparison might be found in what sometimes happens in adolescent and parent relationships. A parent wants to do so much for a child. An ungrateful attitude can shut down the channel between the parent and the child. Frequently, not until the son or daughter leaves home for college or for work is there appreciation for the laundry, meals, housing, and all that mom and dad have provided. Then, a whole new relationship emerges.

This also happens between God and us. When we do not have a grateful and thankful attitude for God's previous gifts, God can't give additional gifts because we are not receptive. The truth is that we have a lot to gain from a spirit of gratitude.

"O give thanks to the Lord, call on his name, make known his deeds among the peoples." (1 Chron 16:8)

My wife comes home almost daily talking about something that occurred in her kindergarten class. Children are phenomenally entertaining and, at times, quite wise. Recently they were discussing what they plan to do as a career when they grow up. There were the usual aspirations of firefighters, police, doctors, and pilots. Jerry immediately spoke up and said he was going to be a garbage man. He wanted to pick up trash. Our first reaction might be to ignore Jerry's comment because, after all, what does a kindergartner know? On the other hand, maybe Jerry should be encouraged to follow his pursuit. It is an honorable one. There is no shame in such an aspiration. We would all be in a mess if those hardworking persons did not come to our homes regularly.

We live in a day of superstars. Society tends to reserve its blessing only for those who pass before us in a successful, often plastic, and highly visible way. The real danger beneath all this glamour is a diminishing respect for those basic services that are so necessary. Some people touch our lives every day, make us comfortable, and keep the daily wheels moving. This is a season of gratitude, and we should offer at least a thought of thanks for these faithful souls. The superstars may entertain us, but many others serve us each day and make life livable. To Jerry I say a big "amen."

"Do not be conformed to this world, but be transformed by the renewing of your minds." (Rom 12:2a)

I made a stop today to buy gasoline. I pumped it, punched some buttons, charged it on plastic, and never saw the first human in the process. Recently I put my money in a soft drink machine. Not only did I get a soda, but the machine talked to me. It wished me a good day then said "it" hoped I would enjoy my soft drink. I really felt like I should say something in response, but what do you say to a machine—"I hope you have a good day, and may no one kick your cans"?

We do banking through instant bankers, buy lunch through machines, and do all sorts of things through our computerized society. Nothing is inherently wrong with high technology. In fact, "high tech" has become the new frontier. Technology has made tremendous progress, but unfortunately this progress is discouraging face-to-face contact. Regardless of how advanced we become in terms of technology, we will always need this personal connection. It is a part of our needs system as much as eating and breathing.

In many of Jesus' healing experiences, a touch was involved on his part. A touch, in and of itself, has a certain healing quality. A follower of Christ must always exercise love and care that cuts through the impersonal nature of our technological society. Look around you today for people whose lives need a gentle touch. It is just another way that we are not "conformed to this world."

November 28

"There is need of only one thing. Mary has chosen the better part, which will not be taken away from her." (Luke 10:42)

Relationships are never static; they never stand still. People are always either moving closer, or they are moving further apart. I believe this will hold true whether one is talking about marriage and family relationships or any everyday friendship. Frequently, marriage partners will assume that they can put their relationship in a holding pattern and give it whatever scraps of time and energy are left over from all of the other demands of living. Unfortunately, even in marriage, a relationship can't be put in neutral. Two people are either moving closer or farther apart. To fail to recognize the need for nourishment of a relationship almost invariably means growing apart.

The same is true with your friends. You are either giving of yourself to that friendship, or you are growing apart. To prevent this stagnation, we must recognize the need in each of our lives for relationships. By nature we are social creatures. We must focus our attention upon a relationship. If you are married, what about your spouse? If you are not married, consider a significant person in your life. Then make a contribution of yourself to that relationship and move closer. Relationships don't stand still.

November 29

"Honor everyone. Love the family of believers. Fear God. Honor the emperor." (1 Pet 2:17)

Recently I was in a funeral procession going from our church to the cemetery. Along the way we passed a small, gray Toyota on the opposite side of the road that had come to a complete stop. The young lady driving the car had paused temporarily as an act of respect for a grieving family and friends. Behind her was a blue van that filled the silence with endless honks from the horn. The driver was screaming verbal insults at the young woman as he waved his arms. Who knows what was going on with the man? He may have been a nuclear scientist, and a reactor was on hold for his presence. Or then again, maybe he was in no rush at all but was just totally insensitive to the pain within the passing cars.

Even in a busy world, room must be left for simple courtesies. Granted, major thoroughfares cannot become motionless, but sensitivity is still needed in a rushed world. Insensitivity is a cancer that will eat away at the heart of a community, reduce man to a feelingless robot, and destroy the image of the creator within us. To the lady in the Toyota: God bless you and your act of courtesy. Don't let a horn-honking world take that away from you. May we all join your ranks.

"See to it that no one takes you captive through philosophy and empty deceit, according to human tradition." (Col 2:8a)

When I was a young boy in LaGrange, Georgia, a number of informal traditions were a part of my home. Most of them were very simple, and we did not even realize that they had become traditions. For example, on Thanksgiving Day we always watched the Macy's parade on television. It was not demanded; we just did it. That night one of the Atlanta television stations always broadcast the lighting of the "great tree." The program had a lot of music and was the signal that Christmas was close.

This year my family was at my parents home in Calhoun, Georgia, for Thanksgiving. Without anyone telling us to do so, we were all together that morning around the television watching the parade in some faraway city called New York. The parade did not seem very different from years long ago. Even our children who are almost grown were watching rather carefully. For a moment, time seemed to have been transcended. In my mind, only a few hours before I was sitting in their place.

This is a season of traditions, and I am convinced that they are God's gifts to cause us to stop and think. They help us to remember how bountifully God has blessed us. Yet, this season is far more than a set of traditions. We do more than just relive the past. We realize that ultimately traditions do not transcend time but rather the God who gave birth to the source of the celebration.

"This day shall be a day of remembrance for you. You shall celebrate it as a festival to the Lord." (Exod 12:14a)

December 1

Advent is that special time set aside by the church for the preparation to celebrate Christmas. A natural question is, "Why all the fuss about preparation? Let's just do Christmas." But preparation is ever so important if celebration is to be meaningful.

The Jewish people of the Old Testament would never think of moving into a time of festivities without giving attention to a time of preparation for that celebration. Remember the eleventh chapter of Exodus that deals with the event of the Passover. The children of Israel always celebrated that great event and sought never to lose sight of what God had done for them through the experience. They learned something that most of us have never discovered: the degree of meaning of an event is very much related to the degree of preparation for that event. God forbid that we move into this season of Christmas in our usual condition of huffing and puffing, frustration and total exhaustion.

Instead, I hope that we will move into this great season with a new sense of commitment, to one another and to our Lord, and that we will open ourselves to new experiences that will add a depth of meaning to this beautiful time of the year. The time to begin this preparation is right now!

December 2

"In the sixth month the angel Gabriel was sent by God to a town in Galilee called Nazareth, to a virgin." (Luke 1:26-27a)

How can we possibly journey through Advent without giving thought to the role of Mary? Of all the characters that surrounded Jesus, Mary was probably the most misunderstood. In Hebrew her name was Miriam, which meant "myrrh." She was betrothed to Joseph. Betrothal lasted for a year and was as binding as marriage, but with no sexual intimacy.

The angel Gabriel came to visit Mary in the city of Nazareth. Imagine a fourteen or fifteen year-old girl whose work was interrupted by someone who said he was an angel. She was told that God had favored her and she would bear His son. (Talk about surprises!) Luke said she was troubles—scared out of her wits is probably a better description. She said, "I don't even have a husband." She must have wondered what Joseph would think and, needless to say, the neighbors. Her response was phenomenal. In everyday terms she said, "Who am I to question God? Let it be as you said." Unbelievable courage!

The story of Mary reminds us that God's finding favor with us is not always an easy task. We see true greatness and courage in the life of a simple peasant girl who was willing to open her life to God's strange ways. Courage was found in her willingness to be used for the divine purpose. True power was found in the arms of a poor maiden who had courage to say to God, "Go ahead."

December 3

"Like good stewards of the manifold grace of God, serve one another with whatever gift each of you has received." (1 Pet 4:10)

At this time of year we are thinking about gift giving, which can sometimes be a tedious task. Maybe there are children on your list, possibly your own or grandchildren. I want to suggest a gift to them that might sound a little strange at first: laugh with them. I can think of fewer things that children need more than honest laughter. Oscar Wilde wrote: "The best way to make children good is to make them happy." Many of the tensions of life, particularly in the family, arise because we take ourselves so seriously. The outside world can be serious enough.

One of the most beautiful sounds I can think of is the sound of children laughing. Laughter does not require a comedian nor paid entertainment. It simply requires a few relaxed minutes together to be open and share in the delights of the moment at hand. I have often thought it intriguing how seldom we have to scold children when they are relaxed enough to laugh. I think God places children, whether ours or those belonging to someone else, in our lives for many reasons, one of which is to enjoy them. They are guests around us for such a brief time. So, quit worrying about the latest Nintendo game, and give children something even more important. Take a few minutes, and give them the gift of your laughter. It could be your best gift of the season.

"Rejoice in hope, be patient in suffering, persevere in prayer." (Rom 12:12) *December* 4

In talking about his personal philosophy, the song writer Oscar Hammerstein once said,

> I cannot write anything without hope in it. When people point out that the world has evil and ugliness in it, I merely point out I know about all of those things, but I choose to align myself to the hope side of life.

As we move into the Advent season, I would like to suggest that to be a Christian means to "align ourselves to the hope side of life." Such a decision must be made consciously and intentionally. The heart of our hope is best described by that beautiful line from John: "The light shines in the darkness, and the darkness did not overcome it."

Hope is more than just a feeling. Hope is a vision, a way of looking at our world, a way of understanding the experiences in our lives. The Christmas story does not proclaim an absence of darkness, but the presence of light. When we know that darkness is not the last word, that in the midst of darkness there is light, then the season of Advent takes on new meaning for us. We all need a little help with darkness. Just follow the star.

"Agree with God, and be at peace; in this way good will come to you." (Job 22:21) *December* 5

The King James Version word for agree is "acquaint." Job's advice is good for the busy days of this season when demands are great and resources become very limited. How blessed are those holy hours in which the soul retires from the world to be alone with God! God's voice, just as with God's self, is everywhere. Within and without God speaks to our souls, if we would only hear. Only the noise of the world or the confusion of our own hearts deafens our inward ear to the divine voice. Learn to commune with God in stillness, and the one whom you seek in stillness will give peace in the midst of a busy world.

In the seventeenth century, Thomas Tryon wrote:

> The great step and direct path to the fear and awful reverence of God, is to dedicate, and with a sedate and silent hush to turn the eyes of the mind inward; there to seek, and with a submissive spirit wait at the gates of wisdom and temple: and then the Divine Voice and Distinguishing Power will arise in the light and centre of a man's self.

December 6   **"I am bringing you good news of great joy for all the people." (Luke 2:10b)**

The Christmas season becomes a very nostalgic time for most of us. One very pleasant thought that comes to my mind has to do with those who were among the first to tell me the story of Jesus and his birth. Having grown up in a family that "camped out" at church, I heard from many who shared the good news.

I remember one special lady who was my Sunday School teacher when I was in the third grade. She wasn't just an average lady. She really believed that the gospel was good news, and she never hesitated to talk about it. We did all kinds of fun things that made Sunday School okay, and not just something you did because you would get a whipping if you skipped out and stayed at Smith's drugstore across the street. (You could always tell who had been to the drugstore. They smelled like bubble gum.)

One year we made a scroll and wrote on it the entire Christmas passage from Luke. The paper was rolled on crooked sticks. As far as I was concerned, it was a piece of art. That same year I gave my life to Christ, having been influenced greatly by that gentle lady. She happened to be my grandmother, but she told the story to lots of other kids as well. I have heard the Christmas story from many different people, but no one told it better than she. I wonder who is listening and waiting for us to tell the good news to them. It's not just a job for grandmothers.

December 7   **"Glory to God in the highest heaven, and on earth peace among those whom he favors!" (Luke 2:14)**

I hope we do not experience this day without giving some thought to the event associated with December 7. Pearl Harbor Day is one of those days we might like to forget, but in all honesty we should not. It should remind us that war is always only a few seconds away. The potential is always great. A few years of peace on our home front causes us to assume life will always be that way. As a country we need to constantly have that threat before us, recognizing that total destruction is the likely outcome of the next global affair.

Our national leaders need to remember that international politics is not a Parker Brothers game but a serious life-threatening time bomb. World peace does not come from isolationism or making a parade of our strength in arms. It does not come from congressional tours or presidential whirlwind trips to wherever. We can never take world peace for granted. If we do, Pearl Harbor will be relived. Some people see world peace as a total impossibility. After all, killing one another is as old as Cain and Abel. Should we not accept war as just a product of humanity? In a few days we will celebrate a special birthday. He came as the Prince of Peace. What he began long ago is still a potential, and I will always believe it is a possibility.

"Joseph also went from . . . Nazareth . . . to Judea, to . . . Bethlehem, because he was descended from the house and family of David." (Luke 2:4)

What does Christmas mean to you? To a child, Christmas often means receiving presents. For parents, it means the joy of watching children opening presents. Christmas may be the only time of the year when a scattered family gets together. To church leaders, it can mean hard work and extra services and programs. To a business owner, Christmas may mean special sales and hiring extra workers. Does Christmas have some deeper meaning, a meaning that comes from beyond ourselves and the commercial world?

The Bible teaches that Christmas has meaning for us that has been designed by God. It means that God can deal with us in unexpected ways. So many members of the original cast were unlikely people. Even Mary and Joseph must rank as two of the most surprised tools of God in all of history. God did the unexpected when He sent His son to redeem the world rather than to judge it. What does this mean for us? It means that God can still do unexpected and good things in our lives.

Christmas means that God really cares. God did not send a messenger, or prophet, or a special sign. God sent His only begotten son. He cares enough to come where we live. He has moved close. Christmas means that God has invaded the world, and we have no choice but to deal with God. The original cast had to deal with God. The members could not evade Him; nor can we today.

"But before they lived together, she was found to be with child from the Holy Spirit." (Matt 1:18b)

As we continue our journey through the Advent season, consider for a moment the role of Mary and Joseph as parents of the Christchild. It was a tremendous privilege but an awesome responsibility. It was not easy for them, but they offered it as their Christmas present to God. Their gift was a magnificent trust in what God said would happen and their willingness to accept their calling. They would take the task regardless. Trust is a present we need to give to God also. This trust says we will follow and love God no matter what. What is involved in this kind of trust?

This trust holds on in spite of ridicule and criticism. We have to admit that God did not give Mary and Joseph very normal circumstances. The chances are good that they suffered enormous criticism from family and friends who were less than kind. Yet, they continued to trust. Trust holds on even in the midst of hardships. I have often thought that if God really wanted Mary and Joseph to be the parents of the Christchild, God could have made it a little easier for them. The truth is that life often does not work that way. Yet, they held on in the midst of uncertainty. God did not tell them all they would face; God seldom does. The details of life always come a piece at a time.

December 10

"In the time of King Herod, after Jesus was born in Bethlehem of Judea, wise men from the East came to Jerusalem. (Matt 2:1)

Nativity scenes are relatively common during this season. Nothing is more entertaining than live nativity scenes, the ones with real animals and "real" children. How would we ever have them without the use of bathrobes? You cannot have shepherds without bathrobes! And there is an unwritten law that the bathrobes must be too large.

Although the shepherds have been dressed in strange ways and reenacted millions of times, their role in the Christmas scene is beyond value. We learn so much from them. For one thing, the visitors acted on the light that they had. The shepherds were hardly theologians, but possibly they knew enough Old Testament to expect a messiah. They did not wait on a full explanation via Federal Express mail. They acted on what they knew, little though it may have been. They may have been seeking out of curiosity, but they went away in joy. They were rejoicing and telling all they met. In current vernacular, "The went for it and came out ahead." There may be a lesson here for us.

The shepherds returned to their world, which was still in a mess. Herod was still king. The baby was a long way from being old enough to do much good. These visitors may not have even lived long enough to see the child grown. Yet, I have to believe that the shepherds were changed as a result of their venture. Christmas is a good time for a little venturing.

December 11

"Where is the child who has been born king of the Jews?" (Matt 2:2a)

The story of the wise men has always intrigued me. I have never been able to settle for the description that these people were just curiosity seekers. They are never to be seen as incidental visitors from the East. One legend suggests they were kings. Another tradition says the magi came from Asia, Africa, and Europe and represented Shem, Ham, and Japheth—the sons of Noah in the Old Testament flood story. Scripture supports none of these conjectures, however. Yet, we do know enough about the wise men to allow them to be of help to us.

- Consider their purpose in this adventure. "We observed his star at its rising and have come to pay him homage." Their motives were pure. They did not seek favors but came to worship.
- I like the way the wise men went about their business. Jesus did not impose his presence on them; the magi searched for Christ. They asked religious officials and probably government officials. The search was important to them, enough to "put them out" a little.
- They were persistent. Not even Herod's deception would derail their progress. Christmas for the wise men was everything they wanted it to be. They set out with the purpose of worship and when they found Christ, that's exactly what they did. Their expectations were fulfilled; their purpose was complete.

Does worship, search, and persistence characterize our Christmas journey this year? There is still time to follow the star.

"The people who walked in darkness have seen a great light." (Isa 9:2b)   *December 12*

Christmas is full of contradictions and none is more obvious than the title of the Christ child: Prince of Peace. The carol speaks of this dissension:

> I heard the bells on Christmas day,
> Their old familiar carols play,
> And wild and sweet the words repeat
> Of peace on earth, goodwill to men.
>
> And in despair I bowed my head,
> There is no peace on earth, I said,
> For hate is strong, and mocks the song,
> Of peace on earth, goodwill to men.

At first it would seem that we have no peace on the world scene. Struggles exist between nations. Communities are a melting pot of anger. The streets are no longer safe to even take a walk. The thermostat of most people is stuck on hot. Peace is more than the absence of conflict, however. Peace includes a sense of wholeness, a healing of that which was broken and alienated. Christ blazes the trail of peace because he has the ability to bring wholeness to our lives and get at the root of so much unrest and struggle.

If we are to ever know anything that even resembles peace, it will come when we are willing to let Christ claim us as his own. Much of the struggle of humankind is but an outward expression of the war that wages within. Settle that conflict and other wars will lose their force. The Prince of Peace comes to bring wholeness and, in so doing, he brings beautiful peace to our souls.

"Look, the virgin shall conceive and bear a son,   *December 13*
and they shall name him Emmanuel." (Matt 1:23)

In 1962 the *St. Petersburg Times* ran a special edition that consisted of two front pages. One contained only good news about the holidays. The other dealt with the more somber matters of world affairs such as riots, robberies, and rapes. The editors explained their arrangement of separating the good news from the bad as a way of honoring the spirit of the season.

I am thankful that the Gospels did not present a special edition. Good news cannot be separated from the bad. Indeed, the beauty of Christmas is this name Emmanuel: "God is with us." The good news comes to us in the midst of the bad. Christmas is the story of an omnipotent and loving God who became intimately involved with sinful humanity. The same narrative that recounts our savior's birth also discloses the strategy of a king and the indiscriminate slaughter of children by a ruthless politician. The same story of a virgin birth also tells of a near divorce. The birth of Jesus is the good news in the midst of such bad news.

Our response to evil is separation. Separation is a faulty solution because it will not redeem. It only creates more darkness and pain. Emmanuel is God's response to evil. God's dealing with evil was not to be found in separation. God only desired to bring us back together in the family. Emmanuel is the good news in the midst of bad. "Come, O Come, Emmanuel; we need good news."

December 14

". . . They offered him gifts . . ." (Matt 2:11)

I am certain that by now you have finished all of your Christmas shopping. Sure! Maybe you enjoy shopping this time of year. The stores are not crowded, the selection is great, the store clerks are not tired, shoppers are not frustrated, everyone has plenty of money in the budget, and no one pushes in the check-out lines! (One concept of eternal punishment is having to spend eternity in a crowded store with a long check-out line.)

Allow me to make one quick gift suggestion that you don't have to stand in a long line to purchase. It may seem like an insignificant item, but don't undercut it before you give it a chance. It could be the most appreciated of all gifts. It is the simple gift of time. We forget its value and ignore its importance to significant people in our lives. Perhaps some family members, such as children or even friends would appreciate this gift more than anything we could send their way. Our world is so hurried and rushed. When you are gift buying, don't exclude the possibility of the personal gift of your time.

One Christmas, my family members gave each other "time gift certificates" and required that they be honored and redeemed. Sounds like a silly thing, but what better gift could you give to your child, spouse, or parent than to say, "Here is the promise of an hour; you choose how it shall be spent."

December 15

"She gave birth to her firstborn son and wrapped him in bands of cloth, and laid him in a manger, because there was no place for them in the inn." (Luke 2:7)

The Christmas tree routine is always an exciting time in our home. Our tree turned out quite well this past year. We followed our usual tradition. Suzanne and I jointly bought it and put it up, but she did the decorating. We have discovered through the years that our marriage is much safer when she does the decorating.

A Christmas tree has a mysterious effect on me. I can sit and stare at it for hours. When I do, my mind is flooded with many good memories. I think of experiences as a boy. My growing-up years were happy ones, especially at Christmas. I remember special gifts: a deluxe Monarch bicycle, a train that eventually burned a hole in my mother's rug, and a go-cart that would outrun everything except the police.

I can think of Christmas experiences of the more recent past, also happy times. I can look into the tree and recall sights and sounds as if they were yesterday. The tree reminds me how much change has taken place over the years: people who are no longer with us and times that might have been simpler, at least for me. Looking into the tree I notice a particular ornament. The ornament is simple and handmade: a medicine cup housing a miniature manger scene with a stable, a young woman, and a tiny babe. A warm feeling moves within me. In spite of life's changes, one part of Christmas does not change: the important part.

"I will greatly rejoice in the Lord, my whole being shall exult in my God;
for he has clothed me with the garments of salvation . . ." (Isa 61:10)   *December 16*

I recently read about a woman who waited until the last minute to send Christmas cards. She rushed into a store and bought a package of fifty cards without really looking at them. Still in a big hurry, she addressed forty-nine of the fifty and signed them without reading the message inside. On Christmas day, when things had quieted down somewhat, she found the lone, leftover card and finally read the message she had sent to forty-nine of her friends. Much to her dismay, it read like this, "This card is just to say, a little gift is on the way." Suddenly she realized that forty-nine of her friends were expecting a gift from her, a gift that would never come.

God promised Israel a messiah and was faithful to that promise. Unlike the lady's forty-nine friends, the people of Israel were not left waiting for a gift that never came. When Christ came, he was not what people expected, however. In fact, the vast majority of people were not willing to take a chance on him. He was not born like a messiah; the town of Bethlehem was certainly no palace. He did not act like a messiah; his actions, clothes, and friends were completely different than the expectations of the messiah. Christ certainly did not die like a messiah; his death was not a pretty site. In the midst of all our Christmas chaos, let's try not to forget that we know the end of the story. This season is about a gift that has arrived, just like "the card" said.

December 17

Gifts are very special. They convey our love, just as the gifts of the wise men expressed love for the Christchild. Although we don't know much about the wise men, the gifts they left were very insightful to the character and nature of the babe they came to see.

Gold was a symbol of kingship. It was thought to be the most precious metal in that day. Whenever one went to see a king, gold was the most appropriate gift to take. With their gold, the wise men were recognizing Christ as a king, a kingly nature yet to be defined.

Frankincense was a symbol of a priest. It was a sweet smelling perfume often used in temple sacrifices. The priest used it in the performance of his duties. Could the wise men have known that the babe would become the priest of all people? The word priest means "bridgebuilder." Christ had come to rebuild the bridge that was broken between God and man.

Myrrh was a symbol of death and sacrifice. It was a precious spice, but its main use was in the embalming of the dead. This gift was the foreshadow of Christ's future mission. He was born to die, and because of his death we are declared innocent.

Above all, the wise men bowed down and worshiped the child. That was their best gift. It should be our best gift as well.

December 18

In spite of our promises to do otherwise, we invariably allow the Christmas season to become so filled with activity and obligation that at times we are almost overwhelmed. We are determined to plan ahead and start early. Yet, we always end up having to rush around and do the things that were on the list to do earlier. Only one week remains before the grand day of Christmas. This week is usually filled with the most hustle. Are the gifts bought? Are the cards mailed? Are the decorations finished? We think that we are going to get everything done, and Christmas Eve will be a quiet relaxed time of reflection and contemplation that should be a natural part of the celebration. Yet, Christmas is not meant to be a time of quiet relaxing.

The event we celebrate has no sense of contentment. With it comes a call, surprising and demanding. There is also a crisis; the entire world, along with our lives, has been turned upside down. Because of this event, commitment is expected. Christmas does not mean sweet nostalgia for a dreamy past. It is a call for action in the present and looking toward the future. So, if you are frustrated because your Christmas is not a time of contentment, don't fret. It wasn't meant for contentment.

"To a virgin engaged to a man whose name was Joseph, of the house of David. The virgin's name was Mary." (Luke 1:27)

Suppose we knew there was a God somewhere of whom we really wanted to know. How would we learn of the divine, assuming we knew nothing? We could look at nature and draw our conclusions, which many people do. Certainly we could get a hint of God's glory in the wonders of nature, for they are the works of divine hands. The breath-taking beauty and amazing complexity of nature bear witness to the omnipotence of God. Yet, nature has an element of cruelty, destruction, and terror. Is that who God really is?

We could also turn to sacred literature for answers about God. The libraries are filled with volumes on the subject. All the world's great religions seek to describe God by way of exalted writings. The Bible is certainly not the only attempt to give form to God through words. While the Bible is my authority, it is not the only book on the shelves. Who is to say with assurance that other books are right or wrong?

Fortunately, another way to know the divine has been provided. Long ago God moved toward a humble maiden in an obscure village and requested her help in bringing God close and recognizable. She would bare a child who would not only become the salvation of humankind, but give us a close look at the God who had previously been distant and holy. If you want to know about God, follow the story of Bethlehem. Look at the Christchild; you're looking at God.

"There were shepherds living in the fields, keeping watch over their flock by night. Then an angel of the Lord stood before them." (Luke 2:8-9a)

Even though we have already talked about the role of the shepherds, I would like for us to consider another important dimension of their role in the Christmas scene. I have always been convinced of their significance because the first announcement of Jesus' birth came to them. We must remember the kind of people that shepherds were in those days. We have become so accustomed to Christmas pageants where children dress up in their mother's curtains and their daddys' oversized bathrobes that we forget who the shepherds really were. In the pageants they always look so humble and mild.

Shepherds were very rugged men and were despised by good, orthodox people. They could not possibly keep the details of the ceremonial law. They could not be bothered by the meticulous hand-washings and rules and regulations. Somebody had to watch out for the snakes and scorpions and keep a close eye on the sheep. They could not prevent the dirt from getting under their nails or keep from working on the sabbath. Life was hard for them, but God chose them as the recipients of the first announcement of Christ's birth. The shepherds were real people doing normal things. Maybe the gospel really is for all people and all types.

December 21

If you wish to enter the Church of the Nativity in Bethlehem and stand at the place where Jesus was born to Mary, you cannot simply walk erect through the entrance. The lintel is low, and you have to stoop to enter. That fact stands as a symbol of something essential for us if we are to penetrate to the real meaning of Christmas. Our proud assumptions must be set aside, along with our conviction that only the prosaic and factual can convey real meaning. The glory of this season is realized only by hearts that are willing to let mystery and wonder take over. The genealogy of Jesus ends with words deceptively simple: "Joseph, the husband of Mary, of whom Jesus was born, who is called the Messiah." Simple words, they are indeed; but they are the simplicity of sublime truth.

The Christmas message comes always as a great encouragement to us. This is especially the case when we grow downcast and so much of what goes on in our world seems to deny our hopes and dreams. Then the fact that Jesus was born to Mary, an ordinary peasant girl, lifts our spirits. We realize afresh what faith teaches: the things that matter most, love and peace and mercy, are not finally at the mercy of the things that matter least. This is God's world. Christmas is the joyous announcement that God will not be kept out of the world. If inns are crowded, God will come in a stable. If the mighty ignore God, God will use a peasant family.

December 22

If you have ever visited Saint Augustine, Florida, then you might have stopped by the so-called fountain of youth. You have heard the story of Ponce de Leon who searched in vain for this fabled fountain. In looking back on his experience, I find it strange that anyone would search for it because most of us know by now that youth is not something you find, but rather something you lose. Could Ponce de Leon have been searching for more than just a symbolic fountain of youth? I think his search really represented the kind of search that exists in the lives of many of us today. It is a search for hope.

Have you noticed how the word "hope" skips across the pages of the Bible? The word has sustained God's people through the ages. Hope has given strength and courage to people in exile, prison, and death. Peter exclaimed that we have been born again to a living hope in Christ. Lasting hope will never be found in external things, whether a fountain or bank account. The news of Jesus' birth brings hope to the world. Like the angels who brought tidings of great joy, I too want you to know that without a shadow of a doubt, a savior is born in the city of David who is Christ the Lord. There alone do we find our hope. Everything else is just a fountain that will sooner or later run dry.

"For as the days of Noah were, so will be *December 23*
the coming of the Son of Man." (Matt 24:37)

The hours are passing quickly as final preparations are being made for our celebration of Christmas. These final days become a time of counting down. We are reminded on television and radio of how many shopping days are left. We just want to be ready when the special day arrives. If we can have everything ready, we can be in control. Keep in mind that we can control these facets of the celebration, but we we cannot control our Lord's coming. The very best we can do is to prepare and make ready.

Much of our efforts are not just to control the various facets of the Christmas celebration but truly an attempt to control the coming of the Lord. We can program our schedules and order our lives, but we have no influence upon the divine coming. We can only get ready. We had better get ready, not for a holiday but for the moment God invades our personal world. We are fooling ourselves if we think we can confine God to one day a year. "When can you least expect the Son of Man to come into your life?" The answer is not December 25; the answer is now. We had better get it together, not our shopping but the ordering of our lives! The calendar does not really matter anymore.

"To you is born this day in the city of David *December 24*
a Savior, who is the Messiah, the Lord. (Luke 2:11)

Even though Christmas Eve seems to roll around so much faster than in years past, there is an incredible sense of reassurance with its coming. It brings us back to a constant point, a point from which everything else is measured in life.

The author Lloyd Douglass told about an old man who gave him violin lessons. One day Douglass asked him, "Well, what is the good news today?" Putting the violin down, the man stepped over to a tuning fork suspended from a silver cord, struck it with a sharp blow with his padded mallet fork, and said, "That's the good news for today. That, my friend, is 'A.' It was 'A' all day yesterday, it will be 'A' all day tomorrow, and it will be 'A' for a thousand years. The soprano upstairs warbles off key, the tenor next door flats his high notes, and the piano across the hall is out of tune. Noise all around me. Noise, but that my friend is 'A'."

Christmas Eve is a reminder that something is constant, something that you can count on. The constant is so much more than just a day on the calendar. It is the historical fact that on a night long ago God sounded a note whose voice would be heard for an eternity and would provide not only sound but light to a dark world. God initiated an act of love that would ultimately prove that love always has the last word. It is a constant. You can count on it. Merry Christmas!

December 25
        "The Word became flesh and lived among us, and we have seen his glory, the glory as of a father's only son, full of grace and truth." (John 1:14)

When rainy days and gray skies surround us, one might raise the question, "How can a being such as God who has no limits to power know what it is like to be weak and limited?" How can one who created time and space understand the dilemma of being a slave to time and space? The people of the Old Testament continually dealt with the problem of feeling distant from God. God was real but also a powerful being to be feared.

You and I have an advantage over people of biblical times. We have a different understanding of God since we are on the other side of Christ's arrival. Because of the incarnation through a man from Nazareth almost 2,000 years ago, everything has changed. No compromise was involved. God lived among us and discovered first-hand that life is not easy. In fact, at times it is downright difficult. God experienced first-hand the pain of rejection and misunderstanding. In the form of Jesus, God laughed, cried, walked, talked, and loved.

Christmas is not just a pretty story; it is a historical fact. Because of the fact of Christmas, one question has been answered forever. How can God appreciate our human frailty? God has been here and, because of Christmas, understands and relates to life's bumps. Now the divine can truly intervene and help us. That is about the best reason I can think of to "deck the halls with holly."

December 26
        "Mary treasured all these words and pondered them in her heart." (Luke 2:19)

We are always a bit sad when we put the Christmas decorations in the attic to collect dust for another year. If only putting them up could be as exciting as getting them down! We prepare for so long and work ourselves into such an emotional high, and then in an instant it's gone. I can remember as a child waking up on the morning after Christmas and thinking, "Oh no, it's all over for another year!" and then came the inevitable childhood wish, "If only every day could be Christmas!" Yet, so much of Christmas is not put away with all the "stuff" that goes to the attic. A ton of memories stay with us and never have to be stored away.

Christmas has a way of bringing to mind many thoughts that at times make the season a bit melancholy, but that's okay. I believe very strongly that our memories are gifts from God. If we use them properly, our memories can keep our chins up and our spirits high. A good memory or two can help out immensely during some dark times. If this past Christmas is a good memory for you, wrap it up very gently and put it in your pocket, not the attic. Then later on this year if times should get touch, pull it out and let a smile come to your face. That's what memories are for!

"When John heard in prison what the Messiah was doing, he sent word by his December 27
disciples and said to him, 'Are you the one who is to come?' " (Matt 11:2-3a)

Today's verse describes a very tired and disappointed John the Baptist. John was in prison and looking for some reassurance that Jesus really was who he said he was. So much had happened to John, and he was beginning to raise questions about Jesus' claim to messiahship. There are several possible reasons for John's disappointment.

The chances are that John had different expectations of what a messiah ought to be and do. He probably expected the same kind of messiah that everyone else did. Expectations are always at the heart of disappointment. When we are disappointed, we should ask ourselves the question, "What are we expecting?"

John was looking for all the wrong signs. When John's followers caught up with Jesus, he answered, "Go and tell John what you hear and see; the blind receive their sight, the lame walk, the lepers are cleansed . . . " In other words, the true signs were being fulfilled. John was simply looking for the wrong signs, just as we do when we question whether God is involved in our lives. In addition to looking for the wrong signs, John had not given God time to fulfill the divine plans. John wanted it done on his timetable. Is a comparison with us even needed?

"She will bear a son, and you are to name him Jesus, December 28
for he will save his people from their sins." (Matt 1:21)

In our concluding of the Christmas celebration, we would be negligent if we did not give some thought to the prediction and accomplishment of salvation. One must understand the collective need of the Jewish people. Salvation was not just a casual concern but an intense need. It was forecast by numerous persons for many centuries. The Jews knew in their hearts that the system was not working. They were totally incapable of saving themselves. They were good but not that good.

They were oppressed politically, but their greatest oppression was spiritual. They were confused about the meaning of salvation. Would military might solve Israel's problems? Even though Jesus was a common name during that period of history, God made this ordinary name unique. Jesus was the messiah. He would would save, bring redemption, and do what laws and rituals never could.

During these past weeks we have celebrated many things. We have enjoyed times with friends, and families have been reunited. Even co-workers who normally stay at odds with each other have called a truce and toasted the season. We have celebrated peace and goodwill, and we certainly need all of that we can get. Let us dare not overlook and forget that we celebrate our salvation. The one who was expected did come, just as the prophets said he would. He came, not to give us a holiday and a break from our work, but to save us from the depths of hell. Salvation has come!

December 29   **"When the time came for their purification according to the law of Moses, they brought him up to Jerusalem to present him to the Lord." (Luke 2:22)**

Most parents have had the experience of being in a public place when their child was young and some particular stranger taking a special notice of the little one. This kind of experience happened to Mary and Joseph as they took Jesus into the temple for Mary's purification rights.

While they were at the temple, a strange old man met them and wanted to hold the baby. Mary might have been a little reluctant, but they agreed. What followed was a very emotional moment, one Mary would always remember. Simeon held the baby toward the heavens and began to pray. As he prayed he began to sob. He made several puzzling statements such as being ready to die in peace. He muttered that he had seen God's salvation and this deliverance was for everyone. Finally he placed the baby back in Mary's arms.

Simeon had been a man of great hope, and he was sensitive enough to recognize when the hope had been fulfilled. He discovered the fulfillment of his hope in a child born to Mary and Joseph. The peace he longed for would finally be his. His eyes may have been old, but he could really see. Of the many characters that wander on and off the stage at Christmas, one of the most intriguing is a man named Simeon—old wrinkled Simeon, peering out of his cataract eyes. He held out his arms to take the baby. Through eyes that could hardly see, he saw.

December 30   **"The shepherds returned, glorifying and praising God for all they had heard and seen, as it had been told them." (Luke 2:20)**

When I was a child, Christmas took ages to roll around each year. Decembers were an eternity apart. Since those days, however, something has happened to the calendar. Now Decembers almost follow each other. In fact, Mastercharge is barely paid off before it is time to use it again. Time seems to be picking up speed and, to be perfectly honest, I am very uncomfortable with its momentum. The older I get, the faster it seems to move. Seems only yesterday that our son Chris was taking his first steps, and now he is a fine young man. I remember some conversations that Suzanne and I had about wanting a daughter. Now Melody is looking at colleges.

The harder I try to put on the brakes, the faster time seems to go. What can we do? Let me make two quick suggestions. First, accept reality. Time is something we cannot relive or alter, but we can change our attitude about it. Remember that it is a gift from God, no more or less than any of the other gifts to us. We are not entitled to any of it. Second, instead of spending energy "putting the brakes on time," live it as a treasured gift. Be alive to every moment, really alive. Don't confuse pace with aliveness. Just do what the shepherds did and return praising God for all we have seen and heard. Slow down, breathe it in, open your eyes; soon it will be Christmas again.

"For a thousand years in your sight are like yesterday when it is past, or like a watch in the night." (Ps 90:4)

Of all the gifts that I received this past Christmas season, the one I have enjoyed most is a battery-operated train that goes with the Dickens Christmas village. Rather than use it for the village display, it was just big enough to put at the base of the Christmas tree. We have watched the little plastic locomotive make lap after lap, pulling the cars on the plastic track.

I was amazed that the same set of batteries "kept on keeping on"—like the pink rabbit in the television commercials. I knew they could not continue forever, for sooner or later they would come to their end, and tonight they did. As we were putting away this year's Christmas decorations, the train finally slowed and then stopped completely. The best of batteries last only so long. This gift included an additional set of batteries and, as a result, the train now awaits its new lease.

Yet, the train's timing was quite symbolic. The year winds down with the final hours of this night. The best or worst of years can last only so long. Unlike the train that goes in the box to await next Christmas, Lord willing, we will get up tomorrow and start our laps again. A brand new set of batteries—and that new set comes as a gift as well. We don't earn it or necessarily deserve it. It is a gift, pure and simple, from the one who owns the whole village.